Architectural
Yangon

Architectural Guide Yangon

Ben Bansal/Elliott Fox/Manuel Oka

DOM publishers

Contents

How to use this guide

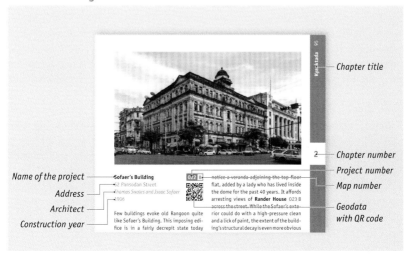

Society and Space

Ben Bansal

This guide presents 110 buildings around Yangon. Collectively they help the visitor—or resident—appreciate the built environment of a fast-changing city. Although we publish this book in DOM publishers' *Architectural Guide* series, we hope to attract a diverse range of readers, and not "just" architecture enthusiasts: this guide is for anyone who wishes to learn about Myanmar and its former capital. As just one of three authors of this book is an architect by training, it will become clear that the built environment is only a lens through which we look at the country's and city's historical, social and economic context.

For me, this project constitutes the culmination of a multi-year intellectual journey. I am a development economist by training, hence I tended to look at the world through the abstract and by approximation. A long stay in Tokyo changed this. As I walked the streets and remembered my classes on the Japanese economic miracle, I found its physical manifestations everywhere, in the many layers of the built environment, prompting my continued research at the interstice of society and space. In early 2013, I took on a month-long assignment in Yangon, researching the investment environment in this rapidly liberalising country. Fascinated by Myanmar's history, the city had a profound impact on me. Traces of the past, far and near, were virtually everywhere. I was hungry for information that linked the many spaces to this most fascinating history. The idea for this book was born.

Of course, there are pitfalls to writing a guide about a city on the cusp of a new chapter in its—and Myanmar's—history. Inevitably information will become out of date, perhaps faster than we expect. Some buildings will disappear. New ones will rise. Their uses will change. Some of our speculations may turn out wrong. Nonetheless, these are exciting times to write such a guide. In 10 to 20 years, much of this city will have mutated beyond recognition. We hope this book helps to record the sheer scale of Yangon's transition at this moment in time.

There are many recurring themes in this book. One is the cosmopolitanism of old Rangoon. Plenty of buildings around the city convey this, and many are featured in our book. Others, which we could not fit in, include the Chinese shophouses in Latha, or a building from the Sikh community—perhaps its *Gurdwara* on Thein Phyu Road. There are also many buildings we would have liked to show in our book but that are no longer standing. A Parsi fire temple near Mogul Street comes to mind. From this angle, a selection of merely 110 buildings falls way short of conveying the true richness of Yangon. To put this in perspective, a new list of notable buildings by the Yangon Heritage Trust (YHT) will reportedly contain more than 1,000 edifices around town.

When telling people that we were writing an architectural guide to Yangon, a typical reaction was to assume we were focusing on colonial buildings only. In fact, the most rewarding moments of research brought us closer to the city's lesser-known, post-independence architecture. The architects—literally building a new country—taught us many lessons. We discovered the lives of Raglan Squire, Viktor Andreyev and Benjamin Polk, among the first foreign architects to work in independent Burma. Of equal if not greater significance, we learned about a small and impressive group of local architects. While U Tin was the most famous among them, U Tun Than and U Kyaw Min left behind important legacies within the cityscape as well.

We hope to provide our readers with more than just information about the buildings. The book contains six thematic chapters, or "insets", covering topics crucial to understanding Yangon's built environment. They make lateral connections that help to place the buildings in a richer context. They may guide thematic explorations in a city that, in many

A street vendor sells his wares on the pedestrian overpass above Sule Pagoda Road, on the corner with Anawratha Road

respects, remains underexplored. Often, reliable information had to come not from within Yangon but from libraries abroad. It can only be hoped that a stronger academic community in Myanmar will soon enjoy greater freedom to explore the urban environment past, present and future. Besides a timeline highlighting the most notable dates and events of Yangon and Myanmar's history, we also included the five favourite buildings of several personalities with deep connections to the city, to add a more personal layer to the book.

We deliberately avoided using old archival photos. For one, we hope that our text builds vivid-enough bridges to the past. But we also wanted the visuals to focus readers on the here and now—and consider Yangon's future too. There are already books that transport you to the days of old Rangoon, and we could not aspire to compete with them (see Bibliography). We only made a couple of exceptions. A 1909 map of Rangoon shows both the continuities and the drastic changes that the city has experienced over the past century. Besides some photos taken by German photographer Adolphe Klier, we also show some snaps from travellers who came through the city between the 1970s and 1980s. While more recent than the black-and-white images of the colonial period, we feel these times are perhaps the most forgotten of all in Myanmar's modern history.

The Road to Yangon

Manuel Oka

Several years ago my interest in Myanmar started to grow. I was mainly intrigued by the stories of a country that seemed to have been almost forgotten by the world. What little knowledge I had only painted a rough picture of Myanmar: on the one hand, of a serene, deeply Buddhist society strewn with ancient temples and monks in red robes; and on the other hand, an autocratic regime with a strained relationship towards human rights and the international community. My interest remained private in nature for many years, fuelled mostly by the bucolic images of an apparently forgotten land that longed to be explored.

As Myanmar gradually started to open up, more stories would reach my ears that painted a wholly different picture. Especially intriguing were the descriptions of the former capital city, Yangon, that was said to exude a vibrancy not unlike that of Havana in its street life as well as its colourful streetscape. Soon, well-known international newspapers and TV stations started to cover the colonial heritage left behind by the British—largely untouched due to decades of international isolation. These media stories would usually highlight the Yangon Heritage Trust's conservation efforts, illustrated with dilapidated and overgrown brick buildings. The journalists would then describe the struggles of combating urban decay, blaming a sluggish and negligent bureaucracy. As a cautionary tale, the audience was reminded of the fates of numerous other Asian cities that had once held a similar cultural heritage. Was a future of indistinct high-rises and mega malls now looming over Yangon, too?

Ben and I had previously collaborated fruitfully on a research project about urban architecture in Tokyo. When he told me about his first visit to Myanmar, I didn't need much convincing. In our own way, we wanted to document this unique assortment of ancient temples, stately brick buildings and crowded tenements before the tides of urban and economic

Street scene in downtown Yangon

Torrential rains flood the city during the annual monsoon

development could threaten them. As a regular visitor to Myanmar with some exposure to its history and politics, Elliott naturally completed the team.

My first trip to Yangon quickly revealed that the city's architectural scope extended far beyond what was left by the British Empire. I would often stumble upon arresting architecture from later decades. But trying to find relevant buildings in a city of seven million was—for lack of written resources such as this very book!—a daunting task. Information about individual buildings I had already discovered was often scarce, if available at all. Yangon, it seemed, was in dire need of an architectural digest.

Research happened on the dusty (but also sometimes flooded) streets of Yangon and in the archives of scholarly libraries overseas. As the team's photographer, my work consisted mostly of the former, which at times could be a laborious task. Even after the torrential monsoon rains had passed and the humidity became less oppressive, shooting hours were mostly limited to the mornings and late afternoons. Soon after the break of daylight, traffic would swell to a stream of roaring metal that wouldn't subside until well past sunset. The midday sun would cast harsh shadows into the narrow downtown alleys, swallowing every detail. In wider areas, it was hard to escape the scorching sun. In the gentler hours of the day, just before sunrise and right after sunset, I became a feast for swarms of hungry mosquitoes.

But these inconveniences pale in comparison to the kindness that I was met with. Access to many off-limits buildings only became possible after getting to know the right people. Personal conversations with architects and artists, but also with shopkeepers and taxi drivers, often revealed important bits of information or anecdotes that ended up in this book. Finally, an active social media community also contributed greatly to our research. I am lucky to have come away with many lasting friendships in another city that I can now call home.

A Troubled History, and Beyond

Elliott Fox

While I was writing, I would often dwell on a curious illustration of Yangon, believed to be from around 1824. In strokes of black ink, you see the **Sule Pagoda** 016 B rising from nothing but swamp and trees. Incredibly, it sits on a small island. A simple footbridge leads to a modest town, population 8,000. To my mind, the story of each building in this city starts with this question: why did the island vanish? Why was the pagoda robbed of its peaceful waters to stand among seven million human lives?

A whirlwind chronology (we offer a proper one, page 16) might go something like this: the British took charge in the 1850s. Yangon became Rangoon. By the 1930s, the docks greeted more immigrants than those of New York City. It was a place for Buddhists, Christians, Hindus, Jews and Muslims, and traders from Baghdad to Glasgow. Churches, temples, mosques, stupas, banks and shophouses stretched from the jetties to the Shwedagon. In other words, a colonial master plan was now a place of flesh, steel and brick: hot and bustling streets, in a tight pattern, wove around the lost island from the illustration—by then, a very British roundabout surrounded the Sule Pagoda. The architecture from those high times was loud and bombastic. But with hindsight, even the loftiest British designs look tired, tragic and mistaken today: inside those vast buildings, with their lions (the **High Court** 021 B) or vaulting towers (the **Secretariat** 006 B) a handful of pink and sweaty men thought they could rule forever. Then came the Japanese and a war that shattered the city, prompting one of the largest human exoduses of modern history, as hundreds of thousands of Indian migrants fled west, by foot, clutching their belongings.

The greatest symbolic trauma in the country's collective memory was a single day, 19 July 1947, when Aung San was shot and killed by jealous rivals inside the Secretariat. The man who embodied the spirit of independence was dead. It took place without him. In 1948, the Union Jack descended the Secretariat flagpole. A new flag, representing the Union of Burma, rose in its place.

Post-independence architecture evokes the hopes of a second boom in the 1950s. Buildings from those days are self-consciously stripped of colonial conceit, wanting to look resolutely modern—I particularly love the downtown cinemas, the **Thamada** 085 B or **Shae Saung** 013 B, whose façades have lost nothing of their optimism. But that boom never came. Myanmar, and the post-colonial world, were too fragile in the throes of the Cold War. So fragile, in fact, that Yangon was de facto isolated from the rest of the country for long stretches of civil war.

Then came 1962, and the dark days of Ne Win. Like poison ivy, barbed wire wrapped around hundreds of buildings. Much of it is still there today, the rusty blades adding yet more historical texture to those fading colonial façades.

Several decades of repression followed, rocked by landmark moments of revolt and bloodshed: 1974, 1988, 2007. The military regime mutated over the period. This led, in the eyes of the world, to an "opening-up" of the country in 2011. While change is palpable in Yangon, it isn't so much anywhere else. For one, the army was at war with the country's dozens of ethnic minority groups for more than 60 years. A draft national ceasefire was signed in April 2015, heralding—perhaps—a lasting peace in the future.

Yangon booms again today. Many pavements are still broken, yet along them, boardings promise gleaming new condos for the swelling international class. But the country's politics remain complicated. Overtures towards democracy seem to lurch—and lurch only—in a fairer direction. And the city dreams again of global stature; many foreign governments and businesses are eyeing Myanmar's resources. This must come with tangible benefits—better jobs, say, or better health services—for all residents, and

This Ferris wheel may look like any other, but for an important detail: it is human powered

not just those in the newest glass towers. I say this because this book has taught me to read pain and injustice on many of the city's most majestic façades. In their shadow, Yangon's residents have shown courage and resilience in the face of upheaval, unforgivable violence and terrible natural disasters. This time around they, and Myanmar as a whole, deserve a better deal. Global actors should do business responsibly. They should heed the visible lessons of the past.

This city is the shared legacy of tangled nations and kindred cultures. In that sense, it is literally an example to the world: as Thant Myint-U points out in his writings, the expression "plural society" was coined to describe the exceptional mix of colonial Rangoon. And in our world, pluralism is often held to be a good thing in general, and a great thing in a global city. The question is whether, and how, Yangon can thrive and move beyond the darker memories for good. I hope the book helps explore this.

To put it another way: it was Clement Attlee, the British prime minister in 1947, who returned the keys to Myanmar's future. But it was Winston Churchill who inadvertently captured Yangon's tumultuous magic, so palpable as you—Burmese or foreigner—wander the streets.

"First we shape our buildings," he once said. "Thereafter they shape us."

Map of Rangoon from the 1909
Imperial Gazetteer of India

RANGOON
AND ENVIRONS

One English Mile

Depths in Fathoms

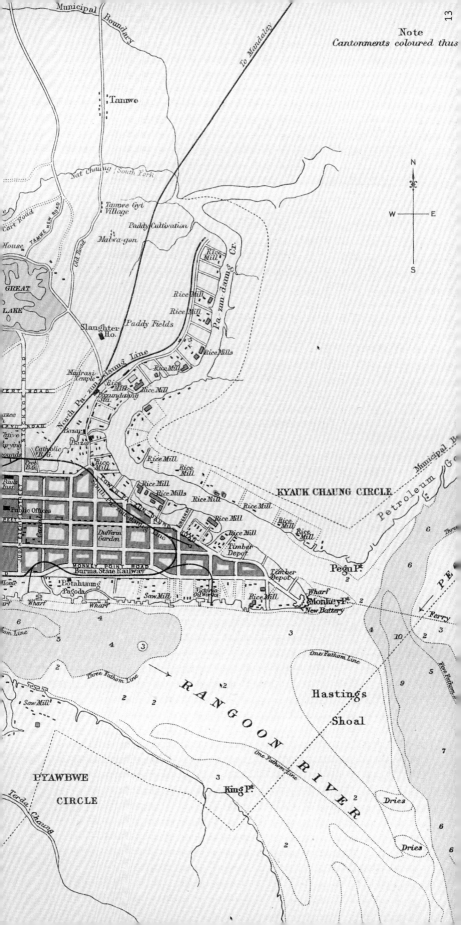

Note
Cantonments coloured thus

13

Municipal Boundary

To Mandalay

Tamwe

N
W E
S

Nat Chaung (South Fork)

Cart Road

Tamwe Gyi Village

TAMWE NEW ROAD

Paddy Cultivation

House

Old Road

Malwa-gon

Rice Mill

Rice Mill

GREAT LAKE

Slaughter Ho.

Paddy Fields

Rice Mill

Pa-zun-daung Cr.

Rice Mills

North Pa-zun-daung Line

ROAD

Madrasi Temple

Rice Mill

Rice Mill

Pazundaung Sta.

Rice Mill

GYI ROAD

Bazar

Rice Mill

Bazar

Catholic B.G.

Native Burying Grounds

Rice Mill

Rice Mill

Rice Mill

KYAUK CHAUNG CIRCLE

Paul's Inst.

Public Offices

Rice Mill

Rice Mills

Rice Mill

Rice Mill

Petroleum

Municipal B

Rice Mill

6

Dufferin Garden

Rice Mill

Rice Mill

Timber Depot

6

Pegn Pt.

8

MONKEY POINT ROAD

Burma State Railway

Timber Depot

PE

Botahtaung Pagoda

Saw Mill

Oil Works

Rice Mill

Wharf

Monkey Pt.

Ferry

2

Wharf

Wharf

New Battery

4

10

3

Mont.

6

5

4

3

One Fathom Line

9

5

4

Saw Mill

2

RANGOON

2

Three Fathom Line

2

Hastings

7

2

2

Shoal

PYAWBWE

Saw Mill

RIVER

Dries

3

King Pt.

CIRCLE

One Fathom Line

2

6

Terda Chaung

2

Dries

Timeline

Circa 600 BC
According to the ancient legends, King Okkalapa begins work on the Shwedagon Pagoda.

6-10th century AD
This is the more likely time period for the Shwedagon's construction, by the Mon people, who reside in present-day Mon State in southeast Myanmar. They also founded the fishing village of Dagon during this period.

1587
Ralph Fitch, a merchant, is the first documented Englishman to set foot in Dagon. He describes the Shwedagon Pagoda as the "fairest place, as I suppose, that is in the world." However, with his trader's mindset, he also notes that if the locals "did not consume their golde in these vanities, it would be very plentifull and [...] cheape".

1612
The first Armenian traders arrive in Syriam (today's Thanlyin, on the opposite banks of what was then Dagon), heralding the start of the city's long cosmopolitan heritage. The **Armenian Church** 041 B is the oldest church in the city today, built in 1862. Its predecessor, Yangon's first-ever church, was built in 1766 along the river shores.

1619
The British East India Company, founded 20 years prior, establishes its first outposts in Myanmar—at Ava, Bhama, Prome and Syriam, dealing in Burmese ivory, oil and timber.

1752
King Alaungpaya founds the Konbaung Dynasty, which unites and rules Burma.

1755
Alaungpaya captures Dagon during his invasion of Lower Burma. He adds several other settlements to the village and renames it Yangon, most commonly translated as "the end of strife".

1824-1826
First Anglo–Burmese War: in 1823 the Burmese Kingdom occupies Shalpuri Island off the coast of Chittagong, in present-day Bangladesh. As the East India Company previously staked a claim to the island, the incident provides a convenient *casus belli* for the conflict, which would last two years and cost 15,000 European and Indian soldiers their lives. The Burmese death toll is not known. The war ends in British victory, forcing Burma into a commercial treaty and relinquishing significant swathes of territory from Assam (in northern India) to Arakan (today's Rakhine State, in Myanmar)—but Yangon remains in Burmese hands.

1852
Second Anglo–Burmese War: Commodore George Lambert blockades Yangon's port in retaliation for perceived breaches of the 1826 treaty. The war ensues, lasting only a few months, and results in the East India Company's annexation of Pegu province, which became Lower Burma—and including Yangon, now officially Rangoon.

All three photos were taken by German-born photographer Philip Adolphe Klier, who lived in Rangoon at the turn of the 20th century, and to whom we owe many stunning impressions from this period

Mogul Street (today's Shwebontha Street) in 1887

Shwedagon Pagoda circa 1890

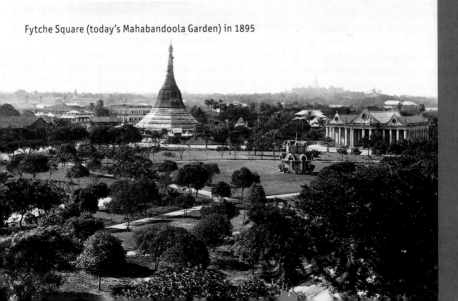

Fytche Square (today's Mahabandoola Garden) in 1895

The Japanese bombing raid on 23 December 1941, here photographed from a reconnaissance plane, brought the Second World War to Rangoon

1885

Third Anglo-Burmese War: in a conflict lasting less than a month, the British take control of Upper Burma in the wake of concerns that Burma's King Thibaw had plotted an alliance with the French. The war completes Britain's annexation of Burma. They make Rangoon its capital. (Thibaw, Burma's last king, is exiled to Ratnagiri, in India, where he dies in 1916. His wife, Supayalat, returns to Yangon in 1919. **Her mausoleum** is featured in this book 078 C.)

1914-1918

First World War: while the war does not reach Burma, it has an economic impact on the cash-strapped colonial administration. Construction of the **City Hall** 018 B, for example, is halted during this period.

1920

In one of the first major acts of local resistance to British colonial rule in Burma, students in Rangoon launch a "Universities Boycott", protesting the British education system's exclusiveness and high costs.

1930

An earthquake of magnitude 7.3, later dubbed the Pegu earthquake, rocks Rangoon and causes damage to many buildings around town, including the **Secretariat** 006 B, causing it to lose 10 of its 18 towers.

1935

The British Parliament passes the Government of Burma Act, which formally splits Burma from India within the British Empire, and devolves greater power to Rangoon. It comes into force in 1937.

1939

Second World War begins.

1940

Japan offers its support to the Burmese nationalist cause, led by a young man named Aung San. He and his "30 Comrades" make repeated visits to Japan for military training over the following three years.

1941

On 23 December, Japan launches its first aerial bombardments on Rangoon.

Shri Kali Temple in 1972

Corner of Sule Pagoda Road and Anawratha Road in 1972.
Today the plot is occupied by Sule Square.

1942
On 8 March, Rangoon falls to a ground invasion from Japanese forces and their allied Burmese nationalists, led by General Aung San.

Several hundreds of thousands of Indian migrants flee Rangoon overland, fearful for their future in a city no longer under British control.

1944
Growing disillusioned with the merits of Japanese support, due to both broken promises and their failure to stem the tide turning in favour of the Allied Forces, General Aung San decides to change sides.

The Allies re-capture Rangoon in December 1944.

1945
Second World War ends.

1947
In January, General Aung San travels to London to negotiate the terms of Burmese independence with Clement Attlee, the British prime minister.

On 29 July a gang of gunmen, instructed by one of Aung San's rivals, storm the Secretariat and murder Aung San along with six of his cabinet ministers and two other people. Today the victims are commemorated at the **Martyrs' Mausoleum** 074 E. Its nine concrete slabs commemorate those killed on that day.

1948
On 4 January, the Union of Burma gains independence.

1949
The government, based in Rangoon's **Secretariat**, struggles to keep the country together: armed groups representing each ethnic minority try to strengthen their leverage over the new government through force. A Karen rebellion actually reaches Insein, in the city's northern suburbs. The Karens are eventually pushed back. (The Burmese army, or *Tatmadaw*, remain at war with the nation's myriad ethnic armed groups—this is the longest-running civil war in modern history.)

King Thibaw's Lion Throne in the National Museum
in 1972, back then located in the former National
Bank of India building, on Pansodan Street

1954-1956

Independent Burma's first prime minister, U Nu, convenes the Sixth Great Buddhist Synod at the purpose-built **Kaba Aye complex** 104 F. The synod, lasting two years, brings together 2,500 monks from countries practising the Theravada branch of Buddhism, including Cambodia, Laos, Myanmar, Sri Lanka and Thailand.

1962

General Ne Win stages a military coup d'état, marking the start of a long period of army-led dictatorship dressed in socialist rhetoric.

1974

Former UN Secretary-General U Thant, a Burmese diplomat, passes away in New York. Ne Win's decision not to grant him a state funeral provokes the "U Thant funeral crisis", which leads to major altercations between the army and Rangoon's students, scores of which lose their lives. Ultimately this leads to the construction of the **U Thant Mausoleum** 077 C.

1988

The pro-democracy "8888 uprising" begins, marking a period of riots, demonstrations and the rise to prominence of opposition leader Aung San Suu Kyi, none other than Aung San's daughter.

General Ne Win resigns in July.

In September, the military-run State Law and Order Restoration Council (SLORC) takes control of the country. They embark on an ambitious public works programme in Yangon, designed to dissuade and more effectively quash further unrest—this is detailed in the inset about post-88 changes to the city on page 332.

1989

Aung San Suu Kyi is placed under house arrest. She will spend 15 of the ensuing 21 years in detention in her University Avenue residence, only freed from 1995 to 2000 and 2002 to 2003. She was most recently released in November 2010.

1990

Having ceded to Aung San Suu Kyi's demands for democratic elections, these are staged on 27 May. Her party, the National League for Democracy (NLD), wins convincingly—although she could not participate herself. The military refuses to recognise the result.

Bus roaring past Shri Kali Temple

1996
Yangon's municipal body, the Yangon City Development Committee (YCDC), designates 189 heritage buildings in the city. The junta declares the "Visit Myanmar Year" in an attempt to attract more foreign investment and tourists. Aung San Suu Kyi supports a boycott of the country.

1997
Myanmar is admitted to the Association of South East Asian Nations (ASEAN). SLORC is renamed State Peace and Development Council (SPDC).

2005
On 6 November, the government moves the country's capital from Yangon to Naypyidaw, 300 kilometres to the north. More about this can be read in the dedicated inset on page 372.

2007
In one of the pro-democracy movement's largest and most iconic protests, up to 50,000 demonstrators, led by thousands of robed monks, take to the streets of Yangon between August and October. The images of the military crackdown shock the world.

2008
Cyclone Nargis, the worst natural disaster in the recorded history of Myanmar, kills more than 100,000 people across the country and turns Yangon into a disaster area. Many buildings around the city still bear the scars, exhibiting permanent damage or makeshift repairs.

Corner of Sule Pagoda and Anawratha Road in 1981. All buildings seen here, including the Sule Pagoda Police Station on the far left, have since been demolished. The corner plot is now occupied by the Naing Group Office Tower II.

While the cyclone rages, the military regime refuse to delay a scheduled referendum on their proposal for a new constitution. According to the junta's tally, 92.8% of the population voted in favour. The constitution provides for general elections, scheduled in 2010, and a nominal return to civilian rule.

2010

On 7 November, Thein Sein, a former military general and prime minister, wins the general election with more than 75% of the vote. He becomes Myanmar's first civilian president since Ne Win's coup in 1962.

On 13 November, Aung San Suu Kyi is released from house arrest.

2012

On 1 April, Aung San Suu Kyi is elected to parliament in by-elections.

2014

In December, the YCDC holds its first municipal council elections. These are marred by low turnout and a controversial "one vote per household" rule.

2015

At the time of writing, general elections were being planned for late October or early November. These were heralded as the next big test for Myanmar's "opening-up". Aung San Suu Kyi remains constitutionally barred from becoming president—an issue seen by many in Myanmar, and around the world, as a major blemish on the government's reform efforts.

"What Are Your Five Favourite Buildings in Yangon?"

Daw Moe Moe Lwin,
Director and Vice-Chair, Yangon Heritage Trust;
Vice President, Association of Myanmar Architects

Shwedagon Pagoda 075 E

My favourite structure, first and fore-most, is the great Shwedagon Pagoda. I think it gives us spiritual strength and a unique sense of security and being in Yangon. It is common for Myanmar people to tell you that their ultimate goal is "to visit the Shwedagon at least once before they die". The stupa itself is a remarkable architectural achievement that was built in various stages through different reigns in history. There are also various fine architectural specimens on the main and lower platforms, including pavilions, smaller stupas, monasteries and image houses. Similarly, these were built across the centuries. The Shwedagon, as one of the larger public spaces in Yangon, has also long been associated with political and social upheavals in Myanmar's history, including the struggle for independence and more recent movements. The plaques recording donations over time would make for fascinating historical or anthropological research.

Sule Pagoda 016 B and surroundings

This historic site has been the centre of the former capital since the mid-19th century. As a result of colonial-era urban planning and design, it is at the heart of the city and has been the most popular site for public gatherings ever since. It is surrounded by a rich architectural land-scape of domes, towers, minarets, spir-als, and lush green trees with seasonal coloured blossoms. This is quintessen-tially Yangon.

Yegyaw High School

An early 20th-century teak structure has served as the local high school in a south eastern corner of the city since the day it was built. The Methodist Burma Mission established it, after purchasing the plot in 1906 to build a boys' school. The mission completed a church, two high schools and a missionary house in the same block of Upper Bo Myat Tun Street (formerly known as Creek Street). Although it was origin-ally a missionary boys' school, it also served as a gathering space and shel-ter for the local community, and became a springboard for social and political organisations. It currently serves over 2,000 high school students. It also fea-tures an indoor court for sports activities such as badminton or the more traditional chin-lone, Myanmar's traditional sport, where players keep a small woven rattan ball in the air by passing it to one another with agile, dance-like footwork.

Scott Market (Bogyoke Market) 059 C

An abiding image of the market I've always had since my childhood is of an old man with a big hard hat dozing off on the street. The market is a single-storey building with a main aisle, flanked by three wings at each side. There are double-storeyed shops lining the peri-meter. The market has always been a gath-ering place, for traders; tourists and the trendy; for youngsters and creatives to hang out; for ladies of all walks of life to show off their fashion sensibilities; where new styles and ideas are introduced.

Central Fire Station 014 B

This fine Edwardian building is a promin-ent piece of architecture on Sule Pagoda Road. It has always complemented the sight of the Sule Pagoda. The road leading towards the stupa, together with the fire station on its right, has been a showcase of Yangon's unique street scenes for dec-ades. It was built in 1913, when Rangoon's municipal government saw the need for the emergency service in a fire-prone city. The Department of Fire Fighting deserves credit for maintaining the build-ing in good condition despite its old age.

Shwedagon Pagoda

Botataung

1

28

Ministers' Building 006 B

019 B Ayeyarwady Bank

Myanma Post and Telecommunications 020 B

008 B St Mary's Cathedral

Printing & Publishing Enterprise 005 B

Basic Education
High School No. 6 007 B

Aerial view of Kyauktada and Botataung townships as seen from Centrepoint Towers

021 B High Court

003 B YMCA

110 A Star City

Sofaer's Building 022 B

Innwa Bank 045 B

Botataung Pagoda 001 B

Armenian Apostolic Church
of St John the Baptist 041 B

Myanma Foreign Trade Bank 046 B

Basic Education High School No. 6 007 B

008 B **St Mary's Cathedral**

Aerial view of the Secretariat and wider Botataung township

Printing & Publishing Enterprise 005 B

006 B Ministers' Building

1

Botataung Pagoda as seen from Yangon River

Botataung Pagoda

001 B

Strand Road
Unknown
5th century BC, rebuilt 1954

By the ever-busy river docks of Botataung Pagoda Road lies this revered Buddhist temple, which lends the township its name. Legends regarding the pagoda's origins abound, all involving various stories of how, and when, relics of the Buddha arrived here. One of them holds that two brothers, Tapussa and Bhallika, landed here after an arduous journey from India about 2,500 years ago. (Although various countries' Buddhist legends have staked a claim to the brothers, archeological findings suggest that they originally hailed from what

is today's state of Odisha in India.) Their arrival was a triumphant one, for they carried with them several of the Buddha's hairs. King Okkalapa, who ruled these shores, ordered the construction of the **Shwedagon Pagoda** 075 E to enshrine these hallowed relics. In the meantime they were to be kept here, at the site of the brothers' landing. Once the Shwedagon was completed, King Okkalapa returned one of the hairs to the brothers in reward for their long and arduous voyage. They decided to erect a pagoda on this site. The 1,000 warriors who were drawn up as a guard of honour to welcome the hair relics from India are what gives the pagoda its name: in Burmese, "bo" means troop and "tataung" is a thousand. Botataung Pagoda, and its tale, became well-known only after it was almost completely destroyed in 1943, in a British bombing raid during the Second World War. During clearance works five years later, several precious artefacts were uncovered, and these seemed to corroborate the ancient legends. The story of these discoveries has a mythical aura of its own: a relic chamber was excavated at the heart of the pagoda. Inside, astonished workers found a treasure vault containing a stone casket in the shape of a pagoda, measuring 60 cm in diameter and 100 cm in height. Within the casket they found almost 700 ancient objects, ranging from precious stones to jewellery. Among these artefacts was a terracotta plaque. Once translated, it helped establish a connection between the Mon people (thought to have built the pagoda, who reside in Myanmar's Mon State today) and the South Indian Brahmi script. After the ceremonial opening of a second, smaller stone casket found inside the first, a golden pagoda-shaped vessel emerged. Within it was a small golden cylinder. When they opened it, Buddhist dignitaries identified two small body relics—each the size of a mustard seed—and a sacred hair of the Buddha. Rebuilding works ensued over following years; they were complete in 1954. As a result, today's pagoda combines traditional temple architecture with post-war construction techniques. It mimics its original shape, at a height of 40 metres, covering

a square of 29 × 29 metres. Unusual for a pagoda of its kind the main stupa is hollow, thanks to the extensive use of reinforced concrete. A circular walkway leads through a sequence of angular chambers. These surround the gold-covered central chamber, where the Buddha's relics lie. The pagoda brings a steady stream of visitors to the adjacent stretch, along the river. This is where passenger ferries dock. Traders' boats can be seen unloading bag after bag of rice, while children play football here until the sun sets and bathes the place in shades of pink.

Myanmar Red Cross Society
Union Bar & Grill

002 B

42 Strand Road
Unknown/SPINE Architects
1959/2012

On a busy Friday night, to step inside the Union Bar & Grill is to forget about Yangon almost completely. The pacey lounge music, the hum of expat conversation, the tinkling cocktail glasses ... The scene is always a far cry from the dark and quiet stretch of Strand Road right outside, not to mention the loud, lurching movements of the cargo docks opposite, which continue well after the bar closes. In daylight, the venue reveals itself to be a straightforward, modern take on the

colonial genre: white brick walls, high ceilings and dark wood finishings bathe in sunlight from large windows. The space was designed by local architects SPINE. What is most striking, though, is the contrast between the bar and the building it occupies. This is a burly, tired six-storey edifice with Art Deco leanings, home to the headquarters of the Myanmar Red Cross Society. (In fact, the space now used by the bar was once a warehouse for disaster supplies.) The Red Cross in Myanmar operates at the forefront of several humanitarian challenges. It has a special division dedicated to Rakhine State, which runs along much of the country's western coast. Rakhine often makes headlines. Stark poverty there has escalated into recurring episodes of deadly sectarian (and often anti-Muslim) violence. When the British colonial administration decided to separate Burma from India in 1937, so did the Burma Red Cross Society (BRCS) peel away from its Indian counterpart. As a newly-independent entity, the BRCS joined the International Federation of Red Cross and Red Crescent Societies (IFRC) in 1946. It changed its name to the Myanmar Red Cross Society (MRCS) in 1989. Today, the MRCS occupies several floors of the building and leases the others to the IFRC as well as some public companies. The income from the rent helps to fund Red Cross activities.

Young Men's Christian Association (YMCA)

263 45th Street
Captain Kyu Kyaw
1960s/70s

003 B

A stone's throw from the **Secretariat 006 B**, the YMCA occupies this large modern complex on the corner of Thein Phyu and Mahabandoola Roads. The entrance itself is in the narrow alleyway behind the petrol station on Thein Phyu Road. Supposedly, a kickboxing centre on the ground floor is the only one in Yangon where anyone—local or foreign—can watch or even join a session. The English YMCA arrived in Burma in 1897; an American branch was set up two years later. These were led by, and gave priority to, the expatriate community rather than the local Christian population. There was a dedicated branch, however, catering to Indians. The YMCA had a number of buildings around town and moved premises several times. A national leadership emerged in the 1940s, before independence. Several other YMCA chapters were set up throughout the country during that period. After independence, the National Council of YMCAs joined the global YMCA structure in 1953. The organisation survived many hardships over the years. It faced generalised mistrust stemming from its colonial origins. (A Young Men's Buddhist Association, or YMBA, emerged a short decade after the YMCA in 1906. A General Council of Burmese Associations, borne out of the YMBA, became a potent vehicle for anti-colonial sentiment in the 1920s.) During the war the Japanese turned one of its buildings into a "comfort station". Their military coerced women from across occupied East Asia here—including some 500 Burmese. As a result of the Second World War, according to YMCA International records, "the damage to YMCA property was devastating; all of the buildings and records were destroyed". The organisation had to begin again from scratch. In the 1960s, the YMCA lost several properties all over again, as a result of the dictatorship's nationalisation programme. Today there are about 25 YMCA chapters throughout the country—predominantly in Kachin, Chin and Shan states, which have significant Christian populations. The YMCA also operates charitable programmes for young people and the elderly. They raise awareness of human rights and environmental issues as well. The building contains a church on the fourth floor. In Yangon, a second YMCA hostel is located on Lanmadaw Road.

Siyin Baptist Church (St Philip's Church)

152 Bo Myat Tun Road
Unknown
1887

004 B

This compact church with its stout, concrete dome is best admired from 49th Street, which it squarely presides from the southern end of the road. Today the church serves Yangon's ethnic Chin population. The mountainous Chin State runs along Myanmar's border with India. Like many of the country's ethnic groups, the "Chin" label is fluid. On the Indian side, Chin people are known as Kuki. Under British rule, the colonial administration adopted the compound term "Chin-Kuki-Mizo". Some people from the region today self-identify as Mizo, rejecting the two other terms. To complicate things, a Kuki-Mizo ethnic conflict in India cost hundreds of lives in the mid-1990s. A further 13,000 people fled their homes. The name of the Church, "Siyin", refers to a sub-group in Chin State—they reside in the Siyin valley. They possess their own distinctive traits, including their own language. The standardised labels of "Kuki" and "Chin", in India and Burma, are due to the success of American Baptist evangelical missions in the early 19th century. A large section of the Chin population today identify as Baptists. Several plaques around the church paint a colourful version of this tale, recounting the journey of the "Chin (...) from headhunters to soul winners". Besides these plaques, the church is sparse. Inside, the pastel-coloured walls have few adornments. First built in 1887 (there have clearly been renovations and alterations since), the building was originally an Anglican church called St Philip's, adjoined by a St Philip's School. At some point after independence, the church was nationalised. It was leased to the Rangoon Christian Chin Association 100 years after its construction, in 1987, and became today's Siyin Baptist Church. (The school was fenced off and became Botataung Basic Education High School No. 2.) The church was bought by the association in 2002. In spite of goodwill gestures such as these, Christian groups have had extremely difficult relations with the Burmese authorities. To name but one example connected to this very building, in the early 2000s authorities detained its former pastor, Lian Za Dal, in the infamous **Insein Prison** 109 A after he had been previously warned not to preach to Buddhists. Today the church has an active community with its own lively Facebook page. Refugee Chin populations in the US and Australia have founded their own Siyin Baptist Churches there.

Printing & Publishing Enterprise (Government Press Buildings)

005 B

228 Thein Phyu Road
John Begg
1906–1912

This large, low-rise complex stands on the northeastern edge of the **Secretariat** 006 B. Built from red bricks, the Government Press' ornaments were cast from concrete—instead of the more usual stone—as a cost-cutting measure. The Secretariat-facing wing, on Thein Phyu Road, features an elegant entrance with Greek columns. Note the continuous loggia across the width of the second floor. At first, the building was a distribution point for official publications arriving from India. Soon after, printing facilities arrived here to produce colonial gazettes and journals. In these publications, the British documented their prized possessions and announced the latest news and official acts. By 1962, 1,300 staff were squeezing into the building. Many travelled abroad to learn the latest printing techniques and worked here with the latest imported machinery. The building later became known as the Printing and Publishing Enterprise, which the Ministry of Information still runs today. It continued to print gazettes and other official publications until 2005, when the facilities, like the rest of the government, moved to Naypyidaw. Like many former government facilities in Yangon today, the Printing and Publishing Enterprise is now mostly vacant. Ideas for future use include a public library—and fittingly, the Myanmar Libraries Foundation already have their offices here. The Government Press was designed by John Begg (1866–1937), who served as the Consulting Architect to the Government of India from 1908–1921. His two other works in Yangon are the **Custom House** 033 B and the **Central Telegraph Office** 020 B. In his works in India, Begg married classical European architecture and Mughal features, a style that became known as "Indo-Saracenic". The Bombay Post Office, which he designed, is a classic example. His works in today's Yangon, however, don't reference any indigenous architectural forms.

Inside the stairwell of the Secretariat's southern wing

Ministers' Building (Secretariat)

300 Thein Phyu Road
Henry Hoyne-Fox
1889–1905

Welcome to the Secretariat, Yangon's iconic colonial building: an epic symbol of British rule; a haunting monument to the broken dreams of Burmese independence. The sight of those glowing red bricks, obscured by forbidding barbed wire, transfixes legions of locals and visitors alike—such that its historic name still sticks, despite being officially known as the Ministers' Building today. As the country launches into a spectacular and uncertain period of change, so will this vast, vacant and delicate complex search for a role in the new Myanmar. Built in several stages between 1889 and 1905, it became the administrative centre of British Burma. Britain annexed Lower Burma in 1852 and Rangoon became the main commercial and political hub for its new colonial possessions. With the annexation of Upper Burma in 1886, the bureaucracy grew such that a vast new building became necessary. (A previous Secretariat stood on Strand Road at the time.) Burma was to remain an administrative subdivision of British India until 1937, when it became a dominion of Britain. The colonial bureaucracy was infamously expansive. It established a firm grip on all aspects of life through its myriad departments and divisions. Policing, prisons, asylums, finances, education, health: the colonists left nothing to chance. Inside the building, rows of officials and clerks hammered away at brand new typewriters. Though a symbol of colonialism, the Secretariat is also central to Burma's independence struggle. The country's first prime minister, Ba Maw, took office here in 1937. This was prescribed by the Government of Burma Act, which led to the separation of Burma from British India. The following year, student protesters in Mandalay demanded the release of anti-British activists. The movement escalated and reached Yangon. When mounted police tried to disperse the protesters, they killed a young man called Aung Kyaw. The street east of the Secretariat bears his name today. Nine years later, the Secretariat bore witness to modern Burma's defining moment. In the morning of 19 July 1947, gunmen entered the Secretariat. They were looking for independence leader General Aung San. They found him on the first floor—along with six other ministers—and murdered them all. A low-key shrine (a table, some flowers and incense) now stands in the Secretariat's northwestern wing, which has been maintained even as the building became derelict. At the time of writing, the room had clearly been renovated, unlike the rest of the complex. Though only 32 years old at the time of his death,

Aung San had already become a legend. He was a driving force behind the 1938 protests and later fought against the British, on the side of the Japanese, in the early years of the Second World War. Later in the war, he threw his lot in with the British and ended on the victors' side. In early 1947, he travelled to London to negotiate the terms of independence, but died in the Secretariat only months later. (For a more detailed account of his life, please see the section on the **Bogyoke Aung San Residence** 092 D.) On 4 January 1948, a few months later, the Secretariat became the stage of another historic event. At 4.20am (an auspicious time, chosen by astrologers) the Union Jack descended from a flagpole to the sounds of God Save the King. The flag of the Union of Burma rose. Thousands of Burmese thronged the streets on the day that marked the end of British rule. The post-independence government used the Secretariat, as did Ne Win's junta post-1962. However, they forbade residents from strolling in the park and declared the place off limits. In 1972, civil servants were placed more firmly under the control of army-appointed ministers. The complex was renamed the Ministers' Office. In the eyes of some, the buildings' structural decay, accelerated by the government's move to Naypyidaw, symbolises the decline of the rule of law in Burma. Henry Hoyne-Fox, an engineer at the Public Works Department, was responsible for drawing up the plans. He

had ample space: the administration earmarked an entire city block measuring 16 hectares. (Hoyne-Fox also designed the **Yangon General Hospital** 061 C.) Baboo Naitram Rambux, a contractor with roots in northern India, oversaw the construction. He had taken over the business from his father (who began the works on the Secretariat, but died in a train accident in 1894). Rambux remained one of the most prominent builders in colonial Rangoon and was still listed in the local trade directories in 1956, aged 74, long after the country's independence. The Secretariat was built in stages, with the south wing erected first between 1889 and 1893. Soggy ground and torrential rainfalls during the monsoon seasons complicated the work and massive timber logs were used to stabilise the soil underneath the building. Drainage problems continue to plague the south wing, with huge puddles forming here during the rainy season. As a result, the building looks slightly uneven in places. Work resumed on the east and west wings in 1903. This time, construction took just two years: the Secretariat as it stands today was thus finally completed by 1905. There was now a veritable colonial palace in the heart of Rangoon: 18 ornate towers marked the corners of both east and west wings. A large dome rose above a majestic staircase along the west wing. The building's structural integrity has been frequently tested by natural disasters. An earthquake reaching magnitude 7.3 on the

Richter scale shook Rangoon in the early afternoon of 5 May 1930. Among the government buildings, the Secretariat fared the worst. Twelve pillars supporting the main dome were cracked; several others of the west and north wings were shattered. The cupola and 10 of the 18 towers could not be saved. Ornaments adorning the original southern wing were also badly damaged and some had to be removed. Here, too, the ceilings had to be dismantled and the fissures in the western wall of the south block were widened. More recently, Cyclone Nargis, ravaging Yangon in 2008, damaged various sections of the roof that have only been repaired with rudimentary fixes. Despite this, the Secretariat continues to impress through its scale and massing. It is more of a complex than a single building. The three wings are complemented by the staff quarters on the northern side. The authorities later added a modest building in the courtyard. It served as Burma's parliament following independence. For the Secretariat's design, Henry Hoyne-Fox drew on various architectural currents, with official colonial-era architecture from Calcutta among them.

Materials were sourced from various locations: the terracotta roof tiles came from Marseilles, France. Large steel beams came from Britain, while smaller steel furnishings were cast locally. The area around the Secretariat is unusually calm: no street vending is allowed on either side of the fenced-off building. After the government's move to Naypyidaw, the military allowed some of its staff to live here with their families. Today, the future of Yangon's most iconic colonial building is slowly taking shape. In 2012, a new and little-known entity called Anawmar Art Group was awarded the lease on the building. It aims to spend a sizeable amount of its own funds on restoration works, but will require additional outside investment to bring the 40,000-square-metre building back to an acceptable state. Estimates for the total price tag differ widely, with the highest being more than 100 million US dollars. The group states that it plans to return the Secretariat to public use. Current plans feature museums, galleries and a cultural centre. Big questions surround the commercial viability of such a huge undertaking.

BEHS No. 6 Botataung
(St Paul's English School)

007 B

Anawratha Road/
Thein Phyu Road
Thomas Swales (extensions)
1885–1922

The school's dry name belies its significance in the history of Burmese Catholicism. Then again, it looks the part. Built in 1885, St Paul's English School (as it was known) was the choice of the European and Anglo-Indian elites. The language of instruction was English. From the south entrance, the school looks deceptively small. The length of the building is revealed from the east, where a football field runs along the side of the road. Beyond the wrought iron fence, commuters at the bus station watch the students kick up clouds of dust during their matches. The school was built by an irrepressible French missionary named Paul Ambroise Bigandet. He became the first Catholic bishop of Burma in 1856, when Rome entrusted its efforts to the Foreign Mission of Paris. Bigandet had first set foot on Burmese soil in 1837. He travelled from Penang, Malaysia to the Mergui peninsula at the southernmost tip of Burma. Starting his new assignment in the country, Bishop Bigandet began what became a legendary effort to convert the Burmese over 40 years, until his death in 1894,

aged 81. In his first year he travelled back to Mergui and onward to Moulmein and then Rangoon. He then ventured further northward. (On a separate trip he went as far north as Yunnan Province in southern China.) He was less than enthused by what he found: despite a century's worth of efforts, there were just a couple of thousand faithful in Burma. Rangoon at that time only possessed a chapel made of bamboo and an unfinished brick church. Bishop Bigandet embarked on a number of ambitious projects, especially building schools, and St Paul's was the apex. Prior to that, he entrusted the construction of a school in Moulmein to three members of the Brothers of the Christian Schools, a Catholic order dedicated to education. He asked them to build another near his home in Rangoon. After several expansions and relocations, it reached its present location. It was later expanded by architect Thomas Swales in the early 1900s. (Swales' other buildings in Yangon include the former **Fytche Square Building** 017 B and **Sofaer's Building** 022 B.) A science laboratory was added in 1922. Although the school

was nationalised in 1965 and given its present name, the wrought iron gate still features the Brothers of the Christian Schools' motto, *Signum Fidei* (Sign of Faith). In the classic *30 Heritage Buildings of Yangon*, Sarah Rooney points out that the symbol of the order, "the five-pointed star of Bethlehem which led the wise men of the East to the Birth of Christ", here features a six-pointed star. Presumably a mistake. The Old Paulians' Association convenes alumni who attended the school before its nationalisation. It continues to meet often, fundraises for charitable activities and holds an annual event at the school. Historically, alumni of the school have included many of the country's upper echelons. These include ethnic Chinese tycoon Lim Chin Tsong (apparently a favourite of Bishop Bigandet's, see **Lim Chin Tsong Palace** 095 F) and Deedok U Ba, who perished at Aung San's side in 1947. Even since nationalisation, BEHS 6 continues to attract the better-off classes of Yangon society. One recent alumnus is Zayar Thaw, a rapper-turned-parliamentarian close to Aung San Suu Kyi.

St Mary's Cathedral

372 Bo Aung Kyaw Road
Jos Cuypers
1899–1911

008 B

The Cathedral of St Mary the Virgin is Yangon's biggest Roman Catholic church. Its neo-Gothic style is reminiscent of cathedrals built around the same time in northern Europe, but the inside sets it apart: the colourful bricks offer a livelier feel than its often austere contemporaries. St Mary's was one of two major Christian churches built at the turn of the 20th century. The other is the Anglican **Holy Trinity Cathedral** 060 C in nearby Pabedan Township. Though consecrated in 1911, St Mary's history goes back to the late 19th century. The

main Catholic church had by that point become too small for the congregation and Rangoon's energetic first bishop, Paul Ambroise Bigandet, wanted a cathedral. He successfully lobbied the government of British India (in other words, the British colonial authority over Burma) for the funds. Henry Hoyne-Fox—who built the iconic **Secretariat** 006 B—made designs for a Byzantine-style cathedral. However, the grounds purchased on what is today's Bo Aung Kyaw Street were initially too swampy; the foundations needed to be strengthened using vertical logs pushed into the ground. As the preparatory work dragged on for longer than expected, Hoyne-Fox abandoned the project and took a long leave of absence. Meanwhile, Bishop Bigandet passed

away. His successor, Alex Cardot, commissioned Jos Cuypers to continue the work. A Dutch architect whom Cardot had met during a trip to Europe in 1895, Jos was the son of Pierre Cuypers, who designed the Rijksmuseum and the central train station in Amsterdam. Cuypers submitted two different designs for the Rangoon assignment. The first one represented a mixture of his Saint Bavo Cathedral in Haarlem with added "oriental" influences as understood at the time. (Dutch architecture during that period made frequent references to a romanticised image of the country's colonial possessions in Asia.) The second—successful—proposal was a more conventional, European-style cathedral in Gothic Revival style. As he had never set foot in Rangoon, Cuypers' designs required revisions for local conditions. Father Jenzen, who studied with Cuypers in the Netherlands, oversaw these adaptations in Rangoon. His close supervision of the untrained staff ensured the foundation's successful stabilisation. The cornerstone of white marble

was laid in 1899. Later Jenzen felt confident enough to add spirals to Cuypers' towers, placing significant additional weight upon the existing structure. Crippled by an accident during construction, Father Jenzen lived long enough—just—to see the cathedral's dedication in 1911. As proof of its structural soundness, it survived the 20th century almost unscathed. The 1930 Pegu earthquake only inflicted minor damage to several vaults and two arches. Aerial bombs dropped on Rangoon during the Second World War missed the cathedral, though nearby explosions did break its glass windows. The damage to the cathedral from Cyclone Nargis in 2008 was similarly limited to shattered windows. The Catholic Church in Myanmar remains split into three archdioceses. (Yangon is the headquarters for the Southern Burma Vicariate.) In January 2015 Pope Francis named Myanmar's first cardinal, Charles Bo, also the Archbishop of Yangon. He is a leading voice of tolerance in response to anti-Muslim sentiment in parts of the country.

Yangon River seen from Centrepoint Towers

Yangon's Waterfront: a City with a View

As river and ocean trade grew, so did Yangon. Historically, industrial port facilities have lined much of Strand Road and sealed off the waterfront from residents. This remains the case today, save for a couple of public access points. With competing visions for riverside development, many hope to see it opened up.

Yangon is within easy access of the Ayeyarwady River, navigable almost as far as the Chinese border 1,400 kilometres north. Only 50 kilometres south, the Yangon River enters the Bay of Bengal and the Andaman Sea; its location was precisely why Yangon became Myanmar's port for river and ocean trade. The country's teak, petroleum products and rice passed through here. Harbour cranes loaded the goods on freighters from the many quays. But it wasn't just trade that kept the port buzzing: the city's growth in the late 19th and early 20th century relied on one of the largest-ever waves of labour migration, chiefly from India. The overwhelming majority of these migrants landed at Yangon's port, in numbers at times exceeding those arriving in New York City.

An 1852 plan designated Strand Road as the southern limit of Rangoon. It allowed ample space along the shore for future developments. Over the years, growing colonial trade led to an expansion of local facilities. The Pazundaung Creek in the east housed numerous rice mills, while much of the wide, south-facing riverfront became wharfs, such as at the southern end of Sule Pagoda Road. Farther to the west, a large number of sawmills processed Burmese teak and prepared it for export. In an age before mechanisation, skilled handlers directed an army of elephants as they carried large shipments.

The Yangon River is too shallow to accommodate today's large container vessels. The special economic zone (SEZ) in Thilawa, some 15 kilometres downstream, will provide relief to Yangon's port once fully operational. However, there are no plans to fully abandon port facilities in the city, as river trade remains important to the local economy. Sizeable investments in facilities have occurred in recent years, for example at the Myanmar Industrial Port in Ahlone Township. There are large port areas further up the Yangon River. Roaring truck traffic along Strand Road is visible proof of this: in order to ease access to the port, it is now partly a toll road.

The modernisation of Yangon's port facilities and the construction of the Thilawa

One rare access point to the river is the jetty at the bottom of Pansodan Street, where Dala-bound ferries dock

SEZ could provide a unique chance to dispense with some of the industrial facilities closer to the city's historic centre, primarily between the Wadan Jetty in the west (close to the **Transit Shed No. 1** 064 C) and **Botataung Pagoda** 001 B in the east.

However there are competing visions and sources of power to reckon with: in December 2013 it emerged that the plans of the municipal authority, the Yangon City Development Committee (YCDC), clashed with those of the Myanmar Port Authority (MPA) which administers much of the waterfront. Its manager told *The Myanmar Times* that they planned to build a "20-floor office block, a 16-storey hotel, a four-storey shopping mall and a three-storey cruise and ferry terminal" as well as "four floating hotels". By contrast, the YCDC is keen to redevelop the waterfront to include green, public park areas.

At the moment, access to the water is limited to the ferry jetties. In the absence of a bridge crossing to Dala on the opposite banks, Yangon will continue to rely on ferries bringing passengers—many of them commuters—between the two shores. Those jetties, primarily Wadan, Nan Thida, Pansodan and Botataung, are lively public spaces. Low-key football games and conversations peter out as the sun sets.

Yangon will gain from turning more areas into public spaces, especially on the waterfront. As the downtown area is by and large built-up, part of this land could be converted into a park—as the Yangon Heritage Trust suggests. The stretch of historic buildings in this part of the city also offers the chance to create a recognisable skyline if the view becomes unobstructed. Finally, old port infrastructure could be converted and adapted for new uses, such as mixed-use commercial, residential and public open space. The old Sule Pagoda wharfs, in particular, would lend themselves to that purpose.

However, the opening of the waterfront also depends on the role of Strand Road in Yangon's future transport grid. YCDC plans, mentioned in this book's section on urban planning on page 206, foresee a flyover serving as the southern perimeter

The iconic red brick warehouses of Sule Wharf, built by Robinson & Mundy in the early 20th century

River taxis at Botataung jetty during rush hour

of Yangon's central ring road. It is hard to argue with the YCDC rationale: Strand Road is already gridlocked at rush hour. However the YHT and other conservation-minded organisations object to these plans, preferring a less car-heavy model. Encouragingly, a tram service, which first operated between 1884 and the Second World War, resumed along Strand Road in 2014, pointing to the potential for public transportation. An alternative to a flyover would be a tunnel along the street. However, Yangon's marshy foundation would present a hugely expensive engineering challenge for a project of that scale.

The highly anticipated new zoning regulations for the downtown area will have consequences for the waterfront, too. In all likelihood, these will restrict the permissible building height and ensure that the **Shwedagon Pagoda** 075 E continues to tower visibly over the city.

To imagine its future waterfront, there are many case studies Yangon can draw upon. In the late 20th and early 21st centuries, many cities have made it a priority to reintegrate their waterfronts into daily civic life. They have come to recognise the waterfront as a significant asset of their particular urban geographies. The redevelopment of Hamburg's *HafenCity*, Buenos Aires' Puerto Madero or London's Docklands may be of limited use, due to their profound social and economic differences to Yangon—and yet they do sound some warning bells, too:

all three cases have led to unbridled gentrification, where private property developers were given free rein to devise lucrative building complexes, sometimes at the expense of the public good. And while these projects contain large, publicly accessible parks, their proximity to affluent residential zones, high-end hotels and grade-A offices have made them less popular with the cities' poorer populations.

Lastly, plans for the flyover could also heed lessons from elsewhere: in the US, Robert Moses' New York City highways over the Hudson and the East River sides of Manhattan are a solemn reminder of the long-term effects of master planning. To this day, large swathes of Manhattan's waterfront remain inaccessible. Elsewhere, and equally controversially, the highways brutally cut through some of New York City's poorest neighbourhoods, which further worsened living conditions for the largely African–American residents there. And San Francisco's demolished Embarcadero Skyway reminds us that transportation infrastructure does not need to be permanent. The question is: how long will Yangon's residents have to wait before they can make the most of their waterfront, and at what expense?

Further reading:

"Studio Yangon" project description, Hong Kong University, 2014. Available at studioyangon.wordpress.com

Botataung jetty

Kyauktada

Innwa Bank 045 B

Strand Hotel 036 B

Botataung Pagoda 001 B

British Embassy 038 B

Myanma Foreign Trade Bank 046 B

General Post Office 040 B

Armenian Apostolic Church
of St John the Baptist 041 B

Strand Mansion 039 B

Bureau of Special
Investigations 037 B

Sofaer's Building 022 B

Internal Revenue Department 023 B

Embassy of India 044 B

Inland Waterways Department 025 B

Myanma Agricultural Development Bank 026 B

B Myanmar National Airlines

027 B Myanma Economic Bank Branch 2

034 B Myanma Port Authority

028 B Yangon Divisional Court

033 B Custom House   032 B Yangon Division Office Complex

030 B Yangon Stock Exchange

029 B Balthazar's Building

047 B Former US Embassy

Aerial view of Kyauktada township as seen from Centrepoint Towers, southeastern direction

022 B Sofaer's Building

025 B Inland Waterways Department

026 B Myanma Agricultural Development Bank

023 B Internal Revenue Departmen

044 B Embassy of India

034 B Myanma Po Authority

Aerial view of Kyauktada township as seen from Centrepoint Towers, southern direction

021 B High Court   City Hall 018 B

046 B Myanma Foreign Trade Bank

Department of Pensions 028 B

THEIN GROUP

059 C Bogyoke Aung San Market

Central Fire Station **014** B

Aung San Stadium **087**

075 E Shwedagon Pagoda

Sule Shangri-La **009** B

Sakura Tower **010** B

058 C FMI Centre

Shae Saung Cinema **013** B

Sunni Jamah Bengali Mosque **015** B

086 B Central Railway Station

016 B Sule Pagoda

089 D Karaweik Palace

018 B City Hall

2

Aerial view of Kyauktada township as seen from Centrepoint Towers, northern direction

Section 1: Along Sule Pagoda Road

Sule Shangri-La and Sakura Tower as seen from the pedestrian overpass across Sule Pagoda Road, at the corner of Anawratha Road

Sule Shangri-La (Traders Hotel)

009 B

223 Sule Pagoda Road
*RSP Architects and Planners Co.
Ltd. and Kanko Kikaku Sekkeisha*
1996

To many Yangon residents this hotel will remain the Traders for some time, although the new name is slowly taking hold. (If cab drivers don't recognise one name, try the other.) Japanese firm KKS drew the designs together with Singapore-based RSP. RSP stands for none other than Raglan Squire & Partners. The British architect left his mark on Yangon in the 1950s and set up an office in Singapore thereafter. (See the **Technical High School** 090 D and the **University of Medicine-1** 099 F for his two works.) One wonders what Mr Squire would think of the Traders: a nondescript tower block with many lookalikes across Asia. Thankfully, its slender width reduces the building's visual impact on the skyline when seen from the south. The large, round tower on the corner of Bogyoke Road only serves a decorative purpose. The Traders' four-storey base is almost windowless, making the building somewhat ominous from up close. The hotel has almost 500 rooms and a large selection of meeting and function rooms. These are named after the country's former kingdoms. The Traders was part of the junta's plan to transform the country into a tourist destination. As the international community began to boycott Myanmar, however, the Traders was very quiet indeed. The fallout of the Asian financial crisis in 1997 also took its toll. Rooms sold at a fraction of today's soaring rates and, ironically, UN agencies and NGOs were able to set up offices there as a consequence. Guests getting off on the wrong floor would find armed soldiers in blue berets. (The sight of busy humanitarian aid offices with thick carpet and en-suite bathrooms was also unusual.) The hotel stands on what was once "Cinema Row". Two theatres from the colonial days, the Palladium and the Globe, were torn down to make way for the building. (Cinema enthusiasts should stroll one minute away to admire the still-standing **Waziya Cinema** 011 B from that period.)

An Armenian cemetery also stood nearby. It was moved to make way for a park, which is now the construction site for Sule Square, a planned 20-storey office complex. The tower will mimic its neighbour with a base similar in height. It will house retail space and overground car parking. One can only hope that this project will provide an occasion to improve pedestrian accessibility of the pavement on Sule Pagoda Road. The Traders was a joint venture between Kuok Singapore Limited and the notorious Lo Hsing Han, a man widely accused in the West of masterminding Burma's opium trafficking networks. He passed away in 2013. His son Steven Law leads their conglomerate which includes hotels, supermarkets, sea ports and Mandalay Beer. The Traders lobby is the most common professional meeting place in the city, especially for expats. Business people, UN officials and journalists eye each other knowingly as they slalom past tourists in the large atrium. In October 2013 a bomb exploded on the ninth floor, in the lead-up to Myanmar hosting its first Southeast Asian Games (often referred to as the SEA Games) in 44 years. The attack injured an American tourist. Several more bombs detonated throughout the country. One month later, authorities arrested three men from Rakhine State. Their reported aim was to target mosques and Western venues.

Sakura Tower

339 Bogyoke Road
Nihon Sekkei, Inc.
1999

`010` B

The Sakura Tower is almost exclusively a Japanese affair, starting with the name. Financed by a Japanese investor, it was designed by Nihon Sekkei and built by Konoike, both Japanese firms. Mitsubishi and Hitachi elevators transport people up and down the 20 floors, and a large and lit Hitachi logo adorns the building's slanted roof structure. In a nod to Japanese expertise, the tower is also earthquake-resistant. Its East Asian pagoda-like roof and recessed top floor are iconic in Yangon's skyline. Built a few years after the **Sule Shangri-La** 009 B across the street, and like most 1990s real estate developments in Yangon, the Sakura Tower battled with high vacancy rates in its early years. In fact low demand for its office space meant the Sakura Tower had to mothball some of the upper floors. Quite the opposite is true today. The building is totally full and one of the few office spaces in Yangon up to international standards. (It has 24-hour generator electricity backup, no small luxury in a blackout-prone city.) Tenants include the Japanese aid agency, JICA, as well as Japanese companies such as Itochu Corporation, Mitsubishi Corporation and Sompo Japan Insurance. A restaurant on the 20th floor offers a breathtaking perspective of the city. This valuable space could do with renovation, though. The slightly kitsch interior is one thing. It would also gain from adding an open-air balcony where customers could fully absorb the exceptional view. As mentioned elsewhere in this guide, this stretch of Bogyoke Road was once colonial Rangoon's entertainment centre, "Cinema Row", lined with many movie houses. The Sakura Tower replaced the Ritz cinema, also known as the Majestic. The only surviving cinema from the colonial period is the next-door **Waziya** 011 B on Bogyoke Road. The area hosts several more recent movie theatres, including the **Nay Pyi Taw** and **Shae Saung cinemas** 013 B down the street, on Sule Pagoda Road.

Waziya Cinema
(New Excelsior Theatre)

011 B

327/329 Bogyoke Road
Unknown
1920s

2

The Waziya Cinema (or the Excelsior, as it was known) is the last remnant of what was once "Cinema Row", an iconic strip of movie theatres opposite the **Central Railway Station** 086 B. Thankfully, it is also the oldest and finest example of that period. A minute's walk from the **Sule Shangri-La** 009 B, right past the **Sakura Tower** 010 B, you won't miss this majestic, cream-coloured building built deep into 33rd and 34th Streets. Traffic permitting, you may want to cross the street to admire it properly. Between its imposing white and gilded Ionic columns hang movie posters for the latest Burmese films. The large space beneath the portico (itself a later addition to the building) always teems with hawkers, betel nut stalls and customers awaiting the next screening. Along the roof of the portico—doubling up as a terrace on the first floor—a second row of columns flanks three open-air arcades. This leads to a holding area outside the main hall, lined with tired-looking leather folding seats. The ground floor lobby features original, if worn, teak panelling and the doors to the screening room are the grandest you are ever likely to find in any cinema. The Excelsior was nationalised and became the Waziya in 1964. Built as a live theatre, the government returned it to its original use in 1985. In 1999 it became a cinema again. The Ministry of Information leased it to the Myanmar Motion Picture Organization (MMPO). Owing to its location and beauty, a restoration proposal by the Yangon Heritage Trust and the MMPO may offer the Waziya yet another lease of life. They aim to convert it into a thriving entertainment and cultural centre, complete with state-of-the-art digital AV equipment. Until then, you can still enjoy the whirring sounds of the old projector spinning its way through reels and reels of Burmese movies—as it did once with those of Alfred Hitchcock, Elvis Presley and Marlon Brando.

The Bible Society of Myanmar 012 B
(British and Foreign
Bible Society)
262 Sule Pagoda Road
Robinson & Mundy
1910

This red brick building became the heart of Christian evangelical efforts in the early 20th century. Being four storeys in height, it reveals the average scale of buildings in the city at the time—and until recently. Although the adjacent Sakura Tower dwarfs it today, the building still stands out thanks to its good condition and simple, graceful form. Robinson & Mundy were the architects and contractors in charge. Their imprint on Yangon is considerable: they also built the **British Embassy** 038 B, the former **Myanma Oil and Gas Enterprise Building** 049 B and **Ayeyarwady Bank** 019 B, as well as the large functional transit sheds at Sule Pagoda Wharf. The latter still dominate the view from the riverside. After Ne Win took power in 1962, foreign missionaries were expelled from the country. In 1964, the Bible Society was reorganised under national leadership. Today it still oversees the dissemination and translation of Christian holy texts into the country's myriad ethnic languages. Today the Bible (or portions thereof) exists in 71 of Myanmar's languages. It all began with an American Protestant missionary named Adoniram Judson. He translated the entire Bible into Burmese and published it in 1835. By that time he had spent more than two decades in the country and mastered the language so well that his translation remains the most popular to this day. When he arrived there were no Protestants in the country; it was several years before he was able to perform his first baptism in 1819. Yet upon his death in 1850 there were as many as 8,000 faithfuls and about 100 Protestant churches around the country. Today about 4 per cent of Myanmar's population is Christian, and three quarters of those Protestant. Most of them belong to the country's ethnic minorities such as the Chin, Kachin, Karen and Lisu.

Nay Pyi Taw Theatre
242/248 Sule Pagoda Road
Unknown
1960/61

 013 B

**Shae Saung Cinema
(Lighthouse Cinema)**
198/200 Sule Pagoda Road
Unknown
Unknown

One long-time Yangon resident consulted for this book dates the Nay Pyi Taw Theatre's construction to 1960 or 1961. After 1962, the cinema was leased to the Chinese Embassy and you could only watch Chinese films there for a time. The Shae Saung, a few doors down the street, seems to be roughly from the same period. The cinemas' patterned façades evoke late 1950s and early 1960s design, which you also find in Thai and Cambodian cinemas from that era. These were usually private ventures by local businessmen riding a climate of post-independence optimism. In that sense, the architecture is clearly forward-looking and, you might say, self-consciously post-colonial. (On the other hand the entrance marquees—a 1930s invention in the West—give the entrances a certain vintage feel.) In this movie-mad city, these are popular stomping grounds for Yangon's young and not-so-young. On any given week, the Nay Pyi Taw and Shae Saung will show the latest Hollywood and local productions. Some Bollywood films are shown here too.

Tourists wanting a piece of the action should get there early. As the captivating Southeast Asia Movie Theatre Project describes on its website, upon visiting in 2010:

"[The films here] drew sell-out crowds. Fast-talking ticket scalpers did their dealings just off theatre grounds, selling tickets at inflated prices to those arriving minutes before show time. The mood was electric as hordes of revellers massed at the gates. The chatter, the excitement, the anticipation of escape into a temporary realm of the artificial was unrivalled."

Both cinemas, like others on this stretch, are owned by the Mingalar Group. The Shae Saung (meaning "Pioneer", and formerly known as the Lighthouse Cinema) has a capacity of 800. The Nay Pyi Taw holds 400. These are modern alternatives to the charmingly neoclassical **Waziya Cinema 011 B** around the corner.

Central Fire Station

014 B

137-139 Sule Pagoda Road
*United Engineers Ltd.
(contractors)*
1912

Fires were a constant threat throughout the colonial period. While its surviving architectural legacy may suggest otherwise, timber was in fact the dominant building material. Rangoon's Municipal Committee established a permanent fire brigade in 1883 and motor fire engines were introduced in 1909. The Central Fire Station on Sule Pagoda Road—still in use today—was built just three years later. Its recognisable octagonal watchtower allowed for panoramic views of the (then relatively low-rise) city. It is set back from the main Sule Pagoda Road on a parallel section of the street. The fire engines park in four bays and have direct access to the thoroughfare. In front of the building is a small stand with a bell struck every half hour. It serves as a clock to those without a watch and still symbolises the fire brigade's watchful eye over the city. The two-storey building was one of the first iron-frame buildings in colonial Rangoon. It was designed by United Engineers Limited, a company formed by British pioneers Richard Riley and William Hargreaves. The men had business interests across Britain's colonial possessions in Asia. The company would later become a major Singaporean contractor and remains in the business today. The glass-fronted building to the right of the fire station used to be the "Diplomatic Stores", run by the Hotel and Tourism Corporation in the days of Socialist rule. In good socialist fashion, the diplomatic corps could exclusively purchase international luxury goods here in exchange for hard currency, preferably US dollars.

Sunni Jamah Bengali Mosque 015 B

93 Sule Pagoda Road
Unknown
19th century

Given its central location, this mosque is one of Yangon's largest and most popular. Built in the 19th century, some believe it was founded by immigrants from East Bengal, today's Bangladesh. Another source states that Bengalis from Calcutta built it and that it was later taken over by the faithful from Chittagong in today's Bangladesh. The same source holds that this mosque was built as early as 1862. If true, this would refer to an earlier wooden structure, with the masonry building coming later. Today, the mosque's façade is covered with colourful tiles. The minarets overlook the central roundabout next to the **Sule Pagoda** 016 B. (Many of

Yangon's mosques are in good condition. As active places of worship, they are often repainted and refurbished.) An adjacent madrasa offers courses in religion, Arabic and other languages. The street in front of the mosque was the site of a rare protest in 2012. About 50 Muslim demonstrators convened here, calling attention to the murder of 10 passengers aboard a bus in Rakhine State. Inter-communal violence between Buddhists and Muslims has flared across the country sporadically. This was especially the case in 2013. Thanks in part to former student leader Mya Aye, a Muslim, the situation in front of the Bengali mosque remained under control. In spite of deadly unrest in other parts of the country, harmonious interreligious relations have always been one of Yangon's defining—and inspiring—features.

The Sule Pagoda grounds

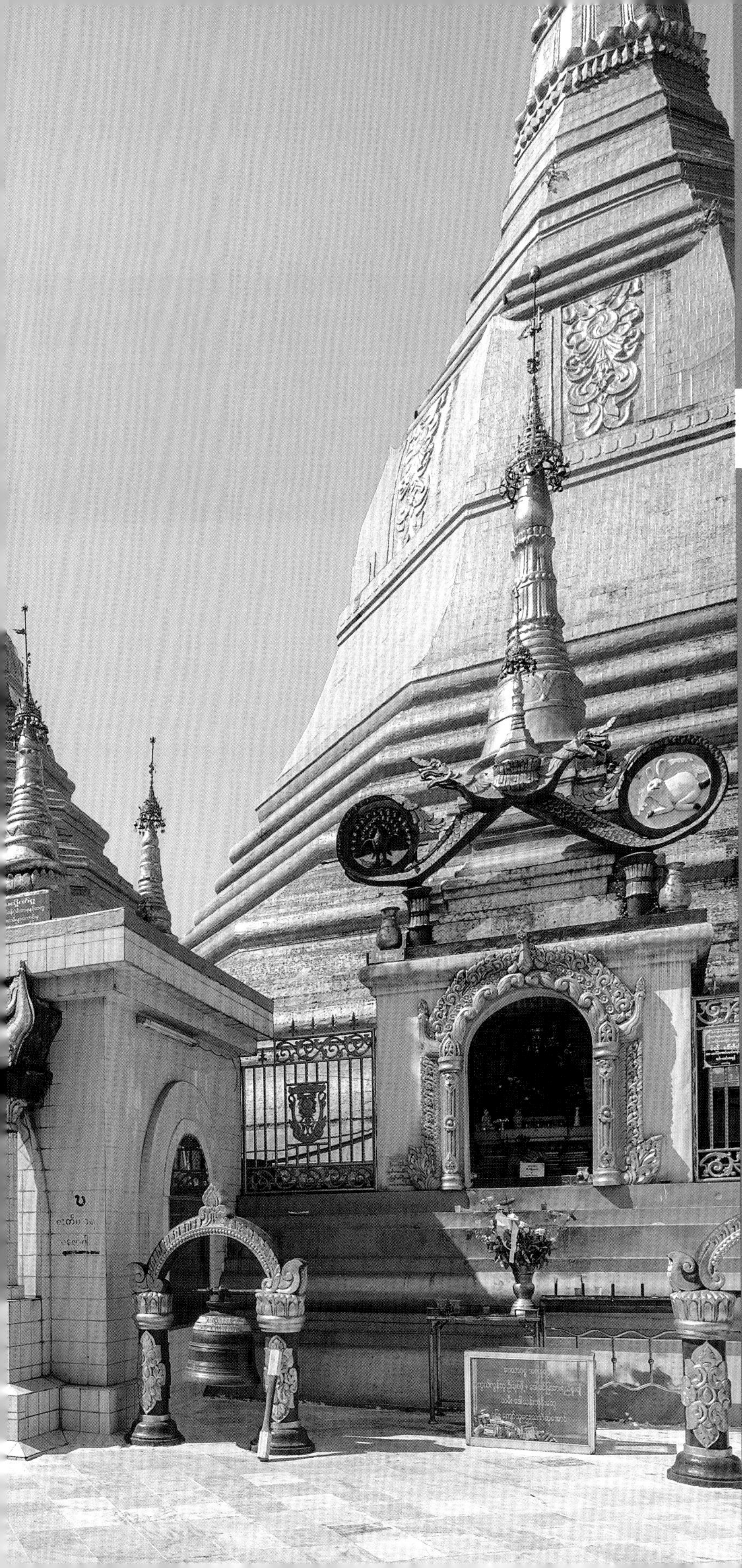

Sule Pagoda

Sule Pagoda Road/
Mahabandoola Road
Unknown
5th century BC

`016 B`

After the Second Anglo–Burmese War in 1852, the British set out to develop Rangoon's port. Lieutenant Fraser of the Bengal Engineers picked the Sule Pagoda to be the heart of the town's new street grid. (Fraser also lent his name to nearby Fraser Street, now Anawratha Road.) At that time, the Sule Pagoda stood on an island on the swampy banks of Yangon River, connected to the town by a small wooden bridge. The British drained the shores to establish downtown Yangon as we know it. This puts into perspective the vast challenge posed by some of Yangon's large colonial constructions. (See for example the **Central Telegraph Office** 020 B, the **High Court** 021 B or **St Mary's Cathedral** 008 B for other mighty swamp-related challenges.) According to Buddhist adage, the Sule Pagoda's construction dates back to the 5th century BC. However, its stupa is typical of Mon pagoda designs. The Mon spread Theravada Buddhism throughout Southeast Asia and were once among the dominant people in the region—naturally, a source of Mon pride to this day. (Now the Mon occupy Myanmar's Mon State, whose capital is Mawlamyine, on the country's southeastern border with Thailand. Like other ethnic armed groups

inside the country, the Mon National Liberation Army still skirmishes with the Myanmar military on occasion, although a draft nationwide ceasefire was signed in April 2015.) The Sule Pagoda's Mon name is *Kyaik Athok Ceti* meaning "stupa where a sacred hair is enshrined". It is said to be older than the **Shwedagon Pagoda** 075 E. According to legend, it also contains hairs given by the Buddha to merchants Tapussa and Bhallika. King Okkalapa—who, according to the same tale, built the Shwedagon Pagoda to host other strands of those same sacred hairs—ordered the construction of the pagoda in the same place where three previous Buddhas' relics already lay.

The octagonal stupa has not changed since those ancient times. But today, a ring of modern construction surrounds it. And far from being an oasis of calm, the place is a scramble of shoulders and elbows, chanting and conversation. Meanwhile, Yangon's increasingly dense traffic grinds its way along the roundabout at its feet. The Sule Pagoda was a frequent and practical rallying space for the country's uprisings. Major rallies took place there in 1988. It was even more central to the 2007 Saffron Revolution. Up to 50,000 protesters and thousands of robed monks took to the streets in defiance of the regime. Some of the photos in this section were taken from the pedestrian bridge at the intersection of Sule Pagoda Road and Anawratha Road. These bridges materialised as part of SLORC plans to redesign the city after the 1988 uprisings. (See page 332 for more details on this topic.) The regime thought soldiers could use them to fire down at protesters during future demonstrations. In an ironic twist, some of the Saffron Revolution's most powerful images were taken from this bridge, which offers an unrivalled view of the Sule Pagoda. A Burmese journalist was on the bridge when he captured footage of a soldier killing Japanese journalist Kenji Nagai. Those images attracted international consternation. Hundreds more died from brutal military repression in these incidents. The Sule Pagoda was not always the heart of a city. For much of its existence, it lay on the shores of a quiet town surrounded by swamp water, not honking and screeching cars. The hallowed stupa has never budged of course, and invites us to reflect on the staggering change that led Yangon to what it is today.

Former Ministry of Hotels and Tourism (Fytche Square Building)

017 B

77-91 Sule Pagoda Road
Thomas Swales
1905

This three-storeyed building is 90 metres wide and displays an impressive, ornate neoclassical façade. It was commissioned by an Indian merchant and later leased to a wealthy Burmese businessman, U Ba Nyunt. He turned it into the first Burmese-run department store, *Myanmar Aswe* (roughly translating as "Burmese Favourite"). With its prime location on the Sule Pagoda roundabout, this building should have pride of place in the area's conservation efforts—especially with the next-door Asia Green Development Bank and **Centrepoint Towers** 048 B impinging on the cityscape. The building's historical significance is hard to overestimate.

Not only was it the first Burmese department store; it also housed the office of the newly established *Dagon* magazine, a springboard for many famous Burmese writers. The office of one of the first Burmese film studios, the "A1 Film Company", was also here. The company closed down in 1983. (Unfortunately many of its historical documentaries, filmed in the wake of Burmese independence, perished in a fire in 1950.) The building was taken over by the government in the 1970s, which coordinated foreign tourism here until the transfer to Naypyidaw in 2005. The building is now almost completely abandoned. It is missing many windows and some of its doors are shuttered. There was speculation about the building's future use, from boutique hotel to office space. You will notice emergency repairs, including new roofing and damp protection that took place following the devastating impact of Cyclone Nargis in 2008.

City Hall

Mahabandoola Road
U Tin, LA McClumpha and AG Bray
(architects), Clark & Greig and
AC Martin & Co. (contractors)
1925–1940

018 B

2

The architecture of Yangon's City Hall tells a tale of rising nationalism in the dying decades of colonial rule. It was built over a drawn-out, fifteen-year period during which the world was changing profoundly. At first this massive complex was not intended to be constructed in its present form, with its overt Burmese features. As Sarah Rooney recounts in *30 Heritage Buildings of Yangon*, initial plans for a new city hall emerged in 1913. Architect LA McClumpha won the tender. British administrators saw in his designs the promise of "the finest group of architectural buildings in Burma". But the First World War broke out, funds froze and construction stopped. When it resumed

in 1925, Burmese nationalists started a debate in the Legislative Council. They demanded Burmese forms inspired by temple architecture from the ancient capital, Bagan. Their campaign overcame Western reluctance. Burmese architect U Tin was invited to revise the designs. But how much leeway was U Tin given? It is easy to imagine the original design without his additions, such as the peacocks, *pyatthat* roofs and purple *nagas* (dragons) on either side of the entrance. The loggia and arcade illustrate the building's competing visions. On the one hand, the lotus flower motif lining the fourth-floor loggia is in keeping with Buddhist heritage. On the other, the design of the three-storey arcade echoes the colonial architecture of Bombay. The building used to be painted a cream colour. Before that it was a striking green, at least for a time. In 2011, it was repainted a shade of "luminous lilac", as Sarah Rooney vividly describes it. A straw poll suggests the

new colours are not to everyone's taste—especially the bright purple *nagas*! Finishing touches aside, this vast edifice is a product of European engineering. Clark & Greig built some parts. (The city also owes them the **Central Telegraph Office** 020 B.) Other parts were built by AC Martin & Co. (who were also responsible for laying the city's asphalt roads and constructing the **General Post Office** 040 B). Architect AG Bray (who also designed the **Irrawaddy Flotilla Company building** 025 B) oversaw the process. Today the building still houses the city authority, the Yangon City Development Committee (YCDC). Its mandate stems from colonial legislation and the 1922 Rangoon Municipal Act; however, the YCDC itself was created by the SLORC government in 1990. The YCDC is independent from the government and raises its own revenue, but the government appoints the chairman/mayor. The current mayor, U Hla Myint, took office in 2011 and is a former brigadier general. He was previously ambassador to Brazil, Argentina and Japan. In December 2014 Yangon held its first municipal council elections, but these were marred by low turnout and a controversial "one vote per household" rule. The YCDC plays an important role in urban conservation efforts. In the 1990s, the SLORC government allowed the razing of several heritage buildings. Following popular outcry, the YCDC drew up a Heritage List in 1996. The list, which contains 189 buildings, was the first of its kind for the city. Although the Yangon Heritage Trust (YHT) deems it incomplete, it remains an important benchmark. The YCDC and other partners (including the YHT and the Japan International Cooperation Agency, JICA) are developing new zoning and planning regulations. For more information about this, please see the chapter on urban planning on page 206.

2

Ayeyarwady Bank (Rowe & Co.) 019 B
416 Mahabandoola Garden Street
Charles F. Stevens (architect),
Robinson & Mundy (contractors)
1908–1910

This building on Mahabandoola Garden Street was once the Rowe & Co. department store, known as the "Harrods of the East". It stands in one of Yangon's most touristic areas, right by **City Hall** 018 B. With City Hall set back from the street, the old Rowe & Co. building stands out by contrast. The building was state-of-the-art: below the three storeys was a large basement, unusual for swampy Yangon. A steel frame, electric lifts and ceiling fans were some of its prized innovations, courtesy of local contractors Robinson & Mundy. Their other commissions include the **British Embassy** 038 B, the former **Myanma Oil and Gas Enterprise Building** 049 B and the **British and Foreign**

Bible Society 012 B. The striking tower on the street corner is one of Yangon's iconic landmarks. Established in 1866, Rowe & Co. was famous for its quarterly illustrated catalogues. A big Christmas tree was put up in December, brought down to Rangoon from the pine forests near Maymyo, today's Pyin Oo Lwin. The store was where high society came to do its shopping. Rowe & Co. branches could be found in Mandalay, Moulmein (today's Mawlamyine) and Bassein (Pathein). After independence, it became a government building, housing the Department of Immigration and Manpower. After the government moved to Naypyidaw, it stood idle for some time before local business magnate Zaw Zaw bought it. His initial plans to turn this property into a luxury hotel got shelved. Instead, his Ayeyarwady (AYA) Bank became the main tenant of this building. Its façade was beautifully restored recently.

Section 2: Along Pansodan Street

View from Pansodan Jetty towards Pansodan Street, looking north

Myanma Post and Telecommunications (Central Telegraph Office)

020 B

125–133 Pansodan Street
John Begg (architect),
Clark & Greig (contractors)
1913–1917

This large and stately building is John Begg's third and last contribution to Yangon's cityscape. It stands beside the **High Court** 021 B, designed by James Ransome, who preceded Begg as Consulting Architect to the Government of India. As Sarah Rooney describes in *30 Heritage Buildings of Yangon*, building the Telegraph Office on waterlogged grounds was a struggle. For the foundation to carry the weight of this four-storey building, wooden piles were sunk across the swampy area. They were then filled with sand, followed by a six-centimetre layer of cement. Today only a smaller portion of the Telegraph Office is accessible to the public on Mahabandoola Road. The rest of the building serves administrative functions. A huge antenna tower marks out the building from many parts of the city. Some of the windows are partially obscured by sunshades made of corrugated iron. In their elegant dark green they—surprisingly— don't really jar with the façade. Book vendors, food stalls and grocers line most of the perimeter. Burma's many rivers and creeks added to the expense of building a reliable telegraph network. (The problem

repeats itself today as newly licensed mobile operators try to build infrastructure across the country. They sometimes use water buffalos to carry telephone relays across rivers.) High masts and cables were needed to overcome these natural barriers. But this did not stop the medium's development. By the late 1930s, there were 656 telegraph offices connected by more than 50,000 kilometres of wire. They covered the entire country, which in turn connected Burma with the world. The fate of the medium is sealed, though. The world's largest remaining telegraphy service, in India, closed in 2013. Meanwhile the building still has counters for sending telegrams, emails and "e-telegrams", a Myanmar-only technology. Myanmar is one of the least connected countries in the world in terms of mobile telephony—but it is catching up. In 2013, Norwegian company Telenor and the Qatari firm Ooredoo won the tender for a new mobile phone and internet network. In exchange, they committed to investing several billion dollars in infrastructure. This will include thousands of transmission towers, often in remote areas without regular electricity supply. Mobile phones and SIM cards, which were so rare they sold for hundreds of US dollars as late as 2012, are now as cheap as in any country—and sold everywhere in Myanmar. In Yangon the service seems to be improving, but slow data downloads remain a common complaint.

2

Mahandoola Garden, with Independence Monument and High Court

2

High Court

021 B

89–124 Pansodan Street
James Ransome (architect),
Bagchi & Co. (contractors)
1905–1911

The High Court is one of Yangon's most iconic colonial buildings. Pictured overleaf with the Independence Monument, it is an inescapable sight as you stroll downtown (or rather, weave through the fumes and traffic). Its architect, James Ransome (1865–1944), was John Begg's predecessor as Consulting Architect to the Government of India. When John Begg took over the position, Ransome's High Court was almost complete. Begg judged the construction "somewhat over-designed". Certainly the building displays a generous dose of pomp. The impression is similar to the one conveyed by Jan Morris about the British colonial High Courts of India: she describes them as "very conscious of their own importance, and into them the architects tried to build the loftiest meanings of empire". The towers and loggia windows feature elaborate brick patterns. The cream-painted arches, rows of balconies and stuccowork echo Renaissance architecture. (But this building is distinctive in its use of pale burgundy bricks, manufactured locally by the construction company Bagchi & Co.) Ransome didn't spare any bombastic detail or British imperial cliché.

On the roof of each wing, a lion faces its opposite number. The tall portico leads into a vast inner courtyard. Loggias run along both the inside and outside of the building. The engineers spared no effort either. This was one of the first buildings in Yangon to have toilet and plumbing facilities as well as electricity. Like many other buildings throughout Rangoon, the construction had to accommodate swampy soils. Sarah Rooney explains: "The clock tower was a risky endeavour and required extensive foundations made of *thitya*, a hardwood that is especially durable in damp conditions."

Prime Minister U Nu's post-independence government maintained—and improved—the British legal system. But Ne Win's coup in 1962 changed everything. The Chief Justice of the Supreme Court was one of several people who were immediately arrested when Ne Win's units rolled into the city. His regime did away with the Supreme Court and replaced it with a socialist variant, the Council of People's Justices. General Ne Win controlled the appointments. The 2008 Constitution states that judges should be appointed on merit. In practice, the president and the speakers of both chambers submit the names to parliament for a vote. Myanmar's Supreme Court moved to the new capital, Naypyidaw, in 2005 and this grandiose building is now a local court. It is only partly occupied.

2

Sofaer's Building

62 Pansodan Street
Thomas Swales and Isaac Sofaer
1906

022 B

Few buildings evoke old Rangoon quite like Sofaer's Building. This imposing edifice is in a fairly decrepit state today but still—despite the years, weeds and grime—retains the grandeur of its young glory days. The four-storey structure occupies the whole width of the block between Pansodan and 37th Street; it concludes the rich stretch of colonial-era architecture on Lower Pansodan Street. Its cream yellow façade features rich ornamentations. These are deteriorating and covered in soot. Its striking dome towers over Pansodan Street. You will also notice a veranda adjoining the top-floor flat, added by a lady who has lived inside the dome for the past 40 years. It affords arresting views of **Rander House** 023 B across the street. While the Sofaer's exterior could do with a high-pressure clean and a lick of paint, the extent of the building's structural decay is even more obvious inside. The courtyard is now a light shaft and rubbish dump. The ceiling is moulding in places. But Sofaer's Building is as bustling as it was in its heyday 100 years ago. And it is seeing some partial renovations. On the ground floor along Merchant Road, an elegant Japanese *yakitori* restaurant, Gekkô, has opened its doors. It was designed by SPINE Architects. When Gekkô's owner, Nico Elliott, paid a stately sum upfront

to take possession of the venue, he discovered a 1.5 metre deep pile of sewage. This took one month and plenty of manual labour to remove. Next door is a branch of KBZ Bank, which decided to split the ground floor into two levels—a highly, let's say, unorthodox take on heritage conservation. In fact, during renovation works, KBZ started to remove the original tiles, which were reportedly imported from Manchester. The Lokanat Galleries, which feature regular exhibitions of contemporary art, are on the first floor. The galleries opened in 1971, making them one of the most established non-profit organisations in Myanmar. Lokanat represents 21 artists today. Its motto, "Truth, Beauty, Love", has vaguely Orwellian connotations. A makeshift teahouse occupies the hallway on the second floor. The building also hosts a basic guest house on the second and third floors, as well as a few government offices and residential units. The whole set-up on the upper floors feels pretty informal and the staircases become more and more fragile as you rise through the building. Isaac and Meyer Sofaer were Baghdadi Jews who came to Rangoon as boys. They set up a trading business together in the late 19th century importing alcohol and specialty foods. Their building opened in 1906. Isaac Sofaer, who was also an architect, made the drawings together with Thomas Swales. By then Swales had already left quite an imprint

on Rangoon despite only being in his early thirties. He designed today's **British Embassy** 038 B, the extensions to the former **St Paul's English School** 007 B in Botataung and the former **Fytche Square Building** 017 B. The opening ceremony of Sofaer's Building was a major event that year. The Governor-General of Burma presided over the proceedings and inaugurated the building by opening its doors with a set of golden keys. Sofaer's Building instantly became one of the city's most prestigious commercial addresses. Tenants included the news agency Reuters, Bank of Burma and China Mutual Life Insurance Company. There were also fine liquor and commodity purveyors. The building featured one of the first electric lifts—only the shaft, cluttered with debris, remains today. The original floor tiles remain throughout the building. (They look their best inside Gekkô, where they've received a good scrub.) The steel beams were manufactured in Scotland. Like in nearby **Balthazar's Building** 029 B, the beams were erected and supplied by engineers Howarth Erskine. No definite plans exist for the future of Sofaer's Building—its fate is complicated by the fact that several parties own it, as is the case for other buildings around the city. More commercial redevelopments are under way on the ground floor. A full renovation, sooner rather than later, is what this magnificent building deserves.

Internal Revenue Department 023 B
(Rander House)
55–61 Pansodan Street
Unknown
1932

With its Art Deco touches, Rander House is clearly from a later architectural era than **Sofaer's Building** 022 B across the road. It also feels more compact due to its height (five storeys), massing and more regular window grid. Remnants of a large portico are visible between the ground floor and the second floor, which was demolished after 1988 when SLORC decided to widen Pansodan Street. In fact, this happened to all buildings with porticos along this stretch of the road. SLORC also cut down a row of tall trees that used to line this street. (For more details on the changes post-1988, refer to page 332.) Rander House was commissioned by traders who migrated to Burma from Rander, a city close to Surat in the Indian state of Gujarat. As Indian Muslims flocked to Rangoon in the late 19th and early 20th centuries, they coalesced into associations according to their towns of origin. One of these, for example, was the Rander Sunni Bohras Soorti Mohamedan Association. The Soorti-Rander community also maintained a Randeria High School on Mogul Street, which admitted non-Muslims as well. The **Surti Sunni Jamah Mosque** 053 C was this group's main house of worship. It is believed that by the 1930s, the owners of Rander House took over the adjacent Sofaer's Building. (Sofaer's is sometimes referred to as Randeria House.) Rander House itself became home to the Pakistani Embassy in Rangoon after India's partition and Burmese independence. This building also housed the Rangoon branch of Dawson's Bank. Economist Sean Turnell explained to the authors of this book that Dawson's was "an extraordinarily successful agricultural bank whose methodologies preceded many of those employed by microfinance today". There were plans to return Dawson's Bank to its glory days after the Second World War; however, the U Nu regime's Land Nationalisation Act of 1954 put the model out of business. The bank shrunk to become a "high-end pawn-broking business," in Turnell's words. It closed down after the 1962 coup. The British Council had their Yangon office in the building from 1947 until it withdrew from the country in 1966. (It returned in 1978 as the "Cultural Section of the British Embassy".) Later, the Internal Revenue Department took over the lower floors. Some of the top floors became apartments for senior departmental staff.

Myanma Economic Bank Branch 1 (Cox & Co.)

024 B

43/45 Pansodan Street
Unknown
1921

The building was originally Cox & Co.'s Burma headquarters. Cox was a tradition-rich company with roots stretching back to the 18th century. It offered banking services to British military personnel. Business boomed during the First World War. Its Charing Cross branch in London had to stay open 24 hours a day to cash cheques for officers returning from the front. The company then opened offices in regions where British or colonial troops were stationed. The Rangoon branch opened in 1921. But Cox's wartime profits were hard to maintain in peacetime: by 1923, the company was forced to scale back its operations abroad and sell its "Eastern" branches to Lloyd's Bank. Lloyd's itself was a latecomer to the colonial business, and the acquisition of Cox & Co. represented its first foray into the region. Lloyd's not only took over the banking side of Cox & Co.'s business, but also its travel and shipping agency. This may explain why this building is sometimes still called the "Bibby Line Building". Since 1889, the Bibby Line Company ran a regular steamboat service between Liverpool and Rangoon. It took about one month and cost GBP 50 at the time (about 5,000 in today's money). By the 1920s, several boats were making the profitable journey and several agents sold tickets in Rangoon, including Cox & Co. (and later Lloyd's) and Thomas Cook & Sons, who had their offices on Merchant Road. Despite a sharp fall in the Burma trade following independence, the Bibby Line service continued well into the 1950s. By then, competition from aeroplanes was already stiff. The British Overseas Airways Corporation (one of the two forerunners to modern-day British Airways) was serving Rangoon from London and other destinations within the former Empire. Today, the building's new lick of baby blue and white paint gives it away as one of Myanma Economic Bank's downtown branches. Most branches received a similar facelift in the last couple of years. The windows on the ground floor are covered with wrought-iron bars bearing the initials MEB. The three-storey building is stately but appears less commanding compared to the later and taller additions surrounding it on Pansodan Street. The only non-colonial building in the vicinity is just to the MEB's right—the Myanma Economic Savings Bank Branch 1.

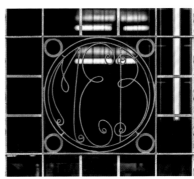

Inland Waterways Department 025 B
(Irrawaddy Flotilla Company)
50 Pansodan Street
AG Bray (architect),
Arthur Flavell & Co. (contractor)
circa 1930

This building stands out from its neighbours due to its recessed façade and twin Doric colonnade. Above the columns are golden clam shells, reflecting the building's maritime connection. All doors and windows on the ground floor are set back too, to protect it from the sun. Like many buildings on the east side of lower Pansodan Street, an enormous entrance canopy stretches across the sidewalk and some of the street. It is suspended by gold-painted rods. Iron elements that can be seen on windows and balconies are painted petrol green. Long-time Yangon resident Harry Hpone Thant told us:

"The pavement in front of the building used to be covered with big black slate tiles. They were slippery when wet, and caused trouble for female office workers when the rain and driving winds made them hold onto their flapping htameins (dresses), the umbrella, their sling bags and their lunch basket all at the same time."

The Inland Water Transport Board building was built for the corporate headquarters of the Irrawaddy Flotilla Company (IFC). The firm's founders, the Henderson brothers from Fife in Scotland, were experienced shippers. They grew their business servicing the "emigrant trade" between Britain and Canada, the United States and New Zealand. On the return journeys from New Zealand, Henderson ships would call at Rangoon, taking on shipments of rice and teak. Before long, they realised the potential of Burma's growing economy and purchased several steamers to profit from the river trade in the 1860s. On the eve of the Second World War, the IFC commanded a fleet of several hundred vessels travelling the country's waterways north to south and vice versa, transporting cargo and passengers. Almost the entire fleet was deliberately destroyed ahead of the Japanese invasion in 1942 to prevent the ships from falling into enemy hands. The Ayeyarwady (today's name for the former Irrawaddy River) flows from the country's north to south. It is navigable all year. Other rivers include the Chindwin (a tributary of the Ayeyarwady) and the Thanlwin. The country also possesses a dense network of canals which, depending on the season, are also navigable. The British connected Rangoon more directly to the Ayeyarwady in the late 19th century by digging the 35-kilometre-long Twante Canal. This infrastructure facilitated the exploitation of Burma's natural resources

and fuelled the colonial project. By 1910 practically all teak and three quarters of rice were shipped by boat. The IFC and the Bombay–Burmah Trading Corporation (both Scottish companies) were instrumental to Britain's northward push. This led to the annexation of Upper Burma in 1885, when the BBTC provided a *casus belli* with King Thibaw over a tax dispute. The IFC readily put its many ships at the disposal of the 20,000 British Indian troops. These took Mandalay with little resistance. Today, almost half of the nation's transported goods still travel on the back of river steamers, some of them several decades old.

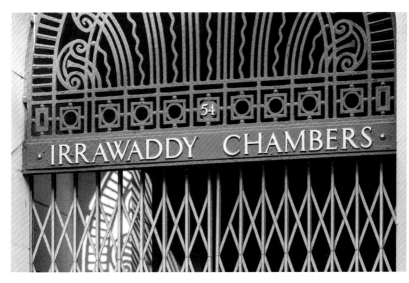

Myanma Agricultural Development Bank (National Bank of India)

026 B

26–42 Pansodan Road
Thomas Oliphant Foster and Basil Ward
Ca. 1930

The National Bank of India (NBI) was one of the main exchange banks of the British Empire. Its Rangoon branch was set up in 1885 and a stately headquarters was erected on Pansodan Street by 1896. In the 1920s, business was booming in this part of the world. The company decided to rebuild its branch from scratch—this time bigger, more opulent—and decidedly more modern. The new building was finished around 1930, designed by Thomas Oliphant Foster and Basil Ward. We cover Foster's legacy in the **Myanma Port Authority** 034 B section. But a few words about Ward are warranted here because his name is practically forgotten in connection with Yangon. Foster was the more experienced member of the short-lived duo but Ward (1902–1976) contributed the flair of a young architect fresh out of school. He leant towards the modern architectural language of continental Europe. A native New Zealander, he studied in Wellington and moved to London upon graduation in 1924. He failed to enrol at the prestigious Royal Institute of British Architects (RIBA) and, after a while, moved to Yangon with his wife. Here Foster and Ward worked on a variety of buildings that are usually exclusively credited to Foster. Apart from the NBI building, these projects include the Myanma Port Authority as well as several buildings for **Yangon University** 101 F. Ward returned to London in 1930, setting up a partnership with his friend from home, noted modernist architect Amyas Connell. They teamed up with London-born Colin Lucas in the mid-1930s to form a short-lived but highly influential partnership. They were among the foremost proponents of pre-war International Style architecture in Britain and designed residential projects in and around London, several of which still stand today. Along with Raglan Squire (see the **Technical High School** 090 D and **University of Medicine-1** 099 F), Basil Ward is one of a small group of architects who used their stints in Rangoon to further their international careers. The National Bank of India building is often known as the Grindlays Bank. What follows is a tale of mergers and acquisitions in high finance, as played out on Pansodan Street in downtown Yangon: Grindlays only entered Burma after it acquired Thomas Cook & Sons in 1942. (Back then, the travel agent also had banking operations—remember travellers' cheques?) Besides Thomas Cook's Rangoon branch on Merchant Road, Grindlays also acquired buildings in major cities in China, India as well as Hong Kong, Ceylon and Singapore. As the

Japanese army had occupied Rangoon, Grindlays had to wait almost four years before it could formally requisition its branch there a few months after the war. Grindlays' owners, National Provincial (later merged into today's NatWest), sold Grindlays to NBI in 1948. Ten years later NBI and Grindlays merged into the new National Overseas & Grindlays Bank. This building was their office. The name change reflected many companies' desire to rid themselves of references to the former Empire. This was, to put it politely, out of fashion in the post-colonial age. After all NBI was no Indian bank and "National and Grindlays", as it became known, sounded more forward-looking. In Yangon popular parlance however, the bank became known simply as "Grindlays Bank". (This revelation concluded the rather arduous task of locating this building for this book's research.) In 1961 National and Grindlays Bank bought Lloyd's Bank, which had a branch just across Pansodan Street, today's **Myanmar Economic Bank Branch 1** 024 B. Eventually, as with all banks in socialist Burma, National and Grindlays underwent its last and final merger, this time a forced one: in 1963 it was nationalised and became the "People's Bank No. 11". From 1970 to 1996, this building housed the National Museum. Its prized exhibit, the Lion Throne of King Thibaw (the last monarch of Burma) stood centre stage beneath a beautiful rotunda with a domed ceiling. Only in 1996 did the entire museum move into its dedicated premises on Pyay Road (now the **National Museum** 067 C). Today parts of the building are occupied by the Myanma Agricultural Development Bank, one of the country's state-owned banks. Perhaps one day, this proud bank building will belong to one of the many offshoots that once owned Grindlays, the National Bank of India or the merged National and Grindlays. Among them are global players such as NatWest, Citibank, Lloyd's and Standard Chartered. In 2000, the latter acquired the bank from none other than the Australia and New Zealand Banking Group (ANZ). It was the only Western bank to receive a coveted licence from Myanmar authorities in 2014. This imposing building, with its strictly geometric façade, is another reason why this stretch of Pansodan Street should be one of Yangon's most treasured and protected thoroughfares. The columns don't follow classical rules: they connect without any capitals. The underside of the protruding roofs is decorated with scales. Lion-headed waterspouts decorate the roofline. The small windows are set back from the columns. They are surrounded by an arched geometric pattern. The large semi-circular entrance canopy cantilevers over the sidewalk and extends onto the street, like most other roofs on this side of Pansodan Street. Remarkably, it also features a mirrored underside. The golden entrance door is worth admiring too. But at the time of writing, entry was not permitted.

Myanma Economic Bank Branch 2 (Chartered Bank of India, Australia and China)
27–41 Pansodan Street
G Douglas Smart (Palmer & Turner)
1939–1941

027 B

This was one of the last edifices built during colonial rule and was originally the headquarters of the Chartered Bank of India, Australia and China, which later became part of Standard Chartered. Its cut-stone tiles used for flooring, steel frame and reinforced concrete made this the most modern building of pre-war Rangoon. Beneath the building is the city's first underground parking garage. G Douglas Smart, who was the Rangoon partner of the regional architectural firm Palmer & Turner, had already designed the nearby **Reserve Bank of India** 030 B. Like other buildings on the west side of lower Pansodan Street, there used to be a portico at the entrance beneath the pagoda-shaped hexagonal tower. All that remains is a cut-back roof over the steps to the entrance, decorated with potted plants. It is painted in baby blue and white, the typical colours of the current

occupant, Myanma Economic Bank (MEB). Long vertical slits in the corner towers contain slim windows. The stylised Greek ornamentation and columns create an Art Deco impression that is rare for Yangon. Try to take a peek behind the main entrance door, where a decorative metal gate references a spider web. The Chartered Bank arrived in Burma around 1860. Founded in London only a few years before by shipping merchants involved in the trade between Britain and its colonies, it focused on foreign exchange transactions and credit. These devices underpinned long-distance trade back then, as they do today. The bank also engaged in direct agricultural financing. While other institutions relied on middlemen like the Chettiar community, Chartered Bank lent against the security of stored commodities such as rice, sesame and groundnuts. This was innovative at the time and remains a key aspect of agricultural reform programmes around the world today. Bank staff held the only keys to the warehouses. They also employed their own security guards. The building was abandoned before Japanese troops entered Rangoon. For a short period it

2

served as the local branch of the Yoko-hama Specie Bank. After independence, Chartered Bank continued to operate in Myanmar. But like most other foreign banks, it scaled back its operations until it was nationalised in 1963. Some of the offices in the building were rented out. For example, the United States Informa-tion Service (USIS) Library occupied the ground floor. Some time after Ne Win's coup, the research department of the Burma Socialist Programme Party (BSPP) took over the premises. During this time, the underground car park was used as a guarded storage for bank notes in transit from the currency presses in Warzi, in

central Myanmar. After the BSPP's dis-bandment in 1988, the building rever-ted back to the Ministry of Finance and Revenue. It later became a branch of the state-owned Myanma Economic Bank. Foreign banks are planning their return to Myanmar. Standard Chartered is thought to be interested in purchasing the historic building. For now though, they have relatively few Yangon-based staff working in nearby **Centrepoint Towers** 048 B. To the surprise of observ-ers, the bank did not apply for a limited banking licence in 2014, casting doubt over its plans for long-term engagement in the country.

Yangon Divisional Court (former Accountant-General's Office)

2

Yangon Divisional Court and Department of Pensions (Accountant-General's Office and Currency Department)

`028` `B`

1 Pansodan Street
AC Martin & Co. (contractors)
1900–1907

This grand, tired and loveable building lies at the southern end of Pansodan Street. It was first the Currency Department and the Accountant-General's Office. In other words, it was the beating heart of the colonial state. While the former oversaw trade customs, the latter handled taxes on production and sales. Together they ensured that the colonial enterprise remained profitable. All revenue collected in Burma belonged to the Government of India and the Secretary of State. But a degree of devolution granted power to provinces in revenue collection and expenditure. To ensure order in these matters, Calcutta (and from 1911 onwards, New Delhi) appointed an Accountant-General. This was a very prestigious position. Some revenues were strategic and thus under colonial control. Salt, customs, railways, postage, telegraphs and opium for example. The colonial policy for opium was particularly interesting. The government permitted opium sales in India, citing strong local demand. They raked in considerable revenues. In Burma however, the government forbade the sale of opium to ethnic Burmese. This echoed a crude racist stereotype that was common in travelogues

and encyclopaedias. Here, Burmese were often portrayed as "weak, child-like, self-indulgent, and peculiarly vulnerable to 'over-doing' opium consumption", as Ashley Wright notes in his study of opium in colonial Burma. Officials were also alarmed by the increase in opium-related crime among young Burmese men. The other function carried out in the building—the Currency Office—provided Burma with both paper and coin currency. As part of British India, Burma used the Indian rupee. Still today, people use the Indian measures *lakh* (100,000) and *crore* (10,000,000) in business transactions. While special Burmese rupee notes were printed here, no coins were minted in Burma. They were brought in from India, England and Australia. The Currency Office became obsolete with the establishment of the Rangoon branch of the **Reserve Bank of India** 030 B in 1937.

The site has not changed much since the Japanese bombings of 1942. Through the trees on Bank Street, it is possible to catch a glimpse of the remains of the wing once attached to the tower. Today this side of the building hosts one-storey shacks with tea and copy shops, as well as legal offices. The original building resumes further along Bank Street, where a third octagonal tower stands. Its adjoining wing is on the corner of Mahabandoola Garden Street. If they are lucky, visitors can peer into the tower on the corner of Strand Road. Inside is a beautifully ornate spiral staircase. (A stunning example of colonial-era architecture interiors, often

hidden from the public and thus overlooked.) Unfortunately the building is in poor condition today. Some of the windows are shuttered with pieces of wood and painted over. Others are just broken. Even the sidewalk is in worse shape here than on the rest of Pansodan Street. The upper levels of the Bank Street tower are almost completely conquered by weeds, but open windows and flying curtains suggest that they are still in use. From a conservation standpoint, however, this building is definitely not beyond repair—just like most other seemingly derelict colonial-era buildings across town. While they suffer from neglect and lack of maintenance, they remain mostly in their original form and are in surprisingly good structural shape. The three original, asymmetric wings of the building were built in stages between 1900 and 1907. The eastern side of the building, on Mahabandoola Garden Street, was first erected in 1900. Further building works took place later in the decade along Pansodan Street. The Currency Department and Accountant-General's Office were built entirely with bricks, causing structural problems. In 1908, a portion of the façade facing Strand Road collapsed. In 1930, a long wall was badly damaged. After independence the building housed a small claims civil court and later a juvenile court. Today, the complex houses the Yangon Divisional Court. The section separated by the Japanese bomb damage—and which is in slightly better shape than the court—is an office of the Department of Pensions.

Balthazar's Building
Bank Street
Unknown
1905

029 B

This faded but beautiful red brick building occupies a stretch of Bank Street that was once downtown Yangon's most desirable address. Its lot is not square: the 34th Street façade is slightly longer than the one on 33rd. A small (and rat-infested) courtyard allows air and light into the inner rooms. Like **Sofaer's Building** 022 B, Balthazar's was once state-of-the-art and featured an electric lift. The building's steel framing was supplied and erected by Howarth Erskine Ltd. The tiles are Italian imports. After decades without maintenance, the inside of the building is in a sorry state: the lift has not worked for decades; the inner courtyard is overgrown with weeds; the staircase is crumbling. Most of the ironwork is rusty. Some offices have attached plates of corrugated iron to their ceilings in order to prevent plaster from falling down. Others have installed plastic sheeting to protect against water leakage. The building's higher floors are partially squatted. Given the short walking distance to the nearby former **New Law Courts Building** 032 B, lawyers' offices have traditionally used Balthazar's Building and several still do so today. There are some tea and copy shops on the ground floor and up the darkened staircase, which curls around the lift shaft. Samuel Balthazar, an Armenian businessman born in Isfahan, Persia (now Iran), arrived in Rangoon in 1866 after making his name in his father's

business. The Burma branch of Balthazar & Son became a reputed import-export, real estate and investment management firm in Rangoon. "Balthazar's Building" was its elegant calling card, a short walk from the port and Sule Pagoda. It also housed the offices of other companies, including the German engineering firm Siemens. The Balthazar family was active in public life. Samuel Balthazar held leadership positions on the Municipal Committee and in the Chamber of Commerce. With his brother, Carapiet, the family donated a statue of Queen Victoria that stood in Fytche Square (now Mahabandoola Square). The statue was removed by the Japanese during the war. The Armenian community was travelling to Burma as early as the 17th century (and like the Balthazars, traces its roots to Persia). In fact the **Armenian Church** 041 B is the oldest Christian church in Rangoon today. Another Armenian family, the Sarkies brothers, built and ran the **Strand Hotel** 036 B. Basil Martin (Martirossian), the last "full" Armenian of Burma, died in 2013. It isn't rare to hear Burmese people claim Armenian lineage. (Mr Martin's brother fled to Dhaka in 1942 following the Japanese invasion. He still takes care of the Armenian Church in the Bangladeshi capital. Similarly, he is often described as the last Armenian of Bangladesh in news reports.)

Yangon Stock Exchange (Reserve Bank of India)

24–26 Sule Pagoda Road
G Douglas Smart (Palmer & Turner)
1937

030 B

An impregnable aura surrounds this heavy cut-stone edifice on the corner of Sule Pagoda Road and Bank Street. Two pairs of Ionic columns dominate the recessed entrance. Imposing iron doors bear the inscriptions "Banking Department" and "Issue Department." Window grilles at the centre further enhance the vault-like impression. Except for two tall patterned windows flanking the entrance, there are no openings on the façade. The Reserve Bank of India (RBI) was founded in 1935 as British India's central bank. The Rangoon branch opened in 1937, the year Burma separated from British India and legally became a dominion of Great Britain. The separation did not lead to the creation of a central bank for Burma; instead, the RBI had to fulfil this function for both countries. The rupee was maintained as Burma's currency, although distinct banknotes were issued for Burma. This parallel system did not operate for very long: the Second World War broke out only a few years later. The RBI's Rangoon branch fell into enemy hands in March 1942, the only one to do so. The bank's staff had time to prepare: all vaults were empty when the Japanese marched into the city. Securities were shipped to Calcutta, coins and notes sent up north (where most were sunk in rivers or burned). After independence, the RBI returned to its former offices. Conditions were tough: the Japanese had used explosives on the vaults and, after their retreat in 1945, lootings occurred. There were no water or electricity supplies. Telephone lines were cut. With independence in 1948, the Union Bank of Burma (UBB) was created and took over the RBI building; however, Burma only achieved monetary independence from Britain in 1952. At that time the post-war currency board, seated in London, was abolished. The UBB then became Burma's central bank, later renamed Central Bank of Myanmar (CBM). In 1993, the private Myawaddy Bank took over the building as the CBM moved to Yankin township. As of late 2014, the building was under renovation. It is slated to host the Yangon Stock Exchange, which is currently being set up—in a twist of history—with Japanese help. This grandiose building is unique in Yangon's cityscape and well placed (in all senses) to serve a financial function in the future. The architects and contractors, Palmer & Turner, later built the **Chartered Bank** 027 B building on Pansodan Street. The Hong Kong-based firm continues to operate in the wider region. Both of these historic Yangon projects feature proudly in their online portfolio.

Myanmar Economic Bank Branch 3 (Bank of Bengal and Imperial Bank of India)

15–19 Sule Pagoda Road
Unknown
1914

2

This building's primary façades were recently repainted in baby blue and white—clearly the colours of choice for MEB's historic branches in Yangon. To some, they accentuate the wedding cake look of this exuberant building. Tall Ionic columns connect the top two floors and an imposing corner tower overlooks Strand Road. There are several pediment designs above the windows—some triangular, others semicircular. The same patterns also feature in the arches at the top. The main arch above the entrance on Sule Pagoda Road is rounded. A corporate insignia probably adorned this space once. There are balustrades at the window balconies and at the edges of the roof. Note the small annex building between the main building and the First Private Bank next door. The Bank of Bengal became the Imperial Bank of India after a merger in 1921. In his fascinating book *Fiery Dragons*, on the history of the Burmese banking sector, Sean Turnell writes that the Imperial Bank was by far the most important in colonial Burma. It took on central bank functions during much of the pre-independence period. For example, it provided the system for clearing cheques. It also offered commercial lending, particularly to the Chettiar community. In turn the Chettiars provided funds to much of Burma's agricultural sector. The bank was renamed the State Bank of India after independence and operated on a much smaller scale after the war. It was nationalised in 1963 and became "People's Bank No. 8". Unlike the parts of Strand Road near the **General Post Office** 040 B or the **Strand Hotel** 036 B, this is a quieter stretch. But the major hotel project at the **Yangon Division Office Complex** 032 B might change the neighbourhood's atmosphere.

Section 3: Along Strand Road

Night-time view along Strand Road, with Strand Hotel, Myanmar National Airlines and Myanma Port Authority

Yangon Division Office Complex (New Law Courts, Police Commissioner's Office) 032 B

Yangon Division Office Complex (New Law Courts, Police Commissioner's Office) 032 B
56–66 Bank Street
Thomas Oliphant Foster (architect), United Engineers Ltd. (contractors)
1927–1931

The photos show this monumental building, which occupies an entire city block, covered in scaffolding in late 2013. After the renovations, pedestrians will once again be able to enjoy the huge arcade covering the pavement along Strand Road. The complex recalls the architecture of Lutyens' Delhi, a part of New Delhi designed by and named after British architect Edwin Lutyens. There is a good reason for this: Thomas Oliphant Foster previously worked in Delhi under Lutyens, whose classicism and monumental tastes inspired many architects. During Foster's time in Delhi, he was also John Begg's assistant. Is it a coincidence that both Begg and Foster moved to Rangoon later? The renovation of the building is due to transform the Yangon Division Office Complex, as it was known until recently, into a 229-room luxury hotel operated by the international Kempinski chain. Initial designs were drawn up by DP Architects, a Singaporean firm. It has since left the project. The plans will no doubt be altered given the involvement of new architects and the passage of time. However, they give us an idea today of how the more ambitious projects involving a heritage building might look. DP foresaw two basement car parks extending away from the building underneath Sule Pagoda Road and Bank Street, to protect the foundation's structural integrity.

On the ground floor, a 1,000-seat ballroom, restaurants, cafes and retail shops would be publicly accessible. The private areas of the hotel, including its reception and lobby, start on the first floor. The proposal also foresaw the installation of glass roofs to cover the two spacious atriums. The fifth and top floors were chosen as the location for the hotel amenities such as its gym, spa and swimming pool. The company behind the project, JL Family Group, won the tender for the site's 60-year lease in 2012 with a bid of 14.4 million US dollars. It also promised to pay 7 per cent of annual hotel revenue as rent. JL operates several hotels in Myanmar and Singapore, but none in the five-star property league. To stem the construction cost, the project will be partly financed by Siam Commercial Bank, a Thai bank. Besides Kempinski, another partner in the project is the Thai furniture manufacturer Kanok. Purcell, a UK- and Hong Kong-based firm of heritage consultants, has been hired to draw up the conservation management plan. Construction is slated to be finished in 2016. The project has attracted major criticism since its announcement in 2012. The Lawyers' Network, a local organisation, says the city would gain from keeping the building as a court. They have fought the project at every opportunity, including through attempted lawsuits. So far the Yangon Region High Court has refused to hear the case. If it does end up becoming a luxury hotel—which seems likely— it would be one with a sinister backstory. The Japanese occupiers used the top floor as torture chambers during the Second World War, as did the military regime in the 1960s and 1970s.

Custom House

132 Strand Road
John Begg
1912–1916

033 B

The Custom House is one of the few colonial buildings still fulfilling its original function. Thanks to continued use in the post-independence era, it is well maintained. It sits on a wide plot on Strand Road, facing the port area and its wharfs. The imposing red brick building, with its towering bracket clock and columned portico, reflects the importance of trade customs to the colonial economy. The window designs are a great example of colonial-era architecture adapting to local weather conditions: note the awnings attached to most first floor windows at street level. The offset oval openings directly above are mainly there for ventilation. They also protect the interior from direct sunlight and torrential rainfalls. A loggia surrounds the second floor, which also features shuttered windows. Again this arrangement offers protection from the harsh sunlight while ensuring good ventilation. The semicircular windows on the third floor feature prominent wooden shutters. The Custom House was designed by John Begg (1866–1937), Consulting Architect to the Government of India. Along with the Custom House, he designed the **Central Telegraph Office** 020 B and the **Printing and Publishing Enterprise** 005 B. Begg was one of the main architects of "the Raj" and a leading proponent of the Indo-Saracenic style (essentially a mix of Mughal architecture with Gothic revival and British neoclassical styles). In Burma, however, his works were European in form only. Officials working in Rangoon's Custom House collected duties and excise taxes from commercial shipping. Although customs in the British Empire were low (even zero for intra-India trade), they were an important source of revenue. Besides collecting customs, officials also tried to prevent smuggling. Some staff were on call 24/7 and assigned apartments on the top floor. Sarah Rooney, in her *30 Heritage Buildings of Yangon*, explains the role of the "rummaging staff" who searched for contraband on ships. The ingenuity of smugglers was astounding, although the officials also knew their trade. Drugs, gold, gems and other contraband goods "were hidden behind bulkheads, inside ventilators, lifeboats, lavatory cisterns, bath and washbasin drainage bends, in remote spaces in cargo holds, the list is endless and they all had to be looked into". As the Custom House continues its work today, there are usually droves of people on the pavement waiting with paperwork in their hands.

Myanma Port Authority (Port Trust Office)

034 B

10 Pansodan Street
Foster & Ward (architects),
Clark & Greig (contractors)
1926–1928

The Port Authority's corner tower is a Yangon landmark. The pitched red tile roof and hand-painted lettering dominate the view from the river and the port. The Corinthian double columns frame arched openings. The enclosed space is covered with green patterns that protect the recessed windows from exposure to the sun. Between the arches, round medallions depict various ships. The entrance is covered by a beautiful entrance canopy similar to the other buildings on this stretch of Pansodan Street. It is slightly arched, increasing its structural height.

A recently constructed pedestrian overpass obscures the view of the building from the Strand Road side. While this may be a good thing for pedestrians and traffic flow on this busy thoroughfare, the visual impact is scarring. In the late 19th century, Rangoon's port became one of the busiest in the British Empire. To reflect its growing importance, the old Port Authority on this site was demolished and replaced with this more spacious and modern building. The architect, Thomas Oliphant Foster (1881–1942), was the Government of Burma's Consulting Architect between 1916 and 1920. His two flagship buildings in today's Yangon are the Port Authority and the nearby **Yangon Division Office Complex 032 B**. Both reflect a modern and monumental architectural style. This relied heavily on imported steel framing and reinforced

concrete. Burma's chief commodities, rice and teak, were handled in the large wharfs facing the Yangon River. A huge flow of people passed across the jetties. For a time, it was the busiest port in the world. In *Crossing the Bay of Bengal*, Sunil Amrith quotes a British official who said in 1933: "Until recently second only to New York in importance as an immigration port, Rangoon now occupies pride of place as the first immigration and emigration port of the world." Most of these passengers were Indian. They became one of the world's greatest but least-known migrations. According to estimates, around 28 million people crossed the Bay in both directions between 1840 and 1940. Half of that human traffic involved Burma. It was common for Indian labourers to stay for three rice-growing seasons

before returning home. Many stayed behind though, and quickly became Rangoon's largest demographic group. In 1881, the Burmese outnumbered Hindus and Muslims from India. But just 30 years later, there were nearly two Indians for each Burmese. The Port Authority still operates today. Its tasks include the maintenance of the harbour infrastructure such as moorings, wharfs and jetties. With the opening of the country and increases in cargo traffic, major investments are under way in special economic zones. The nearest to Yangon is Thilawa, about 20 kilometres south of the city. It's a controversial project. Locals complain that this joint venture with Japan's aid agency JICA has forced people off their land with little consultation and meagre compensation.

Myanmar National Airlines (Bombay–Burmah Trading Corporation)

035 B

104 Strand Road
Unknown
1920s

Besides rice, the grand prize of colonising Burma was teak, a tropical hardwood endemic to South and Southeast Asia. The most successful company in the trade was the Bombay–Burmah Trading Corporation (BBTC). Its Burma headquarters once occupied this building on Strand Road. Built during the 1920s, it replaced an earlier two-storey building. Today's building, slightly taller, has been stripped of its ornamentation. Yet the prominent and covered arcade does lend it some grandeur, and matches the adjacent **Strand Hotel** 036 B. So does a recent paint job of the first floor and arcade, imitating the Strand's light ochre shade.

Teak production grew tenfold between 1859 and 1900, and more than doubled from then until the 1920s. Most teak extracted in Burma was destined for export to India, but was also sent to Europe where it was put to any conceivable use. Just before the onset of the Second World War, Burmese teak accounted for 85 per cent of world teak exports. The cultivation and extraction was mainly undertaken by five European firms, led by BBTC.

The company was founded as the Burma branch of Wallace Brothers, Scottish merchants with their roots in Edinburgh. In the 1860s, William Wallace secured a licence from Burmese King Mindon to extract timber in Upper Burma. A dispute over taxes gave the British a pretext to annex this part of the country in 1885. At times, the income derived from taxing Burmese teak accounted for a sizeable part of all colonial income from British India. Teak camps depended in large part on timber elephants and their skilled handlers. They also required the right level of rainfall to feed the small tributaries of the country's larger rivers, for these were the main transport arteries.

BBTC was nationalised after independence in 1948. The company still exists to this day and is listed on the Bombay Stock Exchange. Despite its name, it no longer operates in Myanmar. During the 1950s, Union of Burma Airways took over the old BBTC building. As the nation's flag carrier, it mainly operated domestic routes and connected provincial towns with Yangon; some international routes, to Bangkok and Singapore, were maintained throughout the years. The international network was taken over by Myanmar Airways International (MAI) several years ago. MAI is a wholly-owned subsidiary of Kanbawza Group, a conglomerate with close relations to the former military regime. It regularly adds more international destinations. But domestic carriers compete with an ever-increasing number of foreign airlines flying to the country.

Strand Hotel

2

Strand Hotel

92 Strand Road
John Darwood (architect),
Catchatoor & Co. (contractors)
1901

036 B

With its convenient location and glamorous pedigree, the Strand was the hotel of choice for affluent visitors to Rangoon in the early 20th century. Its owners, the Sarkies brothers, built and managed two hotels in Penang (in then Malaya, now Malaysia) as well as the iconic Raffles in Singapore. Expanding to Rangoon was a logical choice; the city was booming under British rule. The hotel faces what was then the fast-growing port, but a high wall across the street now hides the docks from view. Like the Balthazar family, the Sarkies traced their origins back to Isfahan, in Persia, where their ancestors were active traders on the Silk Road.

While the hotel retains its elegant aura today, its façade has long been stripped of the rich ornamentation seen in old archive photographs. Windows are combined and the grid structure has been broken up. The hotel's moderate size—it only has three floors—underscores its exclusivity. The 31 rooms are simply but elegantly decorated with Burmese teak furniture. A butler, stationed on each of the two accommodation floors, is on standby at all hours of the day and night. Outside the hotel, a large portico completely takes over the space where a sidewalk should be. Some pedestrians do pass through, but hotel staff seem to keep the passage relatively clear, save for taxis. Also an effort, perhaps, to preserve the hotel's genteel atmosphere in an otherwise heaving city: the worsening traffic is leading to greater noise and exhaust pollution on its doorstep.

Inside, the hotel revolves around a large atrium. In the lobby, several hotel staff take turns playing a Burmese harp or a *pattala* (a xylophone-like instrument made of bamboo) when they are not needed elsewhere. The hotel restaurant is to the left of the main entrance: a light, airy space with large windows, mirrors, rattan furniture and white walls. (Archives show that the restaurant's menu in 1932 was French, and written in French, serving the likes of roast lamb and buttered cauliflower. Not everyone's choice in tropical weather ...) The Strand Bar is on the right of the entrance, with its dark wood panelling, thick columns and heavy leather seats. It is a quiet venue save for Friday nights, when expats from across town hurl themselves at the cheap beer and cocktails for happy hour. At the far end of the atrium is a large, sumptuous dining hall with a skylight. To its right, a hallway stretches along Seikkantha Street, containing a souvenir shop and hotel offices. Don't miss the art gallery at the end of the hall, which features paintings from local artists. (If you are just strolling, you can exit the hotel from a side entrance in the hall and land on Seikkantha Street.) Today the Strand has again become one of the best, if not the best, address to stay at in Myanmar's former capital. Before a major refurbishment in the early 1990s however, the Strand was a shadow of its former self. In 1963, the hotel was nationalised and the property deteriorated as tourists to the country became rare. Tony Wheeler, the founder of the *Lonely Planet* guides, writes this mesmerising description in his first Southeast Asia edition, published in the late 1970s:

"Staying at the Strand is full of amusing little touches—beside the reception desk

there is a glass-faced cabinet labelled 'lost and found'. Most of the articles were clearly lost half a century ago, not many ladies carry delicate little folding fans around these days. The lift is ancient but smoothly operating. The waiters call everybody sir, male or female. Both the bar and the restaurant close at 9pm, but a small cache of Mandalay Beer from the People's Brewery is kept behind the reception area if you wish to continue drinking. By 11pm you are likely to be feeling pretty lonely in the lounge area, just the occasional Strand rat scampering across the floor to keep you company. On the last day of one Burma visit, to my utter amazement hot water came from the shower when I turned on the tap."

The authoritarian SLORC government naively wanted to attract tourists to Myanmar after the slump caused by the 1988 bloodshed. In 1989 a mere 2,850 visitors came to the country. (The number reached more than 3 million in 2014, following the country's opening-up in 2011.) To prepare for international arrivals, the military junta approached legendary hotelier Adrian Zecha, founder of Aman Resorts, in 1990. Though Zecha was only interested in renovating the Strand, the junta insisted he refurbish the **Inya Lake Hotel** 103 F and the **Thamada Hotel** 085 B too. After more than USD 10 million worth of renovations, the hotel reopened in 1993. The entire wiring and plumbing was redone. Many walls and ceilings were partially replaced and strengthened. It is the best example of a successfully restored colonial-era property in Yangon. The hotel also boasts a large "Strand Hall" on the opposite side of Seikkantha Street for functions and other events.

Bureau of Special Investigation (Tubantia Building)

037 B

57 Seikkantha Street
Unknown
1909

2

We recommend a detour up Seikkantha Street to take a look at the Tubantia Building, built by the trading company Stork & Co. in the early 20th century. Its gable and storage facilities on the ground and first floors reflect the original owners' Dutch roots: Frederick Stork was the consul of the Netherlands. The name "Tubantia" is the Latin version of the province of Twente, near the German border, where Stork grew up. His family ran a successful machinery business there, exporting various tools for the textile and sugar industries in the Dutch East Indies. Before the British annexed Burma in the 19th century, the Dutch were already an active presence in the country, particularly during the 17th century. Dutch business ties with Burma remained active during British colonial rule, given their own nearby colonial possessions. As aeroplanes made frequent refuelling stops back then, the Dutch flag carrier KLM was also the first airline to offer regular flights between Rangoon and Amsterdam in 1929 as part of its service to Batavia (Jakarta).

The Rangoon-based Stork & Co. imported "longyees", sarongs, metals, sundries and liquors. The Burmese *longyi* is traditionally worn by men. Counter-intuitively, it is actually a foreign import. Stork & Co. was just one of the companies importing these textiles from India. Even before the arrival of Europeans,

textiles made here fuelled regional trade. The historian Sunil Amrith writes that "in the 16th century 'age of commerce', cotton from Gujarat, Coromandel, and Bengal was traded across South East Asia. (...) Indian weavers' products targeted diverse markets, their weaves, patterns, colours, and designs were all adapted to local tastes." Knowing that Stork & Co.'s mother company in Twente manufactured textile-producing machinery, one can assume that they helped to standardise the cheap production of *longyi* for export to Burma. Today the Tubantia Building is used by a branch of the Bureau of Special Investigation (BSI), one of Myanmar's many secretive security agencies. The origins of the BSI date back to Burma's period of post-colonial democracy. Then-Prime Minister U Nu founded the BSI's predecessor (the Public Property Protection Police, or P4) to—in his words—"eradicate termites from the bureaucracy". With the scale of change now sweeping the country, one wonders whether the security apparatus will change too—and whether it will continue to occupy these crumbling heritage buildings, renovate them or move to modern premises. The smaller building next door also belonged to Stork & Co. It was the company's headquarters before the Tubantia Building opened. Today the BSI occupies it as well.

British Embassy
(J & F Graham Shipping Co.)

038 B

80 Strand Road
Thomas Swales (architect),
Robinson & Mundy (contractors)
1900

Thanks to its wealthy, diplomatic owner-ship, this building is in immaculate shape. Its fine lattice windows and entrance awning, covering the sidewalk, give it elegant airs in a stretch of Strand Road full of impressive buildings. The British Council operates here and offers English language classes. The back of the building is rather unattractive, facing a parking lot that separates it from the **Strand Mansion** 039 B. Both 37th and 38th Street are blocked at the Strand Road end for security reasons. The building, completed in 1900, was first the Rangoon headquarters of Glasgow-based shipping and insurance company J & F Graham. The company already had branches in Bombay and Calcutta when they came to Burma at the end of the 19th century. Like most companies of its kind, J & F Graham Shipping Co. had a litany of exclusive distribution deals with companies from other parts of the Empire. They imported and exported most imaginable products. The British Embassy took over the property after Burmese independence in 1948. Ironically maybe, it became a popular venue for students in the 1980s. They were attracted by the country's only English language library, which offered a regular supply of uncensored Western media as well as the free use of a photocopier. By contrast, the mere possession of an unauthorised typewriter outside the embassy was a punishable offence. On 8 August 1988, dockworkers walked down Strand Road from the port until they reached the embassy. In the present-day lore of the 1988 events, it is said they stopped at the embassy and laid down their tools in symbolic protest. This simple act was the beginning of a national strike that led to the historic uprisings.

2

Strand Mansion

24 39th Street
*PR Designs and Architecture
(renovation)*
1901 (renovation 2014)

039 B

The Strand Mansion was built along with the Strand Hotel in 1901. This nondescript building was a residence for high-ranking British officials, including port commissioners. It occupies a plot 15 × 15 metres wide, wedged between 39th and 40th Streets, with views of the adjacent port and warehouses. The Strand Mansion was completely restored in 2014 and now offers eight residential or office units of about 240 square metres each. The façade and staircases were restored to their original state and the structure boasts vast spaces, as well as four-metre-high ceilings. The entire project, from design to execution, was undertaken by PR (Patrick Robert) Designs and Architecture. Today it serves as an example of heritage architecture renovated to the highest standards for upmarket commercial purposes. In the 1990s, Robert also restored and transformed the **Governor's Residence** 068 C into a luxury hotel.

General Post Office (Bulloch Brothers & Co.)

039–41 Bo Aung Kyaw Street
(corner of Strand Road)
AC Martin & Co. (contractors)
1908

040 B

This red brick structure first housed the office of Bulloch Brothers & Co., the mighty rice trading firm founded by Scotsmen James and George Bulloch. In the shadow of Calcutta's port, Rangoon became an ever-growing maritime hub for the Bay of Bengal in the mid-19th century. The Bulloch brothers, working as a loose subsidiary of the British India Steam Navigation Company (BI), became the largest rice-milling and -trading operation in the region. Although BI's relationship with the Bullochs was tense, they could not afford to alienate these powerful local players. Six decades after its beginnings on the shores of Sittwe (today the capital of Rakhine State, on Myanmar's western coast) in 1840, Bulloch Brothers & Co. commissioned this spacious and elegant building along Strand Road. The design and cream colour of the Lancet-arched windows and ornate stuccowork give the building its distinctive feel. The front, southern side of the building recently enjoyed a fresh lick of paint, with the mortar gaps accentuated with white coating (unlike the other sides). The stunning beaux-arts iron portico is one of the last, if not the last, of its kind in Yangon. Bulloch Brothers & Co. was liquidated in 1933 (although some records show the company trading in some form until the outbreak of the Second World War). At around the same time, the General Post Office suffered terrible damage in the 1930 earthquake. It was a graceful, if delicate, filigreed building with nods to Buddhist architecture. The global ripples of the Great Depression meant plans for a new and improved version were set aside. The Bulloch Brothers building was acquired and repurposed instead. Anyone can venture into the General Post Office today and walk around. The railings of the double-winged stairways are beautifully ornate. The wooden stairs appear to be the original ones, judging by their pattern of wear and the way they creak under your step. The interior mixes some clearly original wooden counters with some new office space made of plastic and steel. At around the time the building became the new General Post Office, a young man named Shu Maung failed his medical exams and began work here as a postal clerk. He was also active in the nationalist struggle and, the story goes, used his job to intercept British letters of strategic relevance. When he rose to become a founding cadre of the Burmese Independence Army, he chose a nom de guerre—Ne Win—that would echo through the ages.

2

Section 4: Along Merchant Road

Inside the Armenian Apostolic Church of St John the Baptist

Armenian Apostolic Church of St John the Baptist

041 B

66 Bo Aung Kyaw Street
Unknown
1863

This is the oldest church in Yangon today. It was built in 1862 and consecrated as the Church of St John the Baptist a year later. The Armenian community first came to Burma from Persia in the 17th century, long before the onset of British colonisation. Sharman Minus, an Armenian genealogy enthusiast, has records of a previous Armenian church "with local bricks and a wooden spire" that stood on the grounds of today's **High Court** 021 B in 1766. Today's church is certainly an improvement on its predecessor, but still modest. It has arched windows and a bell, which is rung by hand. The building features a covered entrance and cane-seated pews to accommodate worshippers during months of searing heat. Besides the altar, with its typically Orthodox depictions of Biblical scenes, the church is sparsely decorated. The makeshift corrugated iron roof, a common feature in this weather-battered city, looks like a temporary solution until repairs can occur. The roof had previously suffered from Japanese shelling in the Second World War. As noted in our description of **Balthazar's Building** 029 B, the country's last Armenian, Basil Martin (a descendent of AC Martin, who built several of the edifices in this book) passed away in May 2013. His death prompted a surge of interest in the otherwise quiet church.

It led the to first-ever trip to Yangon by the head of the Armenian Church in October 2014. For Supreme Patriarch Karekin II's visit, the Yangon Heritage Trust (YHT) unveiled a blue plaque at the entrance, noting the church's historical significance. Inside the church, the YHT also installed storyboards explaining the history and role of Armenians in Myanmar. Karekin II's visit, however, had a more urgent motive than simply to remember Myanmar's Armenians. In an extraordinary tale, he visited effectively to evict the Anglican "priest" in charge, John Felix. As the BBC reported at the time, Felix came across "as a very pleasant, humble man, but unfortunately the Anglican Church says he has never been a priest". When Karekin II delivered his sermon in St John's, Sharman Minus, who was in the congregation, sensed something was afoot. Then Karekin announced: "Mr Felix is not a priest, neither Armenian nor Anglican. Therefore, according to the canons of the Armenian Church and the Traditional Churches, any sacrament officiated by him is not valid. We call on Mr Felix exhorting him to stop violating Church Canons and Holy Traditions and insulting the Armenian Church and nation." After this episode, John Felix refused to vacate the house he occupied on the grounds. He was eventually evicted, and private security guards patrol the church grounds today. There were further allegations that Felix was using his ill-gotten position for financial gain. The Armenian Church now fly in an Orthodox priest from India for the weekly service.

2

Mahatma Gandhi Hall
(Rangoon Times Building)

Merchant Road/
Bo Aung Kyaw Street
Unknown
Unknown

042 B

The *Rangoon Times* was colonial Burma's oldest English-language newspaper. This three-storey building was its main office at the turn of the 20th century. The paper's circulation was always small—as was, in fact, Rangoon's European population. Founded in 1856, it changed hands a few times and went from weekly to daily publishing. In the early 20th century, the newspaper was run by S Williams, who previously opened the first Reuters office in Burma, then located in the brand-new **Sofaer's Building** 022 B. The *Rangoon Times* continued to be published until the retreat of British forces from the city in 1942. In 1951, a few years after independence, this building was purchased by the first Indian ambassador to Burma, MA Rauf. He rechristened it Mahatma Gandhi Hall. It was used mainly for religious, social, intellectual and political gatherings over the following decades. In July 1990, Aung San Suu Kyi's National League for Democracy (NLD) issued its "Gandhi Hall Declaration" after convening here. Having won a stunning victory at the polls just months before, the junta chose not to recognise the results (even though the elections were their idea).

A large crowd greeted the NLD leaders and listened intently as the declaration was read out in front of the building. Heavily armed security forces were on standby next to them. The declaration called for a power transition and the release of jailed members of the party. The call went unheeded. The junta proceeded to annul the vote and declared its sole legitimacy in ruling the country. More recently, Gandhi Hall was in the news when the trustees unveiled their plans to destroy the building and replace it with a new condominium. The Yangon Heritage Trust (YHT) intervened and lobbied—successfully—for the Hall's preservation. The bid was supported by the Yangon City Development Committee and the Indian Embassy. Today the country's main English newspaper is the *Myanmar Times*. (Its offices are across from **St Mary's Cathedral** 008 B.) It was founded by a larger-than-life media entrepreneur from Australia, Ross Dunkley, who also owns the *Phnom Penh Post* in Cambodia. Thanks to connections with Burmese authorities, Dunkley was able to found the *Myanmar Times* as a joint venture with local businessman U Sonny Swe. Swe sold his shares in 2006; he now runs a rival publication, *Mizzima*. Dunkley was briefly imprisoned in 2011 amid what was deemed to be an internal power struggle with Dr Tun Tin Oo, the Burmese shareholder who replaced Swe. (In late 2014, prominent businessman U Thein Tun took a majority share in the paper.)

YCDC Bank
(A Scott & Co.)

526–532 Merchant Road
Unknown
1902

043 B

This three-storey building is diagonally across from Sofaer's Building. It still bears the name of the original owners and the year of its construction on the pediment facing the street. The building's façade and its elaborate cornice above the second floor are worth admiring. A Scott & Co. was a trading house with Scottish roots. Like most of its peers, the firm engaged in a wide range of activities: they were famous for exporting cheroots (Burmese cigars) back to Britain, which were popular at the time. In the 1920s, witty commentators described Rangoon as "a suburb of Glasgow, commercially". Five of the eight members of the Rangoon Chamber of Commerce in 1910 were Scots. Their firms were central to the colonial economy and commissioned many of 20th-century Rangoon's most imposing buildings, such as Graham & Co. (today's **British Embassy** 038 B), Finlay, Fleming & Co. (better known as the former **Myanma Oil and Gas Enterprise Building** 049 B) and the Irrawaddy Flotilla Co. (today's **Inland Waterways Department** 025 B). Nowadays, the A Scott & Co. building serves as the bank of the Yangon City Development Committee. The three long porticos are prime, shaded spots for cars and hawkers.

Embassy of India (Oriental Life Assurance Building)

545–547 Merchant Road
Unknown
1914

044 B

This building began as the offices of the Oriental Life Assurance Company, founded in Calcutta in 1818. The firm served European clients almost exclusively and offered an indispensable service, as colonial postings had high mortality rates due to the climate, tropical diseases and poor medical infrastructure in such far-flung corners of the Empire. Tellingly, the few companies that deigned to insure the local population adopted overtly discriminatory policies: the premiums were usually much higher than those levied on Europeans. Large trees make this whitewashed building difficult to appreciate in its entirety from the Merchant Road side. It is tall for Yangon's heritage buildings, measuring six floors from bottom to top. The building's site is narrow but deep. The demolition of the American Baptist Mission Press building, across the road from 36th Street, has cleared up the space for now and you can enjoy a better view from the idle site. The Indian Embassy moved into the premises in May 1957. By this time, many Indians had already left the country ahead of the Japanese invasion in 1942. As colonial order broke down in the wake of the aerial bombardments of December 1941, Indians became increasingly concerned for their safety. Many still remembered the bloody riots of the 1930s, which pitted striking Indian dockworkers against

their Burmese replacements. This perceived threat—many Indians remained in Burma and were not targeted after the British withdrawal—caused hundreds of thousands to embark on a long and arduous overland trek northwards, to India. The writer Amitav Ghosh collected several accounts of those who took part in his 1942 Burma Exodus Archives (available online, on the author's blog). Collectively they shed light on one of the lesser-known forced migrations of wartime Asia. Upon seizing power in 1962, Ne Win's nationalisation drive led to the expropriation of Indian assets and the expulsion of several hundreds of thousands of Indians. The embassy helped with the logistics of yet another large-scale, and again, little-known forced migration. Planes were chartered and "Burma Colonies" in large Indian cities sprang up, housing the so-called "Burma Repatriates". Indian–Burmese bilateral relations have warmed considerably since the mid-1990s. They reached rock bottom when India supported pro-democracy activists in the wake of the 1988 uprising. The pro-democracy publication *Mizzima*, now based in Yangon, was founded in exile in India. Recently the much-touted "Asian Crossroads" linking China with India via Myanmar have created renewed interest in economic cooperation, with a port and special economic zone in Sittwe designed to better connect India's less-developed

northwestern states to the Indian Ocean. The Indian Embassy was renovated in 1999–2000. Embassy staff today still assist Myanmar's stateless inhabitants of Indian ancestry with obtaining Indian citizenship. A nationwide census was carried out recently; it could help to ascertain just how many stateless "Persons of Indian Origin" (PIO) there are in Myanmar today. However, details have not been published yet for fear of political repercussions. Some estimates put the number of PIOs with neither a Myanmar nor Indian passport as high as one million.

Innwa Bank (Mercantile Bank of India)

554–556 Merchant Road
Unknown
Unknown

045 B

Innwa Bank (S Oppenheimer & Co.)

550–552 Merchant Road
Unknown
Unknown

2

Here are two former bank buildings with distinct looks. The left one is the former head office of the Mercantile Bank of India. Its weathered façade is covered with mildew, moss and weeds. Don't think, however, that this is due to decade-long neglect: the façade looked almost as good as new less than 10 years ago. The heat and monsoon take their toll each year, especially for buildings with a windward façade. This requires more frequent cleaning, or at least more weather-resistant paint. And yet the building still exudes some of the grandeur it shares with the other banks on this street. Stately square columns wrap around the loggia on the third floor. The portico, grilles and balustrades are made of iron and painted in baby blue.

The Mercantile Bank of India was, despite its name, a British undertaking. It was often jokingly referred to as the "Mercantile Bank of Scotland" because of its large contingent of Scottish staff. It mainly financed international trade. The Burmese Innwa Bank took over the premises in the 1990s.

The building on the right is the former S Oppenheimer building, which dates back to the late 19th century. It was recently renovated. The wrought-iron fence and window bars on the ground floor have been replaced with the cheap-looking, shiny metal versions you find throughout the region. Inexplicably, the drainpipes of the awning are now made of blue plastic. Two ATM booths (almost non-existent in Yangon prior to 2012) jut out towards the pavement. In the early 20th century, the third-floor main window extended up to the arch. It was adorned with stained glass. Originally the building featured an iron portico, which was later replaced by two concrete ones. The narrow arcade, which rests on four Corinthian columns, is a relatively recent addition despite its looks. S Oppenheimer acquired the property in 1893 to cope with a rapidly expanding business. The company, whose roots are German, traded in goods as diverse as police uniforms, elephant gear and famous Underwood typewriters. After a 2011 renovation, Innwa moved into these premises.

Myanma Foreign Trade Bank (Hongkong and Shanghai Banking Corporation)
046 B
564 Mahabandoola Garden Street
Unknown
1901

This former building of the Hongkong and Shanghai Banking Corporation (HSBC) was once a Catholic church, creating one of Rangoon's more spectacular—and unusual—corporate buildings of the early 20th century. Not much of this early splendour remains. The building underwent drastic renovations, most likely in the 1920s, to expand and update the premises. It was stripped of its rich Gothic ornaments and the church spire that once rested on the hexagonal tower. The former HSBC office now resembles a sparse, almost fortress-like building. The tight iron bars on the windows reinforce this impression. HSBC opened this Rangoon branch in 1901. (It had opened its first office nine years before, on Bank Street.) At the time the bank was a pillar of the British Empire in Asia. While it was chartered under British banking regulations, its opulent headquarters were in Hong Kong. In *Fiery Dragons: Banks, Moneylenders and Microfinance in Burma*, economist Sean Turnell explains that HSBC's operations in Burma were relatively minor compared to elsewhere in the Empire. And while HSBC worked with Chettiar moneylenders in Ceylon (present-day Sri Lanka), it had little involvement with the Chettiars of Burma, despite their central role in the colonial financial system. Although Rangoon was a minor branch, it was deemed a desirable posting for ambitious young bankers. Today the HSBC building, along with the building next to it on Mahabandoola Garden Street (with its new and questionable glass façade), belong to the Myanma Foreign Trade Bank (MFTB), one of the country's major state-owned banks. As the name implies, the MFTB facilitates foreign trade and used to be the sole conduit

for foreign exchange transactions. The role of the MFTB and other state banks is in flux today, given Myanmar's gradual opening-up. Foreign exchange dealings were liberalised in 2012. The country's currency, the kyat, is now traded relatively freely. Foreign banks are returning: at the time of writing, more than 40 international banks have representative offices in Yangon. In October 2014, nine of these were awarded limited licences to provide banking services, but HSBC was not among them. Nor have they, as yet, re-opened an office.

Mahabandoola Gardens with Independence Monument and Centrepoint Towers

Former US Embassy (Balthazar & Son)

581 Merchant Road
Unknown
1926

047 B

With business flourishing, Balthazar & Son expanded onto these adjacent premises on Merchant Road. This is clearly a more modern building, yet the design imitates its older red brick neighbour. Thanks to long-term use as an embassy, it has been regularly maintained and is in rather good shape today. It is simple and stately, with three floors and a bulky cut-stone portico greeting its visitors. The former tenants made some alterations, including tight window grilles on the ground floor and two walled-up windows on the third floor. Large antennas on the top floor hint at the building's previous diplomatic functions. The US Embassy moved into these premises soon after Burmese independence. Burma was of utmost strategic interest to the Americans, who feared the spread of Communism in the region. They helped the Chinese Kuomintang regroup in the north of Burma, following their defeat by the Communist Party in the late 1940s. They supported preparations for a counterattack on Kunming, but this plan failed to materialise. As an unintended consequence, parts of Shan State became a hiding ground for these Chinese rebels, which led to the growing cultivation of poppy in the region. This haunts the Golden Triangle (the remote border areas between Myanmar, Laos and Thailand) to this day. Although the US ambassador at the time, William Sebald, denied knowledge of covert CIA operations on Burmese soil, Burmese Prime Minister U Nu was enraged and threatened to sever diplomatic ties between the countries. In 1988, embassy staff witnessed the dramatic uprisings outside their window. When Burmese security forces opened fire on the demonstrators, Ambassador Burton Levin ordered the Marine Guards to open the door and let civilians seek shelter inside the grounds. The US did not replace Levin when he retired in 1990, reflecting the frosty bilateral relations that followed. A chargé d'affaires was to represent the United States in the following years. In 2012, Derek Mitchell was appointed the new US ambassador and Myanmar has become an important facet of the Obama Administration's stated "pivot to Asia". President Barack Obama visited the country in 2012 and 2014, both times delivering speeches at **Yangon University** 101 F. The administration began lifting sanctions on Myanmar in 2012 and is pouring aid money into the country, including in sectors that would have been inconceivable to support before 2011. For example, in 2014, the US aid agency committed to spending an eye-catching 20 million US dollars on "strengthening civil society and the media" in the country.

Centrepoint Towers

65 Sule Pagoda Road
Unknown
1995–2014

048 B

At the time of writing, this much-maligned construction project is lurching to its conclusion. Many bemoan its architectural banality and overbearing presence in the city centre. Others breathe a sigh of relief that this 20-year, on-and-off construction is coming to an end. The complex consists of two towers of about 90 metres each. Standing on Sule Pagoda Road's southern edge, they overlook Mahabandoola Park and afford spectacular views (many of this book's aerial photos were taken there). The southern tower's façade is covered with large white tiles, which are reflected in the northern tower's blue solar glazing. Both towers evoke a rather tired architectural language of the 1990s, unsurprising given the project's drawn-out genesis. With a helicopter deck on one rooftop, will private companies offer their rich customers private air taxi services in the not-so-distant future? This might not be far-fetched, given Yangon's increasingly sclerotic traffic conditions. The deal to build this mixed-use project occurred as early as 1993 and construction began two years later. One of the towers was intended to be a luxury hotel operated by the Sofitel Group. The other was earmarked for office and retail space. The Thailand-based investor mothballed the project in the wake of the Asian financial crisis in 1998. It stood idle in a semi-finished state for several years until construction resumed in 2005. By 2009, the investors had to inject another 12.5 million US dollars into the project, taking the overall investment beyond 100 million. This makes it one of Yangon's priciest real estate projects to date. (To put this into perspective, Yoma's "Landmark" project surrounding the **Former Myanmar Railways Company** 057 B will cost an estimated 500 million US dollars, embodying growing investor confidence in Myanmar.) After a considerable period searching for the right partner, the Hilton Group was chosen as the hotel operator in 2013. With 300 rooms, it will add considerable capacity to the city's five-star segment. While the likes of the Canadian Embassy and the Associated Press have already moved into the office tower, the hotel is taking longer than expected. The opening date has been postponed more than once already. The Centrepoint saga isn't over just yet ...

2

Inside the Secretariat's eastern stairwell

"What Are Your Five Favourite Buildings in Yangon?"

U Sun Oo, Principal Architect, Design 2000; Board Member, Yangon Heritage Trust

Buddhist Museum and Library (Pitaka Taik) 106 F

This building is a successful, modern expression of Buddhist religious architecture in a new Buddhist library building design. A foreign architect designed it. You can see how the architect improvised, or modified forms and decorations from traditional religious buildings. And yet this isn't a re-interpretation, but a strongly traditional building.

Thakin Kodaw Hmaing Mausoleum 080 C

This is one of the best examples of progressive architecture design in the history of Myanmar architecture. It features simplified and modified traditional Myanmar design motifs. The basic form is pure and geometric. The daring use of deep red and gold in the interior resembles the traditional colour combination of Myanmar palaces.

YMCA building 003 B

This is a good example of second-wave modern architecture in Burma, exhibiting a style that was popular in the late 1960s and 1970s. It flourished in the socialist period and the style can be seen in a lot of Yangon's residences and in some large towns throughout Myanmar, thanks to the efforts of leading architects of the style, such as U Kyaw Min and Captain Kyu Kyaw.

City Hall 018 B

The City Hall displays a successful expression of Myanmar national character in a civic building design. It features a good composition of Myanmar traditional roof forms and decorative elements, for what was a novel type of building at the time. Architect U Tin designed the City Hall. After its completion, he received the title of "Sithu" (similar to a British knighthood) from the government. He only designed parts of the building; for the rest, he inherited a British colonial design, but was able to nicely articulate the two. It has become an iconic building of Yangon.

Secretariat 006 B

This was a totally new design, brought in by the British at the end of the 19th century. What was an "alien-like" structure at the time became popular and gradually accepted by a majority of Burmese people over time. After a few decades, the building also became part of Burmese architecture's history. Now it is one of the best-loved buildings in Yangon, and acknowledged as one of the country's cultural assets. Religious and civic building designs of later periods in Burma were influenced by this good example of colonial architecture.

City Hall

Façades on lower Shwedagon
Pagoda Road

The Heritage Question:
Building a City or an Open-Air Museum?

Yangon's heritage is the subject of intense global attention. But can the city preserve it in a way that serves the local population, and does justice to a complex and often painful history?

If you are new to Yangon, flicking through these pages will instantly reveal the city's exceptional built heritage. A variety of factors—many explored in our text—have left behind an unparalleled amount of colonial-era buildings. Compare that with the broader region, where the forces of modernity have led to the destruction of similar cityscapes in Hong Kong, Kuala Lumpur and Singapore, especially in the second half of the 20th century. Yangon's surviving edifices embody the city's cosmopolitan nature, a result of the many communities that sought their fortunes at this booming trading port from the mid-19th century up until the Second World War. Afterwards, these buildings provided the backdrop to Myanmar's tumultuous post-independence chapter, when a string of historic events played out before—and behind—their ornate façades. In the same period a small and eclectic body of post-war architecture blossomed, symbolising the young nation's hopes and dreams. As Yangon develops in tandem with a relative re-opening of Myanmar, the heritage debate is growing louder. A multitude of actors are involved in one way or another. Besides the Yangon Heritage Trust (YHT), these include the Yangon City Development Committee (YCDC), Japanese aid agency JICA, a host of embassies, the World Monuments Fund (WMF) and the Turquoise Mountain Foundation, not to mention many research organisations. Self-consciously or not, these organisations bring with them their own heritage vocabulary. In 1996, the YCDC compiled the first list of 189 heritage buildings with the help of the Association of Myanmar Architects, another actor in the heritage debate. This list forms the basis of many heritage debates today. But it omits many obvious candidates by focusing on publicly owned buildings only. The YHT is working on an updated list to address this. In many foreigners' eyes, the discourse is framed by the cursory coverage of newspapers and magazines from around the world. Their dispatches on Yangon's architectural heritage are often similar in depth and sentiment. They usually highlight the imminent dangers of rampant economic growth to some highly visible buildings, such as **Sofaer's Building** 022 B or the **Secretariat** 006 B.

Heritage lists may narrow the journalists' scope. This "heritage discourse", in other words, is often only about the preservation of monuments in the midst of a cityscape that defied late-20th century modernity and evaded market forces in those long years of self-imposed isolation. Sometimes this argument flirts with naïve romanticism and a misplaced—if not downright offensive—sense of nostalgia for the colonial period. What is Yangon's role in modern Myanmar? In response to the 1988 protests, the military rulers attempted to build a new narrative for the nation. It relies on a narrow definition of "Myanmar" language and culture, often synonymous with "Burmese", as well as a rose-tinted view of the "Panglong Spirit" which united the country's various "ethnic nationalities" after the Second World War, at the dawn of independence. Yangon has always been and remains an important spiritual centre, given the Shwedagon Pagoda's long history and glowing dominance over the city. But Yangon's status as a modern city is by and large a colonial invention. (Not to mention the city's pagodas were built by the Mon people, not the ethnic Burmese.) The colonial enterprise was multilingual and multi-ethnic by design.

Sule Pagoda Road Police Station in early 2014

Sule Pagoda Road Police Station being demolished in late 2014

Teak building by Kandawgyi Lake. The depicted part has since collapsed.

The former Rowe & Co. under renovation in early 2014

The cosmopolitan Rangoon of the late 19th and early 20th century, therefore, does not sit easily with this state-led vision of Myanmar culture. Furthermore, the military dictatorship gradually estranged itself from those buildings that embody the legacy of the Burmese independence movement, inescapably tangled with the legendary Aung San. When his daughter, Aung San Suu Kyi, became the figurehead of the opposition during the 1988 protests, the military narrative took steps to marginalise the historic relevance of Yangon's cityscape. (Read more about the changes post-1988 in the dedicated section on page 332.)

While urban preservation debates worldwide have long moved on from a narrow focus on monuments, focusing instead on understanding the history of cities in richer and more complex ways (such as the concept of "living heritage", described in **Theingyi Market** 055 C), perhaps the fixation with buildings in Yangon is unavoidable: in a country like Myanmar, where decades of neglect and isolation have bequeathed a rich body of old buildings but a paucity of records, these bricks and mortar are often the best archive material there is.

In keeping with a more modern and broader definition of heritage, the YHT is more concerned with the wider city, not just the jewels of downtown. Daw Moe Moe Lwin, the YHT's Vice-Chair, describes her organisation's motivation as coming "not from a nostalgia point of view, but the current character of the city". This allows for a much richer appreciation of Yangon. As built heritage conservation specialist Kecia Fong writes, it is "[a] building; a book; an institution; a personal history; political shifts and the economic speculation they incite; the durability of bricks; the spaces in which ideas circulate and transactions occur; and the convergence of international communities [that give] rise to Yangon heritage".

The current economic boom will unavoidably commodify these old buildings. Many restoration projects have begun or are about to begin. While these may be laudable on a case-by-case basis—by, say, giving an old obsolete structure a new lease of life, and providing a home in the process—taken together they will change the face of Yangon. And while cultural elites and community groups often insist on the old city's preservation, this could easily transform the city into an open-air museum. Which way forward, then? Will Yangon fall prey to the "Venice Syndrome" and become over-restored, a gorgeous shell that caters mainly to foreign and well-heeled tourists? And will the celebration of the city's "cosmopolitan past" risk isolating Yangon from a country now led from Naypyidaw, a purpose-built city designed to enforce a narrower and state-led vision of Myanmar identity? What compromise between the need for dynamism, preservation, economic growth and opportunity, while avoiding the pitfalls of raw gentrification and displacement?

As a voice of authority in this important debate, the YHT has a special responsibility. Its leadership and team is itself a mix of educated Myanmar and international elites. As Fong writes, "they are attempting to present heritage conservation as an intrinsic factor in the complex urban equation for a better quality of life and the making of a global city. (...) It is imperative to produce a new vision of Asian modernity that is at once intrinsically Burmese and global, which seamlessly integrates the unknown futures with the continuity of the past".

However you understand it, Yangon's heritage is rich and colourful. Its ethnic tapestry and marvellous monuments have captured time. But much of the city's heritage has also borne witness to painful memories of long and brutal colonial subjugation. Not to mention a harsh and frequently violent post-independence period. This heritage deserves a memory. And yet, you couldn't blame Yangon for wanting to move on.

Further reading:

Fong, Kecia. "Imagining Yangon: Assembling Heritage, National Identity and Modern Futures." *Australia ICOMOS Historic Environment*, 26.3 (2014): 26–39.

Lamprakos, Michele. "The Idea of the Historic City." *Change Over Time*, 4.1 (2014): 8–39.

Pabedan, Latha and Seikkan

051 C Mogul Shia Mosque

055 C

061 C Yangon General Hospital

053 C Surti Sunni Jamah Mosque

062 C Guandong Guanyin Temple

052 C Jain Temple

Aerial view of Pabedan and Latha townships as seen from Centrepoint Towers, northwestern direction

FMI Centre 058 C

Cholia Jamah Mosque 050 B

Shwedagon Pagoda 075 E

Holy Trinity Cathedral 060 C

Bogyoke Aung
San Market 059 C

3

061 C Yangon General Hospital

Aerial view of Pabedan township as seen from Sakura Tower, western direction

Holy Trinity Cathedral 060 C

FMI Centre 058 C

3

gyoke Aung
San Market 059 C

3

Former Myanma Oil and Gas Enterprise Building (Burmah Oil Company)

049 B

604–608 Merchant Road
Robinson & Mundy (contractors)
1908

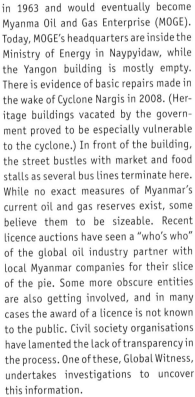

Built as an office for the Scottish trading firm Finlay, Fleming & Co., this elegant building later became the Rangoon headquarters for the Burmah Oil Company (BOC). Two towers flank its sides. The four-storey edifice has two entrances with porticos covering the entire pavement. It once dominated this section of the road—but today, it looks a little lost between a large condominium building and one of the **Centrepoint Towers** 048 B. Along with rice and teak, oil was another of Burma's key resources to become exploited by the colonial enterprise—and BOC enjoyed a virtual monopoly. Before the advent of electricity, the company's candles and kerosene lamps lit homes not just in Burma but around the world. BOC's heyday was in the 1920s, when it was one of Britain's largest industrial firms by revenue. At the time, its operations spanned large parts of the British Empire. BOC's main agent in Burma was Lim Ching Tsong, whose palace in Bahan township was evidence of the riches that oil could already command at the time. After the war, the business was downscaled and the building on Merchant Road shared premises with a nursing home, known as San Pya Clinic. Burmah Oil was nationalised in 1963 and would eventually become Myanma Oil and Gas Enterprise (MOGE). Today, MOGE's headquarters are inside the Ministry of Energy in Naypyidaw, while the Yangon building is mostly empty. There is evidence of basic repairs made in the wake of Cyclone Nargis in 2008. (Heritage buildings vacated by the government proved to be especially vulnerable to the cyclone.) In front of the building, the street bustles with market and food stalls as several bus lines terminate here. While no exact measures of Myanmar's current oil and gas reserves exist, some believe them to be sizeable. Recent licence auctions have seen a "who's who" of the global oil industry partner with local Myanmar companies for their slice of the pie. Some more obscure entities are also getting involved, and in many cases the award of a licence is not known to the public. Civil society organisations have lamented the lack of transparency in the process. One of these, Global Witness, undertakes investigations to uncover this information.

Cholia Jamah Mosque
114 Bo Sun Pet Street
AC Martin & Co. (contractors)
1936

This mosque and its trust occupy several land plots on the corner of Bo Sun Pet Street and Mahabandoola Road. Its history began in 1856 when two men, Gulam Hoosain and Shaik Madar, purchased the first plot and erected a timber mosque. A religious trust, or *waqf*, was created in 1869 to manage the mosque and administer the income from a number of shops built on an adjacent plot on Mahabandoola Road. The first stone mosque opened three years later, but it wasn't until 1936 that the current structure was erected. Of the six tenders received, contractor AC Martin was chosen. Martin, or Martirossian as he was known in the Armenian community, came to Burma from Persia and joined the Public Works Department in 1886. He set up his private firm in 1900 and subsequently built many of colonial Rangoon's buildings, including the **General Post Office** 040 B on Strand Road. That his company built one of the city's central mosques is a tell-tale example of Yangon's cosmopolitan fabric. The new mosque was built in only seven months. Public infrastructure was chronically poor, and the shortage of water prompted the trustees to install a well in the courtyard. Later, a generator-powered well was added. (Note the

large fish swimming in the pond immediately as you enter the mosque.) Whenever there was a shortage of water, the mosque's wells provided for the neighbourhood. The mosque and especially the buildings surrounding it sustained heavy damage in the war. The portico covering the pavement on Mahabandoola Road was built in 1955. A large hall for the trust was opened in 1963. To build it, the trust had to sanction the removal of a minaret on the corner of Mahabandoola Road and Bo Sun Pet Street. The Supreme Court of Rangoon ruled in 1936 that the term "Cholia Muslim" denotes every Muslim whose mother tongue is Tamil. Etymologically, "Cholia" has its origins in the ancient Indian kingdom of Chola (9th–13th century AD), situated in today's

Tamil Nadu. Muslim traders from this part of India have a long history of traversing the Bay of Bengal, which long predates the arrival of Western colonists. Under British imperial rule, they increasingly settled in Burma, especially Yangon. Many returned to India in the wake of the Japanese occupation and after independence. In his *Crossing the Bay of Bengal*, the historian Sunil Amrith points us to the "Burma Bazaar" in Chennai, set up by returnees from Burma in the 1960s, and the fact that "many Tamil towns still have a 'Burma Colony'". By 2004, the Cholia Muslim Religious Fund Trust was run by about 100 well-off Tamil Muslims, although the mosque also welcomes non-Tamil Sunnis for prayers. The charity organisation assists the poor from the Muslim community, notably poor elderly women. It also ran computer classes and a HIV/AIDS awareness campaign. The *lassi* shop between the entrance of the mosque and the corner of Mahabandoola Road is a highly recommended pit stop during your downtown adventures.

Mogul Shia Mosque

051 C

91 30th Street
Unknown
1914–1918

While there are many Shia in India, the majority of Indian Muslims who migrated to Burma were Sunni. Thus, there were only ever a few Shia mosques in Yangon. This is the community's largest. It dates back to the mid-19th century, when Indo-Persian merchant families erected a wooden house of worship in 1854. By the entrance, a well even predates the first mosque: it was dug by order of colonial officer Sir Arthur Phayre in 1852 (at a time when sanitation was a major challenge in the fledgling city). The current structure was built between 1914 and 1918 and remains largely intact in its original form today. The mosque occupies a wide plot between 29th and 30th Streets along Mahabandoola Road. Its main entrance is on 30th Street. Despite the dense urban layout of the vicinity, the two large minarets stand out from afar. The mosque itself is set back from Mahabandoola Road behind the large Mogul Hall, which accommodates worshippers and those on business passing through the city. A recent paint job and interior restoration have kept the entire complex in good shape. The Indo-Persian merchants who set up this mosque hailed from Persia by way of India. The board of trustees comprised men named Kabuli, Ispahany, Sherazee and Khorasanee, to name a few, which give us strong clues about their geographic origin. The history of one family bearing the latter name is exemplary. In his self-published autobiography, S Afsheen explains that his great-great-grandfather, Hasan Ali Khorasanee, came to Burma in the 19th century where he, like other "Iranians", was given preferential trading terms by the Burmese court. Hasan Ali's father, Ashraf Afshar, was an adviser to the royal court in Delhi. The Burma-based Khorasanee family became a powerful family trading firm over the next generations. S Afsheen's

great-grandfather, Backer Khorasanee, owned several villages and other properties in Rangoon as well as a thriving business trading in leather and other merchandise, which he sold in his department store on Mahabandoola Road. His own house stood on 31st Street. S Afsheen's maternal grandfather, Mohammed Hashim Ispahany, was one of the original trustees of the rebuilt Mogul Mosque alongside the adjoining Mogul Hall. Two engineers of a British firm were selected to plan and oversee the construction. According to S Afsheen, they were sent to India to select a design for the mosque.

They were particularly impressed by the Taj Mahal in Agra. The Day of Ashura, the 10th day of the month of Muharram, is regularly observed by the Shia community in Yangon, today about 2,000 strong. The ceremony is held in honour of Hussein, who died a martyr in the battle of Karbala—a historic clash between Shia and Sunni in present-day Iraq, in the 7th century AD. Around the world, Shia mark this as a day of mourning. It involves spectacular and masochistic rituals, mainly by Shia men. For example, they walk barefoot across hot coals or lash themselves with long chains of blades.

Jain Temple

74–78 29th Street
Unknown
1914

052 C

This building on narrow 29th Street may not strike you as a temple at first: its design is closer to the city's official colonial-era architecture. One clue, however, lies in the two golden lion figures on the roof. These represent Mahavira, the most recent of Jainism's 24 Jinas—liberated beings who can help others achieve liberation themselves. The result is an interesting mix of religious carvings on an otherwise neoclassical façade. The signpost on the entrance, "Shree Jain Shwetamber Murtipujak Temple" denotes the sect and sub-sect of Jainism to which this temple belongs. Murtipujaka differs from other Jain sects in that its temples contain idols instead of being empty. Jainism is one of India's smallest but oldest religions, numbering about five million believers. Its most famous principles are nonviolence and strict vegetarianism. During British rule as many as 10,000 Jain lived in Rangoon. The community's first temple, occupying the top floor of a building inside the Surati Bazaar (today's **Theingyi Market** 055 C), was founded in 1899. Most Jain left the country during the Second World War and after the Ne Win coup of 1962. No exact figures exist as to today's Jain population in Myanmar. Some sources state that Myanmar as a whole is home to 2,000 Jain. Others speak of only five Jain families remaining in today's Yangon. Most Jain originally hailed from Gujarat, contributing to the rich mix of people living in Yangon from this part of India. In contrast to India, there is considerable mixing among the various religions. Paris-based writer Mira Kamdar, who herself has Jain roots through her grandmother's line, recounts a visit to Yangon in 2000, while she was tracing her Indian ancestors who had once lived in Burma:

"For the first time in my life outside the rarefied circles of the intellectual Westernised elite of New York, New Delhi, or Bombay, I find myself in a world in which Hindus, Jains, and Muslims mix comfortably and even affectionately in each other's homes, over meals no less. In Gujarat, this kind of easy mixing in people's homes would be quite extraordinary. Whereas Hindus and Jains and Muslims may be good friends in public spheres, such as school or work, in the private sphere of the home it would be unusual to get together. (...) I found none of that in Rangoon. And, as people brought out their wedding albums and photographs of important community events, it became clear these close relationships across religious lines went back many years, for they had been—the men at least—present at all the important occasions of each others' lives."

Surti Sunni Jamah Mosque

053 C

149 Shwebontha Road
Unknown
circa 1860s

Shwebontha Road used to be known as Mogul (Mughal) Street and was at the heart of "Indian" Yangon. India's last Mughal emperor, Bahadur Shah Zafar, was exiled to Rangoon after the Indian Mutiny of 1857—the greatest and bloodiest challenge to British colonial rule at the time. Zafar brought with him a legion of courtiers and attendants. Many of the shopkeepers in this part of Yangon claim descent from the exiled court, as Thant Myint-U explains in his book *Where China Meets India: Burma and the New Crossroads of Asia*. The first mosque in Yangon was built as early as 1826. (It was destroyed in the Second Anglo–Burmese War in 1852.) In the early 1840s, when Colesworthey Grant visited the city, he observed that besides two churches (the predecessor to today's **Armenian Church** 041 B and a Roman Catholic Church), were three "Mohummudan mosques, indicating that intolerance in religious matters, at least, is not amongst the fault of the Boodhists". The Surti Sunni Jamah Mosque was built some time around the 1860s, and some sources refer to its opening in 1871. This makes the mosque one of the oldest still in its original state, although its exterior is covered in tiles today. Two large minarets flank the mosque and its imposing arched entrance tower protrudes above the pavement. The mosque's name suggests that it was built by Gujarati traders originating from or near Surat, quite possibly from the town of Rander opposite the Tapi River. Historical links between Rander and Myanmar survive to this day: many old homes in Rander are built with Burmese teak, and the culinary landscape features specialities brought back to India from "Burma Repatriates" during the Second World War as well as Ne Win's nationalisation campaign in the 1960s. One still finds *Rangooni parathas* (deep-fried pieces of meat enveloped in a thin layer of wheat dough mixed with egg) and *Khow Suey* (traditionally a Shan noodle dish, and a close cousin of Thailand's famous *Khao Soi*) in restaurants in Rander. If this whets your appetite, head to Golden Chetty Restaurant (115–117 Sule Pagoda Road) or New Delhi (on the corner of 29th Street and Anawratha Road) for some authentic Indian dishes. There is another mosque of the same name on 35th Street, worth visiting for its interesting setting on the narrow road.

3

Musmeah Yeshua Synagogue   054 C
26th Street
Unknown
1896

Built between 1893 and 1896, the Musmeah Yeshua Synagogue today serves
only 20 or so Jewish residents of Yangon.
But in the early 20th century up until
the Second World War, it was the spiritual home of the Sephardic Jewish community who settled in colonial Rangoon,
fleeing Ottoman and Iraqi persecution in
Baghdad. Their numbers reached around
2,200. Many of them rose to prominence

as businessmen, such as Isaac Sofaer who
built the iconic **Sofaer's Building** 022 B.
Others served as magistrates, municipal
councillors and commissioners. About
half of the community fled in the wake
of the Japanese invasion in 1942, often
embarking on an arduous overland trek
to India. This "forgotten march" cost tens
of thousands of lives, mainly Indian. As
a result of the war, 1,000 Rangoon Jews
settled in Calcutta. Amid post-independence chaos in Burma, most of the remaining Jews emigrated to the newly created
state of Israel which, like Myanmar, was
founded in 1948. The two countries maintained good relations until Ne Win's coup
in 1962. Burma was the first Asian country to recognise Israel; Burma's first
prime minister, U Nu, travelled to Israel
in 1955, becoming the first foreign head
of state to do so. Israeli Prime Minister David Ben-Gurion spent two weeks
in Burma in 1961. Presidents Ben-Zvi,
Meir, Dayan and Peres would also visit the
country during their terms. Until recently
painted an attractive sky-blue and pale
yellow, the synagogue is now white. Set
back within a tranquil courtyard, the visitor arrives from an entrance on busy 26th
Street, where a menorah adorns the front
entrance on a blue tiled background. The
inside of the synagogue itself is airy and
cool. In a nod to the heat, the benches are
cane-seated and fans (along with chan-
deliers) hang from the ceiling. Note also

the arched windows and stained glass. Although the Jewish population in today's Yangon is minuscule, the synagogue aims to attract Jewish visitors to Myanmar. One of Yangon's Jews, Sammy Samuels, describes spending Fridays inside the synagogue with his father in the hope of meeting foreign visitors:

"Every Friday, my father and I used to wait at the synagogue for Jewish visitors until we can gather the minyan *(requisite ten people) to begin services. (...) It is my father's fervent belief that no Jew should be alone during the holidays—and yet most of the time, the two of us found ourselves alone in the synagogue. But even if only he and I are present, I always feel the echoes of the many Shabbat services that took place in this beautiful synagogue and hear the melodies of the songs our ancestors sang when the community was at its peak."*

Sammy Samuels has founded a travel agency, *Myanmar Shalom*, catering to Jewish tourists.

Theingyi Market (Surati Bara Bazaar)

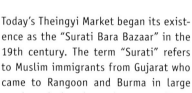

055 C

Mahabandoola Road
Unknown
19th century

Today's Theingyi Market began its existence as the "Surati Bara Bazaar" in the 19th century. The term "Surati" refers to Muslim immigrants from Gujarat who came to Rangoon and Burma in large numbers during the 19th century. (From 1872 to 1881 alone, the Indian migrant population in the city more than quadrupled to 66,000.) Indian cultures and traditions, from religion to music to

food, permeate the streets of this downtown area. Theingyi attracts a broader, less affluent cross-section of Burmese shoppers and fewer tourists than nearby **Bogyoke Aung San Market** 059 C. The market started in the shade of a nearby monastery of the same name, which attracted many traders even before the British. After the British began to expand Rangoon, the market area was handed over to Surati traders who built the bazaar. Between the 1850s and the 1900s the market grew, shrank, and was devastated early on by several fires. (Earlier structures were made of thatch.) Today the market consists of five blocks,

lettered A through to E. They surround the intersection of Mahabandoola and Shwedagon Pagoda Roads. The "A" and "B" buildings date from 1938 and 1905 respectively. The façade of the B building, on Mahabandoola Road, stands out with its vast portico doubling up as a first-floor balcony, patterned perforated walls and louvred windows. Some blocks were rebuilt post-1988 and are clearly identifiable as such. Block D, with its slanted façade, has a distinctly brutalist feel. Theingyi Market was the subject of a German university study on the concept of "living heritage"—in other words, a building that continues to fulfil its historical purpose. As the lead researcher, Professor Frauke Kraas explained: "You will find long-term relationships among the vendors and also beyond the market to other parts of Myanmar and even beyond. There are long historic roots [with] deep economic and social cohesion." A visit to Theingyi Market is a definite must-see Yangon experience as grinding traffic, baskets of fresh fish and hollering merchants seem locked in a seamless choreography controlled by higher forces. The contrast with the sanitised alleys of Bogyoke Market tells more and more of—to use a cliché—a tale of two cities.

Shri Kali Hindu Temple

295 Konzedan Road
Unknown
1871

Among the many Hindu temples in Yangon, the Shri Kali Temple is devoted to the goddess Kali (or Kali Ma, as she is also known). The temple was built by Tamil immigrants at a time when the Indian population of Rangoon totalled around 15,000 people, compared to more than 70,000 Burmese and other "indigenous races", as the census then showed. Only 10 years later, the number of Indians had quadrupled, while the local population remained constant. In the 1870s, then, these droves of new residents required houses of worship for their respective faiths, and in their regional character. Traditionally depicted in black and in fearsome poses (four arms, carrying the severed head of a demon in one and usually a sword in another), Kali is the goddess of time, change, power and destruction. Many praise her as the greatest of all deities. Her sculpture, inside the sanctum, is richly decorated with flowers. The temple is busy with worshippers, many of them bowing before Kali. Temple assistants are there to help place offerings and apply the *tilaka*, the red mark worn on the forehead. The temple's colourful exteriors, especially its characteristic tower (*gopuram*), are recognisable sights. It is richly decorated with sculptures and carvings featuring scenes from Hindu mythology. The power lines above the entrance are usually lined with pigeons, so tread carefully. As in all Hindu temples, footwear must be left outside in the space provided.

Former Myanmar Railways Company during renovation in late 2014

3

Former Myanmar Railways Company

057 B

Bogyoke Road
Unknown
1877

As one of the oldest surviving colonial-era buildings, the former Railways Company predates the Third Anglo–Burmese War in 1885. In 2013, extensive renovations began: these will place the building at the heart of the ambitious "Landmark" project, which is described in the section on the **FMI Centre** 058 C. Eventually Asian luxury group Peninsula will run a five-star boutique hotel within these walls. Local business tycoon Serge Pun planned to convert this building into a high-end office complex when he signed the original lease for the whole plot in the 1990s. However, the Asian financial crisis foiled the idea. This busy intersection of Sule Pagoda and Bogyoke Roads is one of Yangon's focal points: **Bogyoke Market** 059 C is nearby to the west, **Sakura Tower** 010 B and **Sule Shangri-La** 009 B are right across the street. The former Railways Company building can best be admired from that side. The laterite blocks on the first floor and the red bricks used everywhere else give the building its distinctive, glowing shade. The use of laterite also explains the structure's durability compared to other colonial-era buildings. The ornate awnings dominate the façade from the Bogyoke Road side. They are cast from iron and were imported from Scotland. Singaporean firm Lapis, specialising in heritage conservation, has been contracted to oversee the renovation works. The building's lack of maintenance prior to the renovation work was most visible in the inner courtyard. It will likely be covered with a glass ceiling once works are completed in a few years' time. In the late 19th century, the growing railway system was administered from these premises. Coinciding with its completion, Burma's first railway line opened in 1877 and connected Yangon with Pyay (Prome); a distance of 250 kilometres. The railways later became a private company. By 1909, the system expanded to a length of more than 2,400 kilometres, connecting about 250 stations and reaching up to the Chinese border. The famous viaduct across the Gokteik Gorge, north of Mandalay, opened in 1901. Built by US companies and using US steel, its maximum height is 100 metres, symbolising the vaulting ambition of those early railway entrepreneurs.

3

FMI Centre and Grand Mee Yah Hta Executive Residences

058 C

380 Bogyoke Road
Unknown
1995,
renovated 2010
(FMI Centre)

Built in the mid-1990s and opened in 1995, the FMI Centre was Yangon's first major office building up to international standards. (It was followed by the **Sakura Tower 010 B**, which opened in 1999 and remains one of the best office spaces in the city). The rather unremarkable 11-storey building, here seen from 29th Street, hosts the offices of various local and international companies and organisations. The FMI Centre is about 50 metres tall, towering over the low-rise downtown area immediately to the south. The "Parkson" department store in the retail podium opened in 2013, after an extensive renovation by local SPINE Architects.

The Malaysian brand expects to invest in several store projects across Myanmar in coming years. This relatively new building (by current Yangon standards) will soon have to make space for the "Landmark" project, with the former **Myanmar Railways Company** 057 B at its heart. The FMI Centre's twin building, The Grand Mee Ya Hta Executive Residences has already been vacated to make space. (By the time our readers venture through Yangon, it may be gone already.) The owner of the buildings and site is Serge Pun, one of Myanmar's foremost businessmen. His many ventures include a banking group, a hospital, an airline, coffee plantations and domestic real estate. The latter earns the group the most money, and a few key projects provide the financial backbone to the thriving conglomerate. At the time of writing, the group's major cash earner is **Star City** 110 A, a residential project in Thanlyin across the Yangon River. Landmark's completion will fire the starting

pistol for a new phase in the history of Yangon real estate. Budgeted at around 500 million US dollars, it will compete neck-and-neck with the mixed-use project of Vietnamese developer Hoang Anh Gia Lai, on Kaba Aye Pagoda Road, for the priciest-ever real estate deal in the city. Two of Landmark's four projected towers (of about 80-100 metres each) will provide office space, while the other two will house a four-star hotel and serviced apartments. Aedas, one of the biggest architectural firms in the world, will handle the design. Early renderings reveal a generous use of glass and a connected retail area at the base of the four buildings, as well as swimming pools on their roofs. The four towers will flank the former Myanmar Railways Company building. The Washington-based International Finance Corporation (IFC), the private-sector arm of the World Bank, has committed 70 million US dollars to the overall project cost. The Asian Development Bank followed suit, approving the same amount. This sets Landmark miles apart from other major construction projects currently under way in Yangon, especially given the IFC's stated attachment to transparency and accountability. The intention is to signal to foreign investors that the time to invest in Myanmar has come—and that trustworthy local partners await. Parts of Serge Pun's business empire are already being traded on the Singapore stock exchange—to date, one of few ways for Western investors to gain exposure to Myanmar's markets. But all may not be so rosy in the end. At the time of writing, the project is already late by about a year. Serge Pun has so far failed to secure a critical lease extension. The whole four-hectare site still nominally belongs to the Ministry of Railways; it says that it is still studying the application, telling the *Myanmar Times* that it was not "malicious in its intent or purposely trying to prolong the process". Since Serge Pun began leasing the plot in the 1990s, only about 25 years remain on the current lease—too little to secure long-term investments. However, he remains optimistic the deal will come through, albeit in two stages. The first one will include the office, retail and hotel components. Then, once the extended leases are obtained, the residential part of the project will get underway. The big question is whether the international financial institutions will continue to support the project in the absence of this critical lease extension—and if it is granted, on the lease conditions. Yangon's real estate market has run into major capacity shortages and a frenzy of construction activity is taking place throughout Yangon. But conditions are incredibly volatile: in February 2015, several major construction projects for commercial and residential space already under way were suddenly suspended due to concerns over their proximity to the **Shwedagon Pagoda** 075 E. In the meantime prices are astronomical, although the market is showing signs of cooling. Serge Pun himself believes a crash in prices is likely.

Bogyoke Aung San Market (Scott's Market)

Bogyoke Road
Unknown
1926

059 C

Bogyoke Aung San Market, seen here from the west with a view towards the **FMI Centre** 058 C, is one of Yangon's main tourist attractions. It was built by the British and takes its name from the Municipal Commissioner of the time, Gavin C Scott. (It's common to read sources stating—incorrectly—that the market was named after James George Scott, a journalist who wrote *Burma: A Handbook of Practical Information* in 1906. Allegedly, this Scott also introduced the Burmese to football.) It was renamed after Burma's great independence leader in 1948. The market sells gems, local art, western clothes, *longyi* and cloth from Myanmar's ethnic minority states. It features antiques of diverse periods, quality and authenticity, including furniture, vintage glasses, old coins and postage stamps. It also caters to tourists' more immediate needs, such as traditional and plastic sandals and a range of cheap t-shirts. (It's worth noting those depicting Aung San Suu Kyi, or in some way related to the NLD—an unfathomable thing to sell before 2011.) It was also a popular place for visitors to exchange US dollars on the black market at advantageous rates. Money changers still loiter on the market's edges. The market divides itself into various sections, 21 in total. It is roughly organised according to product, with the gem and jewellery section occupying the western wings. Jade is on offer everywhere. Proceed with caution, though: some is unlikely to be authentic. And a much bigger problem is the conditions under which jade is mined in Myanmar. Quarries are mostly in hard-to-reach, northern stretches of the country, inaccessible to the international community and not conforming to ethical mining standards. According to investigations, many of the trade's key players also have close interests in the country's vast drug trafficking networks. In 2014, Al Jazeera reported the official revenue from jade exports to be 1.3 billion US dollars, while an independent study from Harvard University placed the real amount, on the black market, at 8 billion US dollars. Bogyoke Market is set back and separated from the street by a fence and a narrow parking lot. When the market is closed, the fence forces pedestrians to walk along busy Bogyoke Road. All the buildings possess an arcade in front of the shops protecting them from the sun. The main hall features a high arched ceiling and contains numerous small shop booths. The main hall, which faces Bogyoke Road, has undergone a recent paint job. Notable features include the dome, first-floor loggias and the recurring ornate iron arches running along the façade.

As you progress deeper into the market, the original colonial-era features disappear and you discover that most of the market's extensions are made of corrugated iron painted a bright green—and as you go deeper still, the green gives way to rusting iron sheets draped in blue tarpaulin. It's worth noting, however, that while these extensions are clearly intended to be cheap, light and basic, an effort was made to imitate those smaller iron arches that recur on the street-facing façade. Unusually for Yangon, the inner streets of the market are cobbled. The street on the easternmost edge of the market, alongside Parkson Department Store, feature some attractive examples of what the original structures inside the market probably used to look like, before the days of corrugated iron.

3

Holy Trinity Cathedral

446 Bogyoke Road
Robert Fellowes Chisholm
1886–1895

060 C

The Holy Trinity Cathedral is the main Anglican church in Yangon. Its history intertwines with the arrival of the British colonial administration and military. By 1857, only five years after the annexation of Lower Burma by the British, the Church of England accounted for the largest constituency of Christians—far exceeding the numbers of Baptists, Roman Catholics, Orthodox Christians and others. And yet, according to Myanmar history and travel writer Philip Coggan, the number

was still only as small as 169, "not counting the soldiers". The other Christian denominations only had double-digit congregations. It took a long time for the Anglicans to find a permanent home. For a time they worshipped in barracks. Later they used the **Custom House** 033 B. A Holy Trinity Church was built in 1865, but it was a modest affair. As Coggan writes, it "held no bell, no pulpit, no font, no *punkah* (fan), no lamps, no organ or other musical instrument, but at least it was there. It had cost 72,000 rupees, of which 10,000 had been raised by public subscription". But the number of British—and among them, practising Anglican—officials in Rangoon continued to grow and there was

talk of upgrading the facilities to what is today's cathedral. Although work on the redbrick structure began in 1886, it took nine years to get it finished as funds were chronically limited. The church was designed by Madras-based architect Robert Fellowes Chisholm. He was famous for building in Indo-Saracenic style—the merging of European neo-Gothic and neo-Classical styles with Mughal architectural styles. The cathedral is not part of Chisholm's forays into Indo-Saracenic experimentation, though: its neo-Gothic leanings wouldn't look entirely out of place in England. However, you will notice some adaptations to the Burmese climate, including the roofed entrance area underneath the tower, sheltering worshippers from torrential rains. Unusually, the cathedral's entrance is to the side and not facing the central aisle. As you approach it, you will notice that the red bricks are in fact covered with several layers of thick red paint with the mortar joints painted white. (Amusingly, the pattern around the entrance doesn't

3

match the actual brick layout at all.) Inside the cathedral, the pillars are painted an elegant white, cream and burgundy combination, matching the colours of the tiles along the walls and the rows of dark, wooden shuttered doors. Although the church itself survived the Second World War, the altar and furnishings were destroyed by the Japanese. The current set was installed in 1945 by British military officers. The stained-glass windows on the altar as well as the rose window were renovated in 2003 by a retired British couple. It is worth exploring the chapel on the left, called "The Forces" chapel, dedicated to the Allied forces who lost their lives in the Burma Campaign of the Second World War. The crests of various regiments who served in the war adorn the walls, as do a few historical notes. One instructs the visitor, perhaps defensively, to "note that besides British, Australian & Commonwealth Forces, the Regular and Auxiliary Burmese Forces are [also] included". There is also a picture of a regiment of Chindits inaugurating the church's "Regiments Memorial". It is found on the church grounds' southeastern edge. But as you will notice, this monument lists the names of British officers only.

Yangon General Hospital 061 C

Bogyoke Road
*Henry Hoyne-Fox and Henry
Seton-Morris (architects for
main building and additional buildings,
respectively), Bagchi & Co. (contractors)*
1904–1911

Together with the **Secretariat** 006 B, the General Hospital is Henry Hoyne-Fox's major contribution to Yangon's cityscape. The hospital replaced a mostly wooden building that was overcrowded and worn-down by the end of the 19th century. Space was made available on the current site by relocating the Agri-Horticultural Gardens and a museum. The main building was complemented by additional wings and tracts over the next few years, such as the administrative block, matron's accommodation and the morgue. These were designed by Henry Seton-Morris, Consulting Architect to the Government of Burma. Upon completion, the new hospital was cutting-edge, with its electricity-powered operating theatres and anaesthetics rooms. The floors were made of reinforced concrete, a first for Yangon. The main building is more than 200 metres long and has three stories. Its red bricks and yellow plaster create a unique appearance, visible through the trees from Bogyoke Road. But contemporary John Begg (who built the **Custom House** 033 B, the **Central Telegraph**

Office 020 B and the **Government Press Building** 005 B) was not convinced of the hospital's architectural merits. Sarah Rooney, in her *30 Heritage Buildings*, quotes the former Consulting Architect to the Government of India saying:

"Too much 'design' has been expended on certain portions of its external appearance. A hospital ward can hardly be too plain and business-like. Nor is the external very pleasing after all. The colour scheme of light red brick and yellow plaster is distinctly unhappy."

The colonial-era hospital was the front line in the fight against a range of infectious diseases; cholera, typhoid and, above all, malaria were rampant. The General Hospital was also the site of important research into the leprosy bacillus under the head doctor Major Ernst Reinhold Rost, who also happened to be the honorary secretary of the International Buddhist Society. In 1988, the hospital took on a tragic role in the uprisings. The doctors and nurses did their best to care for the hundreds of injured protestors, many of whom arrived at the hospital with gunshot wounds. The bloodshed was severe and tragically, there wasn't enough blood for transfusions. Scores died in the corridors. In response, medical staff took to the street just outside the hospital, carrying a banner calling for an end to the violence. In response, soldiers came to the hospital in three trucks and began shooting indiscriminately.

As well as injuring six nurses, they killed several civilians including two monks. The hospital's buildings are set back from the street by a driveway and parking lot. People crowd the entrance and two small courtyards formed by the building receding next to the central main entrance. Surrounding the main building are a few lower brick buildings. The open hallways along the building façade are covered with chicken wire. Going towards the back of the building, untamed greenery takes over. The General Hospital is the largest hospital in Myanmar today. It has 1,500 beds spread across 29 specialities. Approximately 1,800 staff, including 300 doctors and about 500 nurses, look after the patients. It remains the most reputable public hospital in the country and therefore attracts the best clinicians. People travel from across Myanmar, on what can be painful and uncomfortable journeys for the invalid, because they can only receive treatment here. As a result of this, the hospital is seriously overcrowded: admissions doubled between 2008 and 2012, although no major investment in capacity was made. Wards designed for 20 people routinely have to care for 60 or more patients. When beds run out, desperate staff push chairs together or take tables from neighbouring lecture halls to create additional space. Aung San Suu Kyi and a team from London's Imperial College have drawn up a plan to modernise General Hospital over the coming years. Yangon needs this urgently.

3

Guandong Guanyin Temple

668 Mahabandoola Road
Unknown
1823

062 C

recipe brought over from Guangdong in the 1940s. 'They're just a bit less sweet than in Hong Kong,' he says."

The Guangdong Guanyin Temple traces its origins back to the early 19th century, when Chinese immigrants from Canton (modern-day Guangzhou) settled in Lower Burma together with those from Fukien (Fujian). The latter founded the nearby **Kheng Hock Keong Temple** 063 C. Officially, ethnic Chinese citizens of Myanmar account for 3 per cent of the population, although the true figure may be substantially higher. There are 150,000 in Yangon alone, settling traditionally in Chinatown, here in Latha township, where Chinese restaurants, shops and bookstores abound. The temple is dedicated to Guanyin, the *bodhisattva* (enlightened being) of compassion venerated by East Asian Buddhists. It has long been a cultural hub for the ethnic Chinese community and the area outside the temple always teems with vendors. As the local *Irrawaddy* magazine puts it vividly:

"Every afternoon, hawkers with garlic-fried chilli crabs, steamed dim sum and straw baskets full of strawberries set up their shop around the Guanyin temple, bracing themselves for the onrush of evening strollers. (...) By the time the sidewalk spills into the street, the butcher at Good Diamond Sausages has sold out his daily output of pork sausages he says are made according to a

Every conventional guidebook will also—rightly—tell you to have an evening meal on the rows of plastic tables and stools on 19th Street, though it's becoming more touristy by the minute. Burmese friends of this book also recommend the rice congee with fish on 20th Street, beside the temple, together with a stick of fried dough (*Ei Kyae Kwe*)—sure to attract fewer tourists and reportedly a local institution! Built in 1823, this temple caught fire in 1855 along with valuable records of its early history. It reopened 13 years later, in 1868. At that point a stele commemorating the names of the donors was installed—ostensibly the earliest record of the temple's existence in the city. Its layout differs significantly from the nearby Kheng Hock Keong Temple: it makes less use of its front courtyard and is more open to the road, with street vendors' stalls coming right up to the front steps. The gilded inscribed boards refer to Guanyin. Several rows of altars featuring incense bowls lead to Guanyin's shrine. Note the stunningly detailed scenes depicted on the altars themselves, as well as the golden carvings surrounding Guanyin. Smaller altars in the hall commemorate other *bodhisattvas* including Maitreya who, according to Buddhist belief, will appear on Earth in the future and attain complete enlightenment.

Kheng Hock Keong Temple (Fu Zin Kan Hou Temple)

063 C

426/432 Strand Road
Unknown
1903

Kheng Hock Keong is Yangon's largest Chinese (Taoist) temple, lining the southern end of Chinatown on Strand Road. It is maintained by the local Hokkien community—a fluid ethnic label designating the descendants of Chinese emigrants from Fujian, a province in southeastern China. Many emigrated from Fujian by sea to Southeast Asia in the 19th century in connection with the growth of trade during the British colonial days. Today large Hokkien communities exist in Indonesia, Malaysia, Myanmar, the Philippines and Singapore. The temple is dedicated to the Goddess Mazu, who protects traders, seafarers and fishermen. Hokkien people often emigrated to become merchants— you will note the temple is near the port. In keeping with the temple founders' aspirations, its name means "temple celebrating prosperity". Mazu's statue dominates the main shrine inside, surrounded by lacquered and golden ornamentations. She is flanked to the right by Guan Gong, the god of loyalty and to the left by Bao Sheng Da Di, the god of medicine. A statue of Guanyin, the goddess of mercy, was added later. (**Guanyin** has her own temple at the northern end of Chinatown 062 C.) The temple was spared during the Japanese bombings; according to legend, Guanyin herself appeared on the shore to wave away the bombs. The temple also features guardian spirits along the entrance, together with numerous features of Taoist temple architecture including lanterns, dragons, golden inscriptions, sculpted pillars—and a generous coating of red paint. Burmese author Ma Thanegi quotes a British artist, Talbot Kelly, who visited the temple in 1904 and wrote admiringly about the brand new temple's intricate "beams and joints being completely perforated almost like filigree work, then picked out in gold and vermilion". The courtyard contains large incense-burning ovens where worshippers come to donate "spirit money" made of gold, or silver-plated joss paper. Incense sticks, together with donations of flowers or food, appear every day outside the shrine. The best time to observe the community making these offerings is early in the morning. The temple opens at 5am and locals usually visit on their way to work. The community elders will often be playing a game of chess or simply hanging out by the front court. The local Fukienese Association has its offices here. After 1962, relations between the Chinese community and the authorities took a turn for the worse. A nationalisation programme expropriated many Chinese business owners. Anti-Chinese riots broke out in 1967 when Chinese students defied a ban on wearing Mao badges at university. The ensuing violence would lead to tense bilateral relations between the two countries over the following decades. The temple was founded in 1861— it was then made of wood—and was replaced by this permanent structure in 1903. It saw some renovations in 2011, on its 150th anniversary.

Street vending in front of Transit Shed No. 1

**Transit Shed No. 1
and Port Autonomy**
Between Lanthit Jetty and
Kaing Dan No (1) Jetty
Dominic Leong
2014

064 C

Shortly before this book went into print, and only over a year after its opening, the authorities denied the trendy art gallery and retail space Transit Shed No. 1 (TS1) a lease renewal. We nonetheless decided to keep the project in our pages. The space was an interesting example of adaptive reuse architecture and showed the potential of Yangon's riverside development. The space also gave an interesting insight into the role of art in today's Myanmar. And who knows, maybe the gallery can reopen here or elsewhere someday?

From the outside, TS1 was an unassuming converted old warehouse. Two doors to the right (on a corner plot) stood Port Autonomy, the complex's bar and restaurant. Although beautifully renovated inside, both buildings' corrugated iron exteriors were left largely untouched, and fit seamlessly into the industrial texture of the surroundings. Dominic Leong of Leong Leong, a New York City-based studio, designed the two spaces. Inside the walls of TS1, he built a modern gallery defined by a diagonal wall, creating two symmetrical spaces. Structural changes included new walls and a light well, flooding the space with natural light during the day. The buildings would not look out of place in New York's Brooklyn,

East London or Berlin. Predictably, they attracted a hip and international crowd to this part of the city since their opening in early 2014.

The man behind the gallery and the bar, Ivan Pun, intended this project to be "a demonstration of the possibilities for downtown Yangon's rejuvenation". It would be a place for both art and high-end retail. The latter featured upmarket designer wares, crafts from local creators Myanmar Made and homeware from Hong Kong-based Lala Curio.

Myanmar's political opening makes these interesting times for an art gallery, says Nathalie Johnston, who was TS1's curator: "The artists have always been brave in their ability to express themselves despite challenges, and now more than ever they can use their words and their materials to show they've not only survived, they're thriving." With a group of affluent art buyers in the region, Myanmar art is now getting noticed and purchased across borders. Besides acting as a bridge between international buyers and the local art scene, Johnston thinks events aimed at local audiences had been an important part of TS1's activities. Among them were "Attention, Please!", a night of 10 female performance artists and "I'm Proud", an LGBT exhibition featuring street art and works from local and international artists, as well as an experimental music concert.

Perhaps TS1 could slowly have become an important venue to showcase art that conveys social and political critiques.

Johnston said at the time that local artists were allowed to address contentious issues in the space, but often set the limits themselves. "There are still certain things artists won't touch without the cloak of reverence—like religion and nudity."

And yet, TS1's conflation of art gallery and retail space was questionable. Its ties to the Burmese super-rich (in this case, Serge Pun's business empire) could have limited the space's critical scope—at a time when art should instead test and explore such issues.

These reflections aside, TS1 (and the Port Autonomy bar) were valuable additions to Yangon's cityscape, not least for their interesting adaptive reuse architecture. The changing exhibitions taking place here also made this a cultural hub for residents and frequent visitors to the city.

The vacant space's fate is as yet unknown. If the TS1 project can claim an abiding legacy, it is to have illustrated the potential for opening Yangon's riverside to the public. The nearby jetties make this a busy stretch of waterfront, with commuters using the ferry service to Dala, on the opposite side of the Yangon River. Small cargo boats are unloaded here, their wares filling the nearby storehouses. Tea vendors and other hawkers line the street which is dominated by pedestrian traffic. This is a working port. When asked by filmmakers, locals commented favourably on the presence of an art gallery in the neighbourhood, but also said that they wouldn't have time to go in and browse during the day. Johnston says: "When we had concerts or openings in the evenings, they've shown support by joining us and taking a look around."

Night-time aerial view of Pabedan and Latha townships as seen from Centrepoint Towers, northwestern direction

Boomtown Planning

Yangon's modern age began in 1852 with a master plan cooked up by British colonial officers. Their rectilinear street grid still defines the downtown area. With the country's recent opening-up, Yangon's population is expected to double in the coming decades. A comprehensive urban plan will cause frictions but is undoubtedly needed.

Yangon was shattered by the Second Anglo–Burmese War in 1852. The British then set about turning the small, swampy town into a capital for their latest colonial possession. William Montgomerie drew up a master plan, and Lieutenant A Fraser later amended it. Both belonged to the Bengal Engineers, a corps of British colonial officers. Their plan proposed a wide Strand Road along the river and a grid of streets leading north.

They placed the **Sule Pagoda** 016 B at the city's heart. The city would cover an area measuring about 4.25 kilometres in length, east to west, and a kilometre in width. This is roughly today's downtown—what local planners refer to as the "central business district" (CBD). The northern boundary was defined by the railway planned there in the 1870s, and the land beyond that line was the site of the **Shwedagon Pagoda** 075 E, partially

Grid of downtown Yangon, as seen from Centrepoint Towers

surrounded by the British cantonment areas. Burmese villages dotted the landscape farther afield.

This downtown/uptown distinction remains a feature of today's Yangon. The colonial city first grew within the confines of the downtown area, expanding east and west until it reached the waterways. Large swamps were drained and cleared. Public infrastructure was gradually installed, with sewage becoming a particular challenge in an increasingly overcrowded city. People went around by steam tram, electric tramway and motor buses, often operated by private companies. A large part of the economic activity was concentrated on the southern waterfront with docks, jetties, warehouses and wharfs dominating the shore.

The post-independence era saw much of the new government's scarce resources go to post-war reconstruction efforts rather

Construction site on lower Thein Phyu Road

than a comprehensive overhaul of the urban layout. The city expanded from the downtown core as important public services such as universities, hospitals and cultural institutions were constructed in the northern townships. Because Yangon was Myanmar's capital until the move to Naypyidaw in 2005, national ministries and the armed forces administration continued to operate here. The most intrusive interventions to Yangon's urban fabric occurred when the State Law and Order Restoration Council (SLORC) took power after the 1988 protests. These included extensive slum clearance programmes, the narrowing of pavements and an overhaul of public transport (for more information, refer to the section on post-1988 changes on page 332).

Myanmar's economy is opening, but the bulk of foreign investment remains focused on Yangon. The city's population is set to grow from today's six million to above 10 million in the next two decades. Yangon urgently needs a comprehensive planning framework, including a zoning plan—and the institutional capacity to see it implemented. This plan was about 60 per cent complete at the time of writing.

There are plenty of challenges. Density in the CBD is reaching its limits and new high-rise construction would put even greater pressure on today's overcrowded roads. However, there is a huge need for quality office space and—more importantly—affordable housing. Meanwhile, the city's precious urban heritage begs for protection, and an enviable waterfront is monopolised by industrial zones. (The local conservation and urban planning charity, the Yangon Heritage Trust, proposes to redevelop the waterfront to include public uses.)

Yangon's municipal authority, the Yangon City Development Committee (YCDC), is in charge of urban planning. According to Dr Kyaw Lat, a consultant working for YCDC, we can expect the following: in the short term, traffic management systems and a bus rapid transport (BRT) system will provide immediate relief to congestion. High-rise construction in the CBD has already been frozen to avoid further densification. The more contentious intervention is planned for the medium term. A flyover above Strand Road will become the southern perimeter of an inner ring road highway. From the waterfront, this would totally obscure the view of Strand Road and its stunning line-up of heritage façades. The plans already exist, and the overall project is set to cost about 2 billion US dollars. In the long term, an outer ring road will span the city's wider circumference, reaching all the way south beyond Dala and as far north as Hlawga National Park. A bridge connecting the two sides of the Yangon River will also lead to further development on

Stilt house in Dala, on the opposite shores from Yangon's port

the other side. In the long term, Dr Kyaw Lat foresees a skytrain system operating in Yangon—as it does in Bangkok, Kuala Lumpur and Singapore.

The Yangon Heritage Trust's Director, Daw Moe Moe Lwin, is also the Vice President of the Association of Myanmar Architects. She says flyovers are not the only solution to the worsening traffic problems; there are other options. "Why are vehicle owners privileged?" she asks. "Other cities have shown that increasing the street surface area also increases car ownership. Moreover, construction activities will prove hugely disruptive." While it is true that Yangon is choking on traffic, the resolution suggested by YCDC may only make things worse in the short to medium term. As a non-governmental lobbyist the YHT's power is limited, although it works closely with YCDC in spite of these differences of opinion. Nonetheless, Daw Moe Moe Lwin laments the lack of public consultation, for example in the recent construction of a vast pedestrian overpass on Strand Road.

Many other urban planning questions will need to be answered over the coming years. Japan's aid agency JICA is providing technical assistance in urban planning and has devised a master plan for Yangon's future development stretching to 2040. It sets out a vision of a megalopolis with new sub-centres growing in today's periphery, connected by a much denser grid of transportation infrastructure. While such long-term planning is important, it has two shortcomings in this case: despite rapid growth, Myanmar will remain a poor country for years to come, limiting its financial resources. This will reduce the scope for suggested solutions, such as road tunnels and underground metro lines, and mean more widespread use of cheaper, but eventually more intrusive methods, such as flyovers and skytrains. And while relative political change is accompanying the country's economic opening-up, democratic participation still lags far behind. Local elections for the YCDC were held in late December 2014—a first for Yangon. These were marred by low turnout and a controversial "one vote per household" system, reminiscent of the days before universal suffrage in other countries. But civil society and YCDC seem willing to begin a dialogue. We can only hope that in future, crucial matters of urban planning will be debated in public.

Further reading:

Japan International Cooperation Agency, JICA. *Yangon Urban Transport Master Plan: Major Findings on Yangon Urban Transport and Short-Term Actions.* 2014.

Spate OHK, Trueblood, LW (1942). "Rangoon: A Study in Urban Geography." *Geographical Review*, 32.1 (1942): 56–73.

Dagon and Mingala Taungnyunt

4

075 E Shwedagon Pagoda

Thamada Hotel 085 B

076 E Maha Wizaya Pagoda

Thamada Cinema 085 B

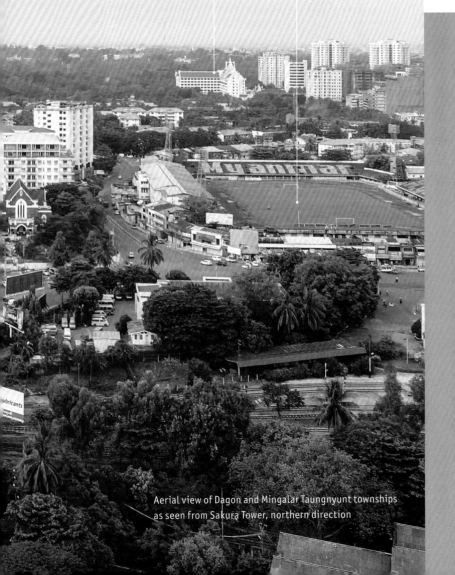

Bogyoke Aung San Stadium 087 B

Rose Garden Hotel 088 B

4

Aerial view of Dagon and Mingalar Taungnyunt townships
as seen from Sakura Tower, northern direction

Pegu Club

Pegu Club
Zagawar Street
Unknown
1882

065 C

The Pegu Club was once the most prestigious gentlemen's club of colonial Rangoon. Today it lies abandoned and decayed. Besides the main teak clubhouse, the compound included residential apartments and tennis courts. To accommodate the sweltering heat, the upstairs living quarters in the main building used louvred doors and windows to allow for cross-ventilation. Note the high ceilings, separate carriageway and carriage porch—all clear signs of elevated social status. The Pegu Club's history goes back to 1871, by which time the British presence in Burma felt irrepressible and permanent and, as in the rest of "the Raj", called for the creation of a colonial members' club. Senior officers came here to relax and mingle, often with a strong drink: today the name "Pegu Club" is better known to bartenders around the world as a gin-based cocktail. By 1882, membership exceeded capacity at the original premises on Cheape Road—today's Ma Naw Hari Street, just behind the **Yangon International Hotel** 071 C. A new site for the club was selected further south, between Pyay Road, Padonmar and Zagawar Streets. This convenient location was within easy reach of the busy, expanding downtown areas and the northern military cantonments around the Shwedagon

Pagoda. By 1910 the club had grown to 350 members, many being high-ranking colonial administrators or businessmen. This gave rise to talk of a "Pegu Club government" running Burma in the early 20th century. Membership criteria at the Pegu Club were strictly racial. The club barred non-whites from entering the premises unless they were servants—usually Indian. Interestingly though, George Orwell's *Burmese Days*, inspired by his time in Burma from 1922 to 1927, chronicles the pressures felt by British clubs to admit "non-whites" (of a certain standing, of course) by the 1920s. In the book, set in the fictional town of Kyauktada, the local club members are petitioned by the

4

club secretary to become more flexible in this regard. But one member, speaking for most, cannot conceal his revulsion at the fact that "natives are getting into all the Clubs nowadays. Even the Pegu Club, I'm told. Way this country's going, you know. We're about the last Club in Burma to hold out against 'em." After a short wartime interlude—when Japanese occupiers used it as a "comfort station", allegedly bringing *geishas* over from Japan—the Pegu Club continued to operate post-independence for almost two decades. Although the strict racial rules were suspended, only a few Burmese joined. Outside the Pegu Club, the tides of change rolled on. Across the street, the Soviet Union moved into the (now Russian) embassy building on Zagawar Street. Burma struggled with the challenges of independence and nation-building. But inside the club, time was standing still. The polished teak bars featured the usual assortment of ice-cold beer, gins and whiskies. Indian staff, still called "boys" in their fifties or sixties, stood quietly in the background, waiting to refill an empty glass. The lawns were still manicured each day. After Ne Win's coup in 1962, the premises were seized and turned into an Officers' Mess by the Burmese army. The last occupant was the Comptroller of Military Accounts, who had a pension office here. Today several families of government employees

All three photos: inside impressions of Pegu Club

live in the surrounding buildings, while the main building is empty and rots away. The roof is damaged and partially collapsing in places. Many of the teak staircases are in hazardous condition; those who venture inside do so at their own risk. A small but increasing trickle of tourists comes to visit the decaying building, though access is reportedly becoming more and more restricted. From a conservation point of view, the Pegu Club is in a remarkable condition given its age, wooden structure and neglect. Much of the original fabric remains, which could guide an informed conservation project, according to conservation expert Kecia Fong. But a full restoration would come with a heavy price tag, fuelling speculation about the building's possible future incarnation. A commercial lease appears a likely option. The Pegu Club would then probably become a luxury hotel, like the nearby **Governor's Residence** 068 C. Some would question whether a building so central to Myanmar's colonial past, with an explicitly racist admissions policy, should end up catering once again to an exclusive clientele.

June XI Business Centre (Prome Court)

066 C

36 Pyay Road
Clark & Greig (contractors)
1921–1922

Built in the early 1920s, Prome Court was one of Southeast Asia's first apartment complexes. One two-storey structure faces Pyay Road. Two other three-storey buildings are on Zagawar and Than Ta Man Streets respectively. Prome was the British name for the city of Pyay, about 250 kilometres northwest of Yangon. (The long road in Yangon bearing the same name will lead you there.) The growth of the colonial apparatus after the First World War called for greater civil service accommodation and many officials used the 28 spacious flats inside this building. No doubt the occupants found the short distance to the **Pegu Club** 065 C convenient. In 1937, the Public Works Department moved into the northern and the southern blocks of the complex. By then, the **Secretariat** 006 B was reaching its capacity following Burma's separation from British India. After independence, the Deputy Prime Minister's Office and the Ministry of Foreign Affairs moved into the building. They remained there for several decades. The building stood empty for some years after the government's move to Naypyidaw in 2005. It received a new, yet controversial, lease of life in 2011 when the government-run Myanmar Investment Commission and a new entity, the "Youth Force Hotel", signed a 60-year lease agreement. These leaseholders first planned to erect a 14-storey condominium on the site, but local conservationists led a campaign in protest. City authorities then changed zoning regulations to allow for a six-storey building only. The colonial-era buildings are now renovated and converted into serviced apartments and high-end offices. It is now called the "June XI Business Centre"—a rather uninspiring reference to the month when the lease agreement was signed... The managing director of "Youth Force Hotel" told the media that rents here will be similar to those in **Sakura Tower** 010 B which, as of mid-2014, was the third most expensive office building in the world. And should the zoning regulations ever change, the business centre can easily expand. The press reported that the foundations put in place for the six-storey building are strong enough to bear the load of a building more than twice the height.

4

National Museum of Myanmar 067 C

66/74 Pyay Road
Public Works Department
1990–1996

The National Museum of Myanmar was founded in 1952. It was first located in the Jubilee Hall on Shwedagon Pagoda Road, which was later demolished. In 1970 the museum moved into the former **National Bank of India** 026 B on Pansodan Street. Its present building opened its doors in September 1996, to mark the eighth anniversary of the SLORC's accession to power after the 1988 uprising. Prior to opening, construction on the two-hectare site went on for six years. The museum consists of three five-storey cubic buildings, with a huge concrete canopy facing Pyay Road. The main entrance, however, is to the side of the museum. The grounds feature bronze statues of three legendary rulers of Burma: King Anawratha (r. 1044–1077), King Bayinnaung (r. 1550–1581) and King Alaung Min Tayar (r. 1752–1760).

At first glance, the façade appears windowless. In fact the regular protrusions have slim windows along the sides, preventing direct sunlight from entering. Despite its relatively young age, the building is already showing heavy signs of wear. Inside, dim lighting, frequently inoperable lifts, poor labelling and large cordoned-off areas highlight the need for major updates. The quality of exhibitions varies greatly. Some sections showcase the political achievements of the current administration. Another room illustrates Myanmar's great diversity via a rather tokenistic, wide-ranging display of ethnic minorities' traditional costumes. The museum's main exhibit is the Lion Throne, made of local *yamanay* wood and completely gilded: it was the throne of Burma's last king, Thibaw, who was driven from his Mandalay Palace during the Third Anglo–Burmese War in 1885. Removed to Kolkata during colonial times, it was promptly returned to newly independent Burma in 1948.

Governor's Residence Hotel (Kayah State Governor's Residence)

068 C

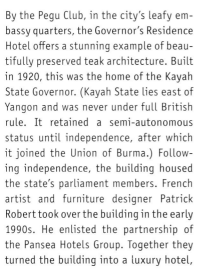

35 Taw Win Road
Unknown
1920

4

By the Pegu Club, in the city's leafy embassy quarters, the Governor's Residence Hotel offers a stunning example of beautifully preserved teak architecture. Built in 1920, this was the home of the Kayah State Governor. (Kayah State lies east of Yangon and was never under full British rule. It retained a semi-autonomous status until independence, after which it joined the Union of Burma.) Following independence, the building housed the state's parliament members. French artist and furniture designer Patrick Robert took over the building in the early 1990s. He enlisted the partnership of the Pansea Hotels Group. Together they turned the building into a luxury hotel, which opened in 1997. The restoration was painstaking: the edifice was taken apart completely and put back together, with each piece being numbered and then re-assembled. A large amount of concrete now reinforces the walls—enough, apparently, to withstand a major earthquake. A swimming pool was added to the compound with tiles imported from Spain. In 2006, the Residence's owners sold it to Orient-Express Hotels (today's Belmond Ltd.). The London-based company runs the hotel to this day. The venue and its surrounding gardens are a sanctuary of quiet and luxury. All 48 rooms use local teak furniture. The place conjures up images of the colonial days, from the fan-cooled terrace to the Kipling Bar, where well-heeled sightseers retreat for a quiet cocktail after a long day in the heaving city. But must stunning conservation efforts always transform Yangon's heritage into enclaves for the rich?

Children's Hospital

Kha Yay Pin Street
U Tun Than
1970–1978

069 C

Original plans for this functional hospital building foresaw a much bigger structure, but scarce funds and rampant inflation imposed this scaled-down version. The Canadian government provided wheat to Burma at heavily discounted prices in the 1960s. The proceeds of the onward sale were earmarked for the construction of this hospital building; a typical Canadian aid practice at the time. The hospital's architect, U Tun Than, is now in his eighties and retired long ago.

He was among the first batch of architecture students at Yangon University after the country's independence, graduating from the institution in 1958. Initially, many of the professors came from abroad. Upon graduation, U Tun Than worked for a short time with U Tin (of **City Hall** 018 B fame) and spent several years working on public housing projects, for example in Yankin township. In 1965 he was offered the chance to travel to the UK for further studies. He first gained a postgraduate diploma in architecture and then spent a year as an architect-apprentice at the British Ministry of Health. When he returned to Burma in the late 1960s, he focused on building hospitals, with

the Children's Hospital being his first major assignment. The façade modelling is designed to create shade and provide cooling. Its structural honesty and stylistic unity make this an exemplary public building from that period, adapted to local conditions and the limited availability of building material. The building's two identical wings are connected on the western side by a third wing, clad in a semi-permeable pattern visible from the inner courtyard. U Tun Than continued working for the Public Works Department for more than 20 years. In the 1980s, he began building and renovating schools with UNICEF, a job that took him mainly to rural areas. To him, Burmese architecture should focus on the country's harsh climate conditions first and foremost: extreme heat and heavy rainfalls are a constant issue. Such a vernacular Burmese architecture would also be more environmentally friendly and energy-efficient. However, a cursory look at Yangon's construction sites shows rampant use of glass cladding. New power plants will no doubt be needed just to keep the AC units humming.

4

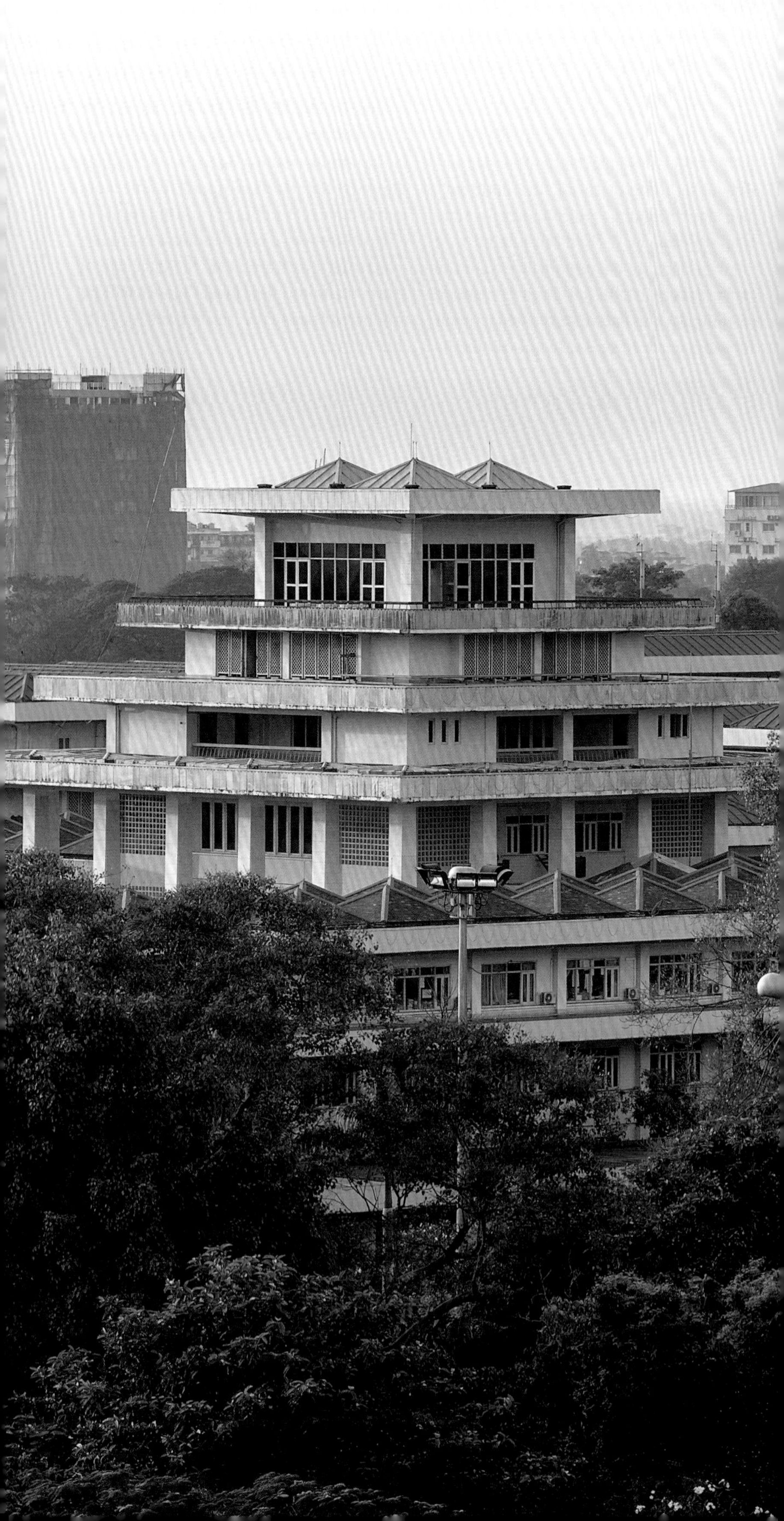

Yangon Region Parliament 070 E
Pyay Road/Ahlone Road
Public Works Department
1986–1996

Most visitors to Yangon—and residents, for that matter—have probably not had the chance to take a close look at the local parliament building (Hluttaw). Sometimes known as the "Congress Building", it is set back deep from the busy thoroughfares of Pyay and Ahlone Roads. Already difficult to observe through the security fence that lines the perimeter, the tall trees of the generous park area that surrounds the building further shield it from view. These photos taken from the **Yangon International Hotel** 071 C, however, reveal an austere structure that displays perhaps one of the bulkiest and most rectilinear interpretations of temple design. This can be seen for example in the tallest wing, measuring six storeys. Its tiered structures mimic that of the traditional pyatthat roofs. You can also make out the use of the perforated wall designs often seen in modern Yangon architecture, for example at the **U Thant Mausoleum** 077 C. Throughout the structure, the roofing consists of a gridded (and rather odd) series of consecutive low roofs. The roof of the westernmost wing sets itself apart with a design that vaguely echoes that of East Asian temples. Aerial views reveal a spacious and grassy internal courtyard, on the model of the wide park and fountain facing the building on the Pyay Road side. Traditionally, the word hluttaw referred to the council of advisers to the court of a Burmese monarch. The term was repurposed during colonial days to refer to a parliamentary structure. The British Parliament's Government of Burma Act, in 1935, separated Burma from British India and provided for the creation of a local parliament inside the **Secretariat** 006 B. This parliament consisted of a 36-seat Senate and a 132-seat House of Representatives. Some seats were reserved for specific political constituencies, reflecting Rangoon's cosmopolitanism at the time. Indians, Europeans and the "Anglo–Burmese" all had their quota of seats, as did labour organisations and the wide range of chambers of commerce operating in the city, from the Chinese to the Chettiars. The Karen also had seats, although other ethnic minorities, such as the Shan, were not entitled to elect members of parliament. (In a reminder that the Burmese military have in many ways perpetuated the habits of the country's former British rulers, half the Senate seats were nominated by the Governor directly, not unlike the 25 per cent of seats reserved for the army in Myanmar's current parliament.) The parliament remained inside the Secretariat grounds after independence in 1948, and sat there until Ne Win's coup in 1962. The country did not have a functional parliament from 1962 until 2011, although an army-appointed legislative branch did operate from 1974 until 1988. This building was a government office until 2011, when it became the regional Hluttaw for Yangon. The national Hluttaw sits in Naypyidaw.

Yangon International Hotel ⌄ » `071` `C`
330 Ahlone Road
Unknown
1990–1995

The Yangon International Hotel's construction started in 1990 and finished five years later. Its endless rows of rounded balconies wouldn't look entirely out of place in Las Vegas. The Japanese Minatsu Construction Group initially planned a more ambitious project on this site, opposite the People's Park. During the 1990s, several Japanese firms had their representative offices in this building, which explains the hot bath on the upper terrace, as well as the Japanese restaurant and the karaoke venue on the premises. The location may be the best thing about the hotel. An elevator ride to the ninth floor rewards the intrepid explorer with unhindered access to an airy but largely abandoned roof terrace overlooking this leafy part of Yangon, and affording good views of the **Shwedagon Pagoda** 075 E. The hotel management has begun building an almost identical-looking annex, set to open in 2016.

Summit Parkview Hotel ⌄

350 Ahlone Road
Unknown
1994

4

Just like the neighbouring Yangon International Hotel , the Summit Parkview was built in the mid-1990s. However, it rose at a much faster pace, visibly leaving little time to draw up meaningful designs. It received a facelift recently, although compared to its more exuberant neighbour, the hotel's façade remains pretty bare. One of the few notable features is its driveway, which imitates Burmese temple design. You may not be entirely surprised to learn that the Singapore-based Summit Hotel Group no longer owns this property—it now runs the five-star Sedona Hotel instead.

Planetarium

57 Ahlone Road,
inside People's Park
Unknown
1986–1987

073 E

A stroll through People's Park is a welcome distraction from Yangon's hustle and bustle. Several unique sites greet the visitor, including a decommissioned Fokker propeller plane, a locomotive, some tree-top observation platforms—and the Planetarium. The windowless white building is near the Yangon Gallery in the southwestern end of the park. You could easily miss it amid the trees. It is open most days from 10am to 3pm. Inside, the building features Japanese stargazing equipment. Former military dictator Ne Win took an interest in astrology. He was reportedly quite pleased with this Japanese gift and used it to coincide his strategic moves and political plots with auspicious times. He told his astrologers to perfect their horoscopes using these modern electronic devices. As a result, the Planetarium was allegedly off-limits to the public, although Japanese officials denied this at the time. The fates of Japan and Myanmar were tangled in the 20th century. Though their motives differed, Japan supported General Aung San's nationalist movement in its fight against the British. Burma was of strategic interest to wartime Japan, which desperately sought oil and other natural resources to counteract the effects of Allied sanctions. Japan also wanted to cut through the Allied supply lines supporting Chiang Kai-shek's government in Chongqing, China. At the time, Japan was also locked in conflict in Manchuria and beyond. Almost 200,000 Japanese soldiers perished on Burmese soil during the Second World War. Despite the humiliating retreat of Japanese forces after their defeat in 1945, Japan's influence remained strong during Burmese independence. Take its national army, the *Tatmadaw*: it started life strongly

modelled on Japan's army, since Aung San and his fellow *Thakins* received the best Japanese training. Japan and Burma entered into diplomatic relations in 1954 and Japanese development—or reparation—payments were a welcome source of funds for the fledgling and troubled democracy. After a short cooling-off period during the first years of the Ne Win regime, Japan resumed its role as the most generous donor to the country, providing two-thirds of total bilateral assistance between 1973 and 1988. Japan's aid was strategic and natural resources still topped the agenda. As is often the case with Japanese aid, a lot of the money was tied to public procurement contracts that were hugely advantageous to Japanese firms. Eleven of them had offices in Yangon in the late 1980s. Controversially, Japan was also one of the few countries to maintain diplomatic ties with the military junta after 1988. Today Japan has become a major investor in Myanmar's opening-up and regards strengthened bilateral cooperation with the country as an important facet of its foreign policy, not least to keep China's regional aspirations in check. To this end, Japan has forgiven hundreds of millions of US dollars worth of debt, generously supports a major deep sea port project near Yangon and is involved in a myriad of projects throughout the country. A real community of Japanese businesses has settled here; contrary to more cautious Western investors, they are not afraid to put their money to work in Myanmar. The Japanese development agency JICA is also the most active of the major bilateral aid bodies. Critical voices point out that Japanese aid is often tied to public procurement projects that benefit Japanese firms: look out for Japanese rolling stock on Yangon's railway tracks. A rough headcount suggests there are more than 60 Japanese restaurants around the city, many of them perfectly authentic down to the gaggles of homesick *salarymen* who appear at dinner time.

4

Martyrs' Mausoleum

4

Martyrs' Mausoleum

Ar Zar Ni St
U Sun Oo
1984

After more than 20 years of restricted access, the Martyrs' Mausoleum opened to the public again in 2013. This is where the victims of the 19 July 1947 assassination in the **Secretariat** 006 B, including General Aung San, are entombed and commemorated. A previous mausoleum to honour the victims of the 1947 assassination was erected in the early 1960s on a nearby site. In 1982, architects from all over Burma were invited to submit designs for a new commemorative structure. U Sun Oo, at the architecture faculty of the **Institute of Technology** 108 A at the time, submitted a design on behalf of the school. The design's main idea was to create an informal covered space for ordinary Burmese to pay respect to their heroes while at the same time learning about the recent history of the country. The architecture was to be simple and elegant, using locally sourced timber. Alas,

the existing memorial became the scene of another brutal assassination on 9 October 1983. A high-level delegation from South Korea was visiting the mausoleum when a bomb planted inside exploded, killing 21, including South Korea's minister for foreign affairs and its deputy prime minister. South Korean President Chun Doo-hwan got away unscathed because his car was delayed in traffic. The bomb was planted by North Korean agents and destroyed much of the earlier structure. This was seen as an omen. U Sun Oo and his 12-strong team were asked to redesign their monument to be bombproof, and to do it fast! Over a two-month period, the plans were completely reworked. They now featured nine curved—and staggered—upwardly pointing cantilevered reinforced concrete ribs. Based on a study of similar monumental sites in Burma, U Sun Oo and his team carefully considered the approach that visitors would take to the site, opting for a processional route arriving from the south to the feet of the buried heroes. But then Ne Win personally got involved. Following his intervention,

the design was watered down, weakening its architectural integrity. A road for official cars was instructed. Now there were to be two tiers of visitors, ordinary people and the elite. The road approached the site from the northeast, arriving at a handy drop-off point at the steps of the podium. Plans for a cut-out star adorning the left-hand rib were ditched. The elegant cantilevered ribs were deemed too daring, structurally, and a supporting wedge was added behind them. The materials were cheapened too, such as the floor surface: the one eventually used is unbearably hot in the sun, making it impossible to stand barefoot. Visitors have to wear shoes—highly disrespectful in Burmese tradition. While U Sun Oo is credited as the architect of the project, you couldn't blame him for wanting to disown it. His original idea for an egalitarian and elegant place of respect, mourning and education has become a bombastic and lifeless monument to the authoritarian cheapness of Ne Win. In addition, the architect wasn't paid for the commission—it was deemed part of his work as a university lecturer.

This is a story of broken dreams, one with which many architects will sympathise. U Sun Oo still works today and chairs the local architectural firm Design 2000. He is also a board member of the Yangon Heritage Trust and an outspoken supporter of urban conservation projects. Although the monument is perhaps an architectural disappointment and certainly fell short of its creator's ambitions, it retains symbolic power. As his daughter became the opposition's figurehead, the cult of General Aung San was repressed by the military junta after 1988. The mausoleum became off limits to the public and the site was patrolled by soldiers. With the country's recent opening-up, the authorities lifted these restrictions in 2013. Martyrs' Day celebrations were once again held at the site of the mausoleum, involving Myanmar's top political leadership from both government and opposition. Although President Thein Sein declined to attend, his Vice President Sai Mauk Kham represented him. Aung San Suu Kyi was reported to have "appreciated the manner in which the government had marked the day".

Lights illuminate the Shwedagon Pagoda at night time.
The glow can be seen right across Yangon.

Shwedagon Pagoda

Ar Zar Ni Street
Unknown
Since 2,500 BC/
6th–10th century AD

075 E

Yangon's most majestic landmark towers over the city from the top of Singuttara Hill. The pagoda is 99 metres high and covered with shining gold plates. It has been the centre of religious life in this part of Myanmar for many centuries. The pagoda's layout is intricate, while the complex surrounding it is vast, occupying almost 50 hectares. Apart from being the most important centre of Buddhism in Myanmar, the Shwedagon Pagoda has been a focal point for military occupation during colonial times and a rallying place in Burma's quest for independence. It would later become an important civic space for political resistance. It continues to—and forever will—hold a unique position in Yangon's urban fabric. In local legend, the two merchant brothers Tapussa and Bhallika offered the Buddha alms in the 6th century BC. They received eight strands of his hair as a blessing before they travelled to today's Lower Myanmar. Then-king Okkalapa enshrined the hairs in what was to become the present-day pagoda. As Buddhism is thought to have come to Burma later, and from South India as opposed to North India, it is more likely that the original Shwedagon was built by local Mon people between the 6th and 10th century AD. The main stupa itself is a more recent addition, dating back about five centuries. Queen Shin Sawbu raised the structure and, before her death, had her own weight in gold added to the stupa as gilding— thus starting a long tradition. The pagoda was raised again to its current height of just under 100 metres by King Hsinbyushin in 1774 after an earthquake caused some serious damage to the previous structure. Over the centuries, many additions were made to the compound of the pagoda, such as dozens of shrines, assembly halls, monasteries and four monumental stairways, or *zaungdans*, which ascend Singuttara Hill from all four cardinal directions, with the one from the west being the longest. The 20th century saw a number of local Burmese merchants rising to considerable wealth. Many of them became benefactors of the Shwedagon Pagoda. One of them was U Po Tha, who donated the funds to build **Chaukhtatgyi Pagoda** 094 E in Bahan township and contributed the Shwedagon's Northern Devotional Hall in the late 1920s. Most of this early 20th century architecture was traditional in form but relied on European engineering advances to increase the height and elaborateness of tiered roofing, for example at the southern entrance. Woodcarving also became more extensive. Many structures surrounding the stupa have been built and rebuilt over the last decades, especially since a

devastating fire in 1931 destroyed most of the wooden elements at the eastern and western sides of the platform. Three out of the four *zaungdans* are lined with stalls selling Buddha statues and devotional flowers, among many other items. Visitors can also use the elevators such as the one conveniently located at the southern entrance. Footwear is not allowed anywhere beyond the base of the hill, where provisions are made for its storage. As this limits the freedom to exit the pagoda via another stairway, you are advised to carry shoes in your rucksack.

Guides will approach foreign visitors—their tours generally offer decent value for money, especially if you are visiting the pagoda with a group. For those on a shoestring, the map given at the entrance is very detailed and informative. The best way to experience the Shwedagon is to forget about the facts and history for a while: simply appreciate the spirituality of the place, especially in the early morning hours or late in the evening, when the heat is less torrid and fewer tourists visit. Upon entering the main terrace, the stupa looks even more impressive at close distance. Many smaller stupas, pavilions and tall prayer posts surround it, creating a labyrinth of built structures on the outer ring of the encircling passageway, which is about 50 metres wide and covered in marble. Each local visitor has his or her own path when visiting the Shwedagon. As Professor Elizabeth Moore of the School of Oriental and African Studies describes in her paper about "unexpected spaces" at the Shwedagon, each of them creates "a personal narrative in the physical and poetic space of the pagoda". (The paper is worth reading for those interested in the practices and rituals in more detail. For bibliographic information, turn to page 396.) Many choose the clockwise walk around the stupa (circumambulation). Others venerate one of the four Buddhas of the current era (of which Gautama is the most recent; his hairs are also enshrined at the Shwedagon), while still others offer their wishes before planetary shrines and those dedicated to the eight Buddhist days of the week (with Wednesday partitioned into am and pm). Lastly, there are visitors who seek out cult images on display here. The Shwedagon Pagoda is the living presence of the Buddha. Some see the lower, middle and upper levels as the Buddha, the teachings (*dhamma*) and the monkhood (*sangha*) respectively. Others think of the whole stupa as the Buddha in a seating position, with the umbrella (*hti*) at its top being its head. The amount of gold covering the pagoda is the subject of some speculation. Regardless of how many tons there already are, new layers of coating are added every five years alongside a renovation and re-polishing of the stupa. For this, an intricate scaffolding is installed, in itself an elaborate work of art performed by experienced contractors—seemingly unafraid of the dizzying heights. The Shwedagon Pagoda was occupied by British forces during the Second Anglo–Burmese War. It would remain under colonial administration for almost 80 years before being returned to the Burmese in 1929. Much of the adjacent land was used for military purposes, as the pagoda was located in the cantonment area of Rangoon. A map from 1914 shows the Shwedagon surrounded by rifle ranges in the north, *coolie* lines (denoting imperial soldiers from India) and artillery barracks in the west as well as European infantry barracks to the south. The spiritual importance of the Shwedagon Pagoda—and its insulting re-appropriation as a strategic military location by the colonial authority—made it a focal point of the independence movement. In 1920, students from Rangoon College met here to launch the University Boycott, which we describe in the section about **Myoma National High School** 081 C. A small plaque in the southwestern section of the middle platform commemorates the students who took part in the protest. In 1938, striking oil workers established a camp at the foot of the pagoda, firmly establishing the Shwedagon as a symbolic site of political protest. After the war, and on the eve of Burmese independence, General Aung San gave a rousing speech to a nationalist meeting convened here. Forty-two years later, his daughter would address several hundreds of thousands of demonstrators at a pivotal moment in the democracy movement's struggle against dictatorship. In 2007, the Saffron Revolution largely led by monks saw thousands converge towards the pagoda, too. Today the Shwedagon's position above Yangon is challenged by tall construction projects. In an attempt to safeguard its towering symbolism, buildings constructed within

a one-mile radius of the pagoda must be no more than six storeys high. To further protect the skyline as seen from the downtown area, buildings in the line of sight beyond this radius, to the south, must not exceed the total height of the hill plus the pagoda (approximately 160 metres). This begs the question of where the skyline can best be admired. Downtown's narrow streetscape prevents clear views in most directions anyway; only from the top of tall buildings and closer up can you really take in the Shwedagon. The top of the **Sule Shangri-La** 009 B or the **Sakura Tower** 010 B offer compelling views. Buildings of a similar height are being built between the Shwedagon and the waterfront (though some of these projects were suspended in February 2015, precisely due to concerns over their proximity to the pagoda). Vista Bar, on West Shwegondaing Road, is a popular venue to watch the stupa glow from up close in the night time. While Yangon's skyline is likely to change dramatically in the coming years, one thing is sure: none of us will ever experience the magic of the Shwedagon as 19th-century travellers did, slowly approaching the city's port on ships.

4

Maha Wizaya Pagoda
U Htaung Bo Road
Unknown
1980–1986

Just opposite the **Shwedagon Pagoda's** 075 E southern entrance lies another arresting Buddhist place of worship. But the Maha Wizaya Pagoda differs markedly from its bigger and much older neighbour. The main approach from Shwedagon Pagoda Road takes visitors to a rectangular pond with a bridge leading to the pagoda. The hti crowning the golden stupa has 11 tiers, which is two more than the Shwedagon. The pagoda contains Buddhist relics given to Burma by the King of Nepal. Like the **Botataung** 001 B and the **Kaba Aye** 104 F Pagodas, the inside of the stupa is hollow. The Nepali relics are displayed here, in a central shrine. The light-blue dome is adorned with depictions of animals. Painted trees grow up the walls, their leaves made from plastic. Carpets surrounding the shrine are there for visitors to sit on. The Maha Wizaya Pagoda was built on Ne Win's orders. As he grew older, the General distanced himself from his earlier commitment to secularism. To some, this was a clear attempt to portray himself as a pagoda-building leader in the style of Burmese kings. Before the "General's Pagoda" was finished, rumours circulated that upon its opening, Ne Win would be overthrown. He in fact stayed in power for two and a half years after the pagoda's opening ceremony in February 1986. The pagoda was built by scores of Burmese people from all walks of life. The regime of the time called this "meritorious voluntary service". Human rights activists called it forced labour.

4

Mausolea on Shwedagon Pagoda Road

Each of these four buildings honours a woman or a man with a proud—but fraught—place in Burmese history. During the dark days of dictatorship, these monuments were neglected and people discouraged from paying their respects. And yet, the fact that the generals never dared remove them—and in some cases, grudgingly authorised their construction—showed the limits of their influence even at the height of their power.

U Thant Mausoleum

Shwedagon Pagoda Road
Unknown
1975

077 C

Here lies one of Myanmar's most cherished sons. U Thant was the United Nations Secretary-General for two terms, from 1961 to 1971. He was at the helm of the organisation at the height of the Cold War, including the Cuban Missile Crisis, one of history's most dangerous geopolitical standoffs. Somewhat secluded, this building stands to the far right of a row of tombs near the southern entrance of the **Shwedagon Pagoda** 075 E.

The front walls of the mausoleum are perforated, letting in light and air. A park with a manicured lawn and short hedges surrounds the building. U Thant was a member of the post-independence and democratic government led by Prime Minister U Nu. After the 1962 coup, relations between U Thant and General Ne Win's military dictatorship were tense. Ne Win was reportedly convinced that U Thant was using the United Nations as a stage to connive against him and support the deposed U Nu. After U Thant's death in New York in 1974, his body was sent to Rangoon for the funeral. Ne Win decreed that no official protocol should meet

the coffin's arrival, prompting widespread anger. Students seized the coffin from **Kyaikkasan Race Course** 096 F, where it lay, and brought it to the campus of **Yangon University** 101 F, where the body was guarded by protesters for seven days. The government finally proposed to place the body at its current site, but the students refused and buried it at the Student Union compound. Two days later, at night, troops came to dig up the coffin and placed it here, where the mausoleum now stands. Tragically, scores died when the military raided the university shortly afterwards, on 11 December 1974. This was an overt attempt to punish the students and deter them from launching further protests. The mausoleum was quickly erected by government engineers—too quickly, perhaps. "U Thant deserves better than that," says Yangon-based architect U Sun Oo. U Thant's grandson, Thant Myint-U, is a writer and diplomat. Raised in the United States, his first visit to Rangoon was to accompany U Thant's remains. Now a former UN official himself, he moved to Myanmar several years ago and became an adviser to President Thein Sein's government on the peace process with the country's ethnic armed groups. He also chairs the Yangon Heritage Trust and plays a crucial role in efforts to preserve the city's iconic heritage buildings. He has written several popular books on Myanmar's history and frequently comments on Myanmar affairs in the Western media. His books feature affectionate portraits of his grandfather and their life in New York. Of his passing, he writes that U Thant was "unwell from exhaustion and the stress of work" by the end of his tenure at the helm of the United Nations. In his writings, Thant Myint-U also recalls his grandfather's life on the other side of the planet, in New York, in a "red-brick house, partly covered in ivy and set on a grassy six-acre hillside along the Hudson River. On the map it was part of Riverdale, but in most other ways it was a small slice of Burma."

4

Queen Supalayat Mausoleum 078 C
Shwedagon Pagoda Road
Unknown
1925

The whitewashed brick monument was erected after the death of Burma's last queen in 1925. It is built in traditional style: the square base containing her ashes is topped by a stone-made imitation of a multi-tiered *pyatthat* roof. Its top is crowned by a golden *hti*. The designers may have "wisely divined that Supalayat would be happier in a tomb reflecting the past rather than the present", as Donald Stadtner writes in his book *Sacred Sites of Burma*. Supalayat was born in 1859 and ascended to the throne as King Thibaw's wife. The two were half-siblings, their father being King Mindon. Unusually for polygamous Burmese royal households, Supalayat was Thibaw's only wife. This,

it was said, could be attributed to the queen's domineering attitude and stormy temper. Her most notorious acts included the execution of a rival with whom the King had fallen in love and, though she denied knowledge of the plot, the assassination of up to 100 royal family members in one brutal slaughter. The royal family was sent into exile by the British following the Third Anglo–Burmese War in 1885. Along with their three daughters and a small entourage, they ended up in Ratnagiri, halfway between Mumbai and Goa along India's western coast. Thibaw died here aged only 57. For those interested in a literary account of Burma's history and the royal family since their 1885 exile, Amitav Ghosh's *The Glass Palace* is a pleasing page-turner. Supalayat was permitted to return to Burma in 1919, and spent her last years in seclusion in Yangon, in today's 24 Komin Kochin Road.

Daw Khin Kyi Mausoleum

Shwedagon Pagoda Road
U Kyaw Min
1989

079 C

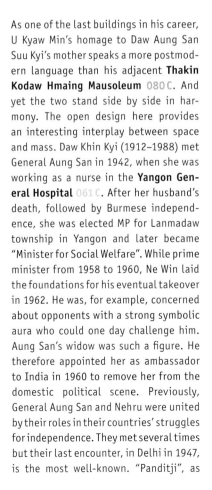

As one of the last buildings in his career, U Kyaw Min's homage to Daw Aung San Suu Kyi's mother speaks a more postmodern language than his adjacent **Thakin Kodaw Hmaing Mausoleum** 080 C. And yet the two stand side by side in harmony. The open design here provides an interesting interplay between space and mass. Daw Khin Kyi (1912–1988) met General Aung San in 1942, when she was working as a nurse in the **Yangon General Hospital** 061 C. After her husband's death, followed by Burmese independence, she was elected MP for Lanmadaw township in Yangon and later became "Minister for Social Welfare". While prime minister from 1958 to 1960, Ne Win laid the foundations for his eventual takeover in 1962. He was, for example, concerned about opponents with a strong symbolic aura who could one day challenge him. Aung San's widow was such a figure. He therefore appointed her as ambassador to India in 1960 to remove her from the domestic political scene. Previously, General Aung San and Nehru were united by their roles in their countries' struggles for independence. They met several times but their last encounter, in Delhi in 1947, is the most well-known. "Panditji", as

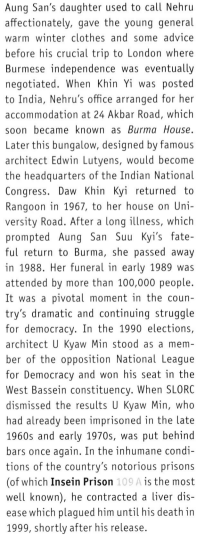

Aung San's daughter used to call Nehru affectionately, gave the young general warm winter clothes and some advice before his crucial trip to London where Burmese independence was eventually negotiated. When Khin Yi was posted to India, Nehru's office arranged for her accommodation at 24 Akbar Road, which soon became known as *Burma House*. Later this bungalow, designed by famous architect Edwin Lutyens, would become the headquarters of the Indian National Congress. Daw Khin Kyi returned to Rangoon in 1967, to her house on University Road. After a long illness, which prompted Aung San Suu Kyi's fateful return to Burma, she passed away in 1988. Her funeral in early 1989 was attended by more than 100,000 people. It was a pivotal moment in the country's dramatic and continuing struggle for democracy. In the 1990 elections, architect U Kyaw Min stood as a member of the opposition National League for Democracy and won his seat in the West Bassein constituency. When SLORC dismissed the results U Kyaw Min, who had already been imprisoned in the late 1960s and early 1970s, was put behind bars once again. In the inhumane conditions of the country's notorious prisons (of which **Insein Prison** 109 A is the most well known), he contracted a liver disease which plagued him until his death in 1999, shortly after his release.

Thakin Kodaw Hmaing Mausoleum

Shwedagon Pagoda Road
U Kyaw Min
1966

080 C

Thakin Kodaw Hmaing is one of Myanmar's most celebrated poets. His mausoleum was finished in 1966, two years after his death. The tomb is located inside a strikingly simple and square-shaped concrete building. The dim interior is illuminated mainly by the tall door openings, as well as a skylight. The perforated walls allow light and air to enter. After a period of long neglect, the mausoleum was recently renovated. Thakin Kodaw Hmaing (1876–1964) moved to Rangoon in the late 19th century. He started out as a playwright and later turned to journalism. He joined the Burmese nationalist cause and became one of its leading public intellectuals. An active proponent of reconciliation between the warring factions in post-independence Burma, he earned the "Stalin Peace Prize" in 1954; this explains the hammer and sickle on the façade of the mausoleum, alongside symbols of a book, a peacock (Myanmar's national symbol) and a peace dove. The mausoleum's architect, U Kyaw Min, also designed the adjacent mausoleum of Daw Khin Kyi. U Kyaw Min was born in 1933. Upon entering his third year at Yangon University's Engineering College, he was offered a scholarship to study in the US, at the Massachusetts Institute of Technology, from where he obtained an engineering degree in 1957. Upon returning to Myanmar, he spent some time as a lecturer and then set up his private practice in the early 1960s. As the country took a dark turn under Ne Win, this was not a time for lavish private commissions. However, U Kyaw Min built many residential projects for business people who appreciated his expertise and understated style. He was able to incorporate local design elements in his modern architecture, seen here in the mausoleum's subtle ornamentation.

BEHS No. 2 Dagon (Myoma National High School)

081 C

353 Myoma Kyaung Street
U Tin
1929–1931

Today's Basic Education High School No. 2 was once the Myoma National High School. It holds a special place in the story of Burma's quest for independence. When the Universities Act was passed in 1920, it foresaw that Rangoon College was to become a higher education institution—now the totemic **Yangon University** 101 F. But it was prohibitively expensive for most Burmese. Students in the nationalist movement staged a boycott which went down in history as one of the first acts of defiance against the colonial regime. In the wake of these protests, nationalists created a parallel schooling system with a heavy emphasis on Burmese language, culture and history. Most of these schools folded under great financial difficulty. Myoma National High School, however, survived the 1920s. By 1922, the school was nothing more than a few makeshift wooden structures in today's Bahan township. The main building was described by those studying and teaching in the school back then as "one big hut". The school moved twice before reaching its current location.

The cornerstone for a more permanent building was laid on 25 November 1929, the ninth anniversary of the University Boycott. The day continues to be celebrated as National Day. In a deliberate break with British colonial tradition, the building was designed by a Burmese architect, U Tin, whose signature style married classical elements of Burmese temple architecture with European forms and building techniques. His approach is visible at the **City Hall** 018 B, built around the same time. At Myoma, Burmese features include a five-tiered *pyatthat* roof above the main entrance. Its carvings are echoed in the dormers. Fittingly, the ceremonial opening of the school occurred on National Day 1931—falling on 4 December that year, according to the Burmese calendar. A statue of the school's headmaster, Ba Lwin (1892–1968), still greets visitors at the entrance. His celebrated dedication to the school's cause and donations from parents ensured the institution's survival. Ba Lwin remained an important figure in Burmese education. After independence, he became ambassador to Sri Lanka. The school was nationalised in 1965 and given its typically generic current name. It remains a prestigious school offering kindergarten up to tenth-grade education to more than 4,000 students.

National Theatre of Yangon

082 C

Myoma Kyaung Street
Unknown
1987–1991

When China's then-President Li Xiannian visited Burma in 1985, he offered the country this theatre building. Plans were drawn up and construction began in 1987 with the help of Chinese engineers. Construction work stopped during the 1988 uprising, but resumed the year after. The building was finished in December 1990 and opened the following month. Although construction was agreed before the State Law and Order Restoration Council (SLORC) took power in 1988, the theatre became a mainstay of the authoritarian regime and its emphasis on "safeguarding" Myanmar culture and heritage to mould a sense of national identity. Thus the theatre was principally used for traditional cultural shows such as dance and musical performances. With a capacity for about 1,300 spectators, the National Theatre is one of the best-equipped theatres in the region and features comparatively modern stage technology. China remained one of Burma's few allies post-1988. When visiting the construction site in 1989, SLORC First Secretary Khin Nyunt remarked that his government "sympathise[s] with the People's Republic of China as disturbances similar to those that took place in Myanmar during 1988 broke out there". He thanked China for sending engineers while Myanmar suffered from the consequences of the "disturbance". Chinese Secretary-General of the State Council Luo Gan attended the opening ceremony in January 1991. The Chinese government also provided manpower and equipment for maintenance of the theatre during the following years and granted 1.5 million US dollars to renovate the building in 2004, just 13 years after its completion. Another Chinese gift nearby is the Tatmadaw Hall, an exhibition centre on U Wizara Road.

Yuzana Tea Shop
Nawaday Road
SPINE Architects
2013

083 C

SPINE Architects is an architectural firm founded by Stephen Zawmoe Shwe and Amelie Chai. After graduating from Columbia University, both worked in New York for close to a decade before setting up shop in Myanmar in 2004. Today they boast an enviable portfolio of clients here. The Yuzana Tea Shop on Nawaday Road is one of the best examples of their work. Its open layout creates a small, light-flooded environment where customers can purchase varieties of packed tea. The shop is connected to the business owner's residence, a renovated colonial-era mansion, set back from the street. This busy stretch of Nawaday Road is a travellers' favourite, given the ample supply of bars and restaurants in the vicinity.

4

Methodist English Church
65 Alan Pya Pagoda Road

084 C

BEHS No. 1 Dagon (Methodist English High School)
57 Alan Pya Pagoda Road
Unknown
Circa 1894/1948–1949 (reconstruction)

This school, adjacent to the Methodist English Church, is one of the most prestigious institutions of secondary education in the country. Its alumni include many major figures in Myanmar's history. The most famous one, of course, is Nobel Peace Prize laureate Aung San Suu Kyi, who attended the school in the 1950s until 1960 when her mother was appointed Burmese ambassador in New Delhi. The main three-storey school building is set back from Alan Pya Pagoda Road. Access through its main entrance can prove difficult: school buildings are generally and understandably off limits to visitors in Myanmar. The site is densely built-up, with several other building wings providing space for the pupils. A large open ground at the rear of the school is variously used for parking cars, and as a sports ground. The building's post-war appearance belies its age and importance. The history of Dagon's BEHS 1 goes back more than 100 years, to 1881. The Methodist Women's Foreign Missionary Society was granted land and funds by

the government of British India to build a girls' school. The location of the school was in the downtown area, in today's Seikkantha Street. Methodist education at the time was strictly along "national" lines with separate English, Chinese and Burmese schools. The school was successful and attracted a steady stream of pupils. By 1894, it was "full to overflowing", a problem that was partially addressed—in good colonial fashion—by shortly displacing the Burmese Girls' School. Space remained an issue and by 1924, the school gladly accepted the government's offer of 300,000 rupees for the land, having been gifted it some 40 years earlier. The school immediately invested the money into a new, bigger school on the current site, on the corner of Alan Pya Pagoda and Nawaday Roads. It already owned the land. Japanese bombs destroyed the new school building in the Second World War. The adjacent church survived relatively unscathed. There is some debate about whether this was a conscious choice, for Subhas Chandra Bose's Indian National Army, which was allied to Japan, used the church as its Rangoon headquarters. (That said, Japanese bombs were probably not precise enough to target, or avoid, a building with such accuracy.) The school reopened in 1947. The few students who returned received their lessons inside the church. A new main building was

built under the direction of Methodist missionary Frank Manton and former principal Doreen Logie. Using 1 million US dollars from their "Crusade Fund", the Methodists completed the new, and current, main building by 1949. With a prime location opposite the British Embassy residence, this was the school of choice for Rangoon's westernised intellectual and social elite. When young Aung San Suu Kyi entered MEHS in the 1950s, her father's fame barely conferred her special status, as Peter Popham notes in his biography of the Burmese democracy icon. As one alumnus told him, "the children of three out of four of our presidents, of Prime Minister U Nu, of many branches of the royal family, of most politicians, of diplomats before there was an international school, and of old

money Rangoon aristocracy—they all went to [the] school". By this time, and as the only missionary school in Rangoon, MEHS was already co-ed. This meant, as the same ex-pupil told Popham, that "our parents were the most progressive, liberal-minded and westernised in Rangoon". This came at a price—MEHS was a very expensive school, with a tennis court and all the modern amenities. After Ne Win's nationalisation campaign, the school received its current name in 1965. It retained its reputation as one of the country's elite institutions. A new three-storey building facing Nawaday Road was added in 1986. Today the school has more than 6,000 pupils, making it one of the biggest in Myanmar. Its alumni are scattered around the world and hold regular reunions.

4

Thamada Cinema at night

Thamada (President) Hotel and Cinema

5 Alan Pya Pagoda Road
Unknown
1956–1964

The Thamada Hotel and Cinema is one of the city's best examples of modern post-war architecture. The four-storey cinema features rounded corners and, unusually for its time, an oval cinema hall. The hotel is directly to the north, set back slightly from the street to allow for drive-way access and parking. Its seven storeys repeat the cinema's rounded features on the corner of Yaw Min Gyi Street. The downstairs Café 365 features floor-to-ceiling windows, as does the first-floor hall which was being renovated at the time of writing. The Thamada was built by ethnic Chinese businessman U Kyaw Sein. He built the cinema first, to sub-sidise the construction of the adjacent hotel. When the cinema opened its doors in 1958, it immediately set the stand-ard for viewing and seating comfort in this movie-mad city. Most of Rangoon's cinemas, on "Cinema Row", were just a ten-minute walk away. This is where today's **Sule Shangri-La** 009 B and the **Sakura Tower** 010 B stand and where some cinemas, such as the **Waziya** 011 B, still remain. The Thamada boasted a fully air-conditioned hall. Its most expensive and plushest seats were at the front of the balcony. The cinema is still in opera-tion today and draws sell-out crowds, especially at weekends. It was renovated and upgraded only a few years ago. It is operated by the Mingalar Cinema Group,

Myanmar's largest movie screen company. The next-door Thamada Hotel was not yet completed when the government nationalised the whole complex in 1962, and only opened in 1964. It then came under the management of the inimitably named "Trade Corporation No. 20 - Hotels & Tourism Trade Corporation" under the Ministry of Trade, which mainly catered to foreign tourists. Not much is known about the complex's foreign architects. What we do know, however, is that a Japanese craftsman involved in the technical drawings inspired a young U Sun Oo (who designed the **Martyrs' Mausoleum** 074 C) to become an architect. After the SLORC assumed power in 1988, the Thamada became the unlikely choice for a renovation by one of the world's most exclusive hoteliers. Adrian Zecha, founder of the fabled Aman Resorts (a collection of five-star properties in plush, palm-lined locations) had his eyes set on the **Strand Hotel** 036 B. But in exchange for the privilege of renovating and operating the colonial-era gem, Zecha was required to upgrade the **Inya Lake Hotel** 103 F and the Thamada too. The SLORC wanted to improve tourist accommodation in preparation for an influx of foreign visitors—one that would, in reality, take many more oppressive and sanction-filled years to materialise. Zecha was not too impressed with the two extra properties that were forced upon him. He described the Inya Lake Hotel as a "Russian bunker", whereas the "tatty" Thamada could only become, at best, a two-star venue in his eyes. And in fact, that's exactly what it is today. This is assuredly not a luxury hotel and yet it has its charm. The curious traveller may enjoy taking a closer look.

Central Railway Station

Kun Chan Road
U Hla Gyaw
1947–1954

086 B

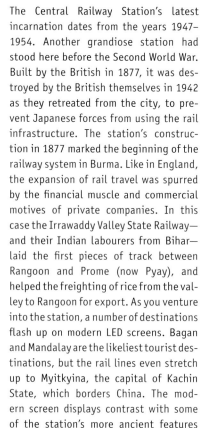

The Central Railway Station's latest incarnation dates from the years 1947–1954. Another grandiose station had stood here before the Second World War. Built by the British in 1877, it was destroyed by the British themselves in 1942 as they retreated from the city, to prevent Japanese forces from using the rail infrastructure. The station's construction in 1877 marked the beginning of the railway system in Burma. Like in England, the expansion of rail travel was spurred by the financial muscle and commercial motives of private companies. In this case the Irrawaddy Valley State Railway—and their Indian labourers from Bihar—laid the first pieces of track between Rangoon and Prome (now Pyay), and helped the freighting of rice from the valley to Rangoon for export. As you venture into the station, a number of destinations flash up on modern LED screens. Bagan and Mandalay are the likeliest tourist destinations, but the rail lines even stretch up to Myitkyina, the capital of Kachin State, which borders China. The modern screen displays contrast with some of the station's more ancient features

and its tired, post-war feel. (It's worth seeking out the old machine by the ticket office, which both measures your weight and gives your horoscope.) That feel may not last forever: several developers are competing for the contract to redevelop the station, though discussions remain in the early stages. The footbridge at the eastern end of the main building affords clear views of the platforms, including their green corrugated roofing, which has echoes of pagoda design, and the concrete heptagonal seats that encase some pillars. Traditional *pyatthat* roofing covers the four towers that punctuate the main building. Two wide porticos double up as generous balconies on the western and eastern wings, facing a wide expanse of tarmac between the station and **Bogyoke Aung San Stadium** 087 B, often the scene of wildly creative car manoeuvres. From platform 6 and 7 runs Yangon's circular railway, used by the city's rail commuters and a steady stream of tourists. The railway winds up the northwest of the city, past Insein, before looping eastwards and south back towards the railway station. Sit by the large windows and watch Yangon life, the commuters and betel nut vendors, weave in and out of the train cars and flow with the city. (For more about the circular railway, read its dedicated chapter on page 274.)

Bogyoke Aung San Stadium (Burma Athletic Association Grounds)
Zoological Garden Road
Unknown
1930/1958

087 B

The Bogyoke Aung San Stadium was once Yangon's greatest sports stadium, with a capacity of about 40,000. It opened in 1930 as the grounds for the Burma Athletic Association (BAA). After independence in 1953, authorities renamed it to honour Burma's national hero Aung San. (Bogyoke means general in Burmese.)

A PA system and two-storey stand were added in 1958. The stadium was also renovated in 1959–1960 for the second Southeast Asian Peninsular Games, which Yangon hosted in 1961. The games brought together more than 800 athletes from Burma, Cambodia, Laos, Malaysia, Singapore, Thailand and Vietnam. Today the stadium is home to one of the Myanmar National League's major football clubs, Yangon United FC. The club was founded by ubiquitous tycoon Tay Za, who also owns Air Bagan and has myriads of business interests in the country. His son is the club's chairman. The league

replaced the Myanmar Premier League in 2009 but, like its predecessor, suffers from underfunding and poor facilities. The pitch appears barely playable, especially during the rainy season when a thick layer of water floods the grass. The games are poorly attended. However, the growth of internet access in Myanmar promises a greater audience for football clubs in a football-mad country. On Facebook, YUFC counts several tens of thousands of followers who can watch video clips of the latest match highlights. In 2014, the team had several Brazilian outfield players and an Australian goalkeeper. Except during organised events, the ageing sports complex is accessible to the public. It contains small indoor facilities including a gym. An impoverished community lives beneath the stands. The stadium is bordered to the south by ticket stalls for long-distance bus companies. A supermarket, restaurants and other retailers line the stadium to the north. A series of portraits of Aung San and his daughter, Aung San Suu Kyi, feature at the entrances. Can you think of another country where a portrait of the political opposition adorns the country's biggest football stadium? (Or indeed, *any* stadium?)

4

Rose Garden Hotel

171 Upper Pansodan Road
Unknown
1995–2015

088 B

Parts of the hotel still remain under construction at the time of writing and only two floors are being rented out in what the management calls a "soft opening". Work on this site began as early as the mid-1990s, but was delayed by the Asian financial crisis, suffering similar struggles to the **Centrepoint Towers** 048 B. Once finished, the five-star hotel (financed by a Hong Kong-based investor) will have more than 300 rooms, adding much-needed capacity to Yangon's market. Although it gives the impression of belonging to an international chain, this is an independently operated hotel. The rooms on offer are more spacious than those of competitors in the same price range, and tastefully furnished. But—for the time being, at least—you may be unsettled by the hotel's "construction site" feel: for example, the current entrance leads through a tunnel to the makeshift reception area. The architects deserve credit for their ambition. This is a fearless and exuberant take on Myanmar architecture, differing from the all-too-common faceless tower blocks. Unfortunately, stone-made *pyatthat* roofs do not convey the same lightness and elegance as traditional temple designs. On Upper Pansodan Road and only a short walk from Kandawgyi Lake, the hotel is set against the greens of the adjacent Zoological Garden, apart from the hustle and bustle of downtown Yangon. An open sewer in front of the hotel illustrates that infrastructure remains a big challenge in the city.

Karaweik Palace

Kandawgyi Compound
U Ngwe Hlaing
1972–1974

089 D

Returning from the 1970 World Exposition in Osaka (Japan), General Ne Win was so taken with the Burmese pavilion displayed there that he decreed a vast replica be built in Yangon, on Kandawgyi Lake. The Burmese pavilion in Osaka itself was inspired by the Pyi Gyi Mon Royal Barge used by Burmese kings for ceremonial processions in Mandalay, seat of the royal court in the second half of the 19th century. Kandawgyi Lake was created by the British colonial administration to provide clean water to the city. It sources its water from nearby Inya Lake through underground pipes. Karaweik Palace was built between 1972 and 1974, off the eastern shore of the lake. Its dimensions are impressive (82 × 39 metres). Its gold coating glistens at night, illuminated by massive spotlights. It is bulkier and less delicate than the two versions that inspired it, in Mandalay and Osaka. The name Karaweik is derived from the mythical birds adorning the front of the boat. The seven-tiered *pyatthat* roof is a classic display of traditional Burmese architecture, echoing the royal palace in Mandalay. A pavilion in front of the palace contains a restaurant hosting dinner shows featuring traditional dances. The venue can also be hired for special celebrations and events. Karaweik

Palace is visible from almost anywhere around the lake, the shore of which is split into two sections accessible to visitors. The larger one contains a few small temples reached by foot along wooden boardwalks. The smaller one features Karaweik Palace, a children's playground and areas for music festivals. Just like most venues catering to foreign tourists and Yangon's high society, the Palace was run by the Ministry of Trade before it was leased to a local entrepreneur in the late nineties. Although tourists these days have rather mixed views of the dinner buffets, the Karaweik's kitchen used to be famous for the quality (and exorbitant prices) of its breads and ice creams. During the violent scenes in August 1988, the Palace's staff invited monks from nearby monasteries to spend their nights here in safety.

4

"What Are Your Five Favourite Buildings in Yangon?"

U Hpone Thant (Harry),
Senior Advisor, Myanmar Tourism Federation

Old Police Court Building
(New Law Courts Building) 032 B
The engraving on the façade says the Governor of Burma erected the building in 1931, in time for Queen Victoria's Jubilee. Since then it has lived through some of the most interesting periods of Myanmar's history. It became the headquarters of the dreaded Japanese secret police, the *Kempeitai*, during the Second World War. After the war it was the main police court building in Yangon. It was also used as offices by the socialist regime after 1962.
But this isn't just a lifeless concrete structure. The old building shared in the joys and sorrows of the people under its roof. The walls would reverberate with laughter and songs during the Myanmar New Year staff parties every April. It cried in silence when a young female employee drowned in the Yangon River in a ferry mishap, right under its nose. And there was the mysterious case of the old rusty iron safe on the veranda: nobody knew when or who put it there, or why, let alone what was inside. Another time, a night duty officer saw a snake on his rounds and when he captured it, found it was a female cobra with eggs in her belly. Oh my God!

Lim Chin Tsong Palace 095 F
It is an imposing structure with spires constructed in Chinese style. There were rumours of a tunnel under the main building to connect it to another similar, but smaller, structure on the other bank of Inya Lake. Some say there was a secret basement. There was also talk among envious locals who claimed Chin Tsong was so rich that he burned banknotes to boil his tea kettle. Although not in Myanmar architectural style, it shows the cultural diversity of the city.

Boat Club and Kandawgyi Lake
The Boat Club was strictly the domain of the "whites". No local Myanmar members were accepted; they were even forbidden from entering the building. After independence in 1948, the lake reverted from "Royal Lake" to its Myanmar name of Kandawgyi, which means "Great Lake". The Boat Club was renamed the Pyidaungsu Club ("Union Club") and the doors of the clubhouse were opened to local people (if they were elite or powerful).
The lake's origins are shrouded in mystery. Legend says it was formed when King Okkalapa used the earth from this place to make bricks for the great Shwedagon Pagoda. Others suggest the lake was formed when the Head Minister of Dagon (Yangon's historical name) dammed a small creek draining into the Pazundaung River to water his war elephants. But however the lake actually emerged, it has become Yangon residents' favourite spot for rest and relaxation.

Rangoon Turf Club 096 F
Sundays were race days: Rangoon's high society would gather at the Rangoon Turf Club in all their fineries, sitting in the Members' Stand on the western side of the grounds. The lower classes had to enter by the eastern gates. General Ne Win, who took over the country in 1962, was a regular visitor at these Sunday meets even before he took power. Later he decided to abolish horse racing. But the former Members' Stand found a new life. They became a stage for delegates from the country's 14 States and Divisions to give glowing speeches and extol the virtues of socialism. Today the grounds are overgrown with weeds and tall grasses but the ancient crumbling walls of the Members'

Rangoon Turf Club (today's Kyaikkasan Race Course)

Stand might still be remembering the voices cheering the winning jockeys—or are they cheering the glories of socialism? Who knows what they might tell us if they could speak!

Ministry of Hotels and Tourism 017 B

First built by Indian investors, the building was partly destroyed during the Second World War—suffering extensive damage to its façade in particular. After the war the Ministry of Commerce had some of its offices here. After 1962, the Revolutionary Government substituted the Ministry of Commerce with the Ministry of Trade and created state-led corporations to boost the economy, notably in the tourism sector. Tourist Burma had its offices here. Although it was the sole authorised tourism agency, it never really looked busy. The counters were silent and covered with faded and frayed pamphlets.

Fortunes changed when the building became the Ministry of Hotels & Tourism (MOHT) in the early 1990s: the halls were filled with eager entrepreneurs hoping to attract international visitors to the world-famous Golden Land. Investors were lining up to build new hotels and resorts, new airlines and cruise ships, hoping for a boom in tourist arrivals. When the whole government machinery moved to Naypyidaw, the MOHT of course followed. Now, sadly, the once majestic building stands forlorn and forgotten in the shadow of the Sule Pagoda.

A train pulls into the Central Railway Station

Yangon's Public Transport: Squaring the Circle?

Taking the railway full-circle requires the best part of three hours. The trains squeak and grind along old and often bumpy tracks—a journey that offers unique insights into the fabric of the city. Many believe this creaking railway will hold a central place in Yangon's future as a rising megalopolis. Could it?

Only about 100,000 of Yangon's daily trips are made by rail, compared to about two million by bus. This is owed to the trains' slowness and infrequency. But some—including foreigners—appreciate the railway's bumpy charms. Some staff of the Japan International Cooperation Agency (JICA), for example, told the authors that they commute by train each morning from their homes a few kilometres northwest of

their offices, in the **Sakura Tower** 010 B. This makes for a somewhat slower commute, undoubtedly—but one more relaxing than Yangon's inevitable rush-hour gridlocks. The train is also cheaper than travelling by bus, and traders can transport larger quantities of goods from market to market on the spacious wagons. The circle contains 39 stations along 45.9 kilometres, with the **Central Railway**

Station 086 B at its heart. Services run clockwise and anti-clockwise. Important stops include Lanmadaw, Kemmendine, Kamaryut and Insein stations, all of which are townships and former towns and villages in their own right, lying outside Yangon's historic core. Going clockwise, the train makes a right turn after the market of Danyingon. From here, the setting becomes more rural; the train passes a golf course, military facilities and Yangon International Airport. It then returns to built-up areas as it approaches downtown. Mingalardon, Okkalar, Kanbe, Tamwe and Pazundaung are the next major stops before the train pulls back to the Central Railway Station, where your journey probably began.

Because of the city's peninsular setting and the lack of bridges—which could have

Ancient Japanese busses carry passengers through the city at perilous speeds

Passengers getting ready to disembark shortly before arriving at Central Station

aided concentric growth away from the centre—the downtown area is nestled at the southernmost end of the city. As a result, traffic flows south towards the centre and north towards the periphery, according to the timings of the working day. Even before the war, this was a known problem, although traffic was, of course, only a fraction of today's. Back then the city counted about half a million inhabitants and only had three road and two rail exits. Prome Road (today's Pyay Road) was the main outlet, and despite having three lanes, heavy traffic here caused frequent accidents.

The number of cars has soared since import restrictions were lifted, and the situation has worsened considerably since those days. Pyay Road continues to bear the brunt of the traffic until Insein Road splits off at the southern end of Inya Lake. Kaba Aye Pagoda Road is another main north–south artery. The authorities are investing in traffic management systems, and the city would gain from more efficient signalling. Meanwhile, flyovers on Pyay Road and Kaba Aye Pagoda Road have alleviated some of the congestion around crucial intersections. But they don't solve the fundamental problem of excessive car traffic flowing north to south and vice versa.

Public transport can provide at least a partial solution. An operable Bus Rapid Transport (BRT) system may still be years away: the challenge is to unify the constellation of small independent bus operators (with their often old and roaring Japanese-made buses) into a modern, single system using designated priority lanes.

An upgrade of the circular railway could make a huge difference too: in its master plan for Yangon's future development, JICA assigns a key role to a modernised circle line that would operate at faster speeds and with greater frequency. The challenge is significant: the 1,000 mm gauge tracks are on soft soil and require major civil works to strengthen the bed. The rolling stock consists of about 200 coaches and 21 trains, some of them dating back to the 1960s. Unsurprisingly, these are also in dire need of major upgrades. Numerous railway crossings

further reduce the average speeds the trains can reach. Station facilities are old and often obsolete (although the combined weight scales and horoscope machines at the Central Railway Station must surely be preserved!).

Early cost projections for a comprehensive overhaul assume 10 million US dollars per kilometre of track, bringing the overall tally to 400 million US dollars. But that would just be the beginning. More investments are needed over the next decades to make JICA's predictions a reality: by 2040, the agency estimates 30 per cent of Yangon's public transport will become rail-based. The circular route will be enhanced. Additional lines would bring the total length of track to more than 300 kilometres. One of these extensions would connect the circular line to the special economic zone and deepwater port in Thilawa.

JICA's role in master-planning Yangon's future is understandable: Japan is by far the largest provider of soft loans for infrastructure development in the region, from metro lines in New Delhi, Bangalore and Chennai to the Skytrain in Bangkok. Frequently (although not always), Japanese firms end up winning the tenders for construction or provision of rolling stock—or both. While Japan has been criticised for such instances of "tied aid", the country's expertise in urban transportation is undeniable.

Meanwhile, Myanmar Railways has begun the tender process for a complete transformation of the Central Railway Station and its vicinity to the south and southeast. The responsible ministry estimates the project to cost as much as 2.5 billion US dollars. This entails the construction of several tall buildings on an area primarily occupied by sidings and maintenance facilities. Meanwhile, Japanese computer-aided design visualisations of the station foresee it becoming a hub at the heart of urban rail, the BRT and—someday—underground metro lines. As you travel around Yangon's circular railroad, you may wish to take photos of the life teeming around the wagons and stations. If all goes to plan, the pace of change in the coming years will be profound.

Japanese-made train on the circular railway, near Mingaladon Airport

Bahan and Tamwe

5

Western wing, Technical High School

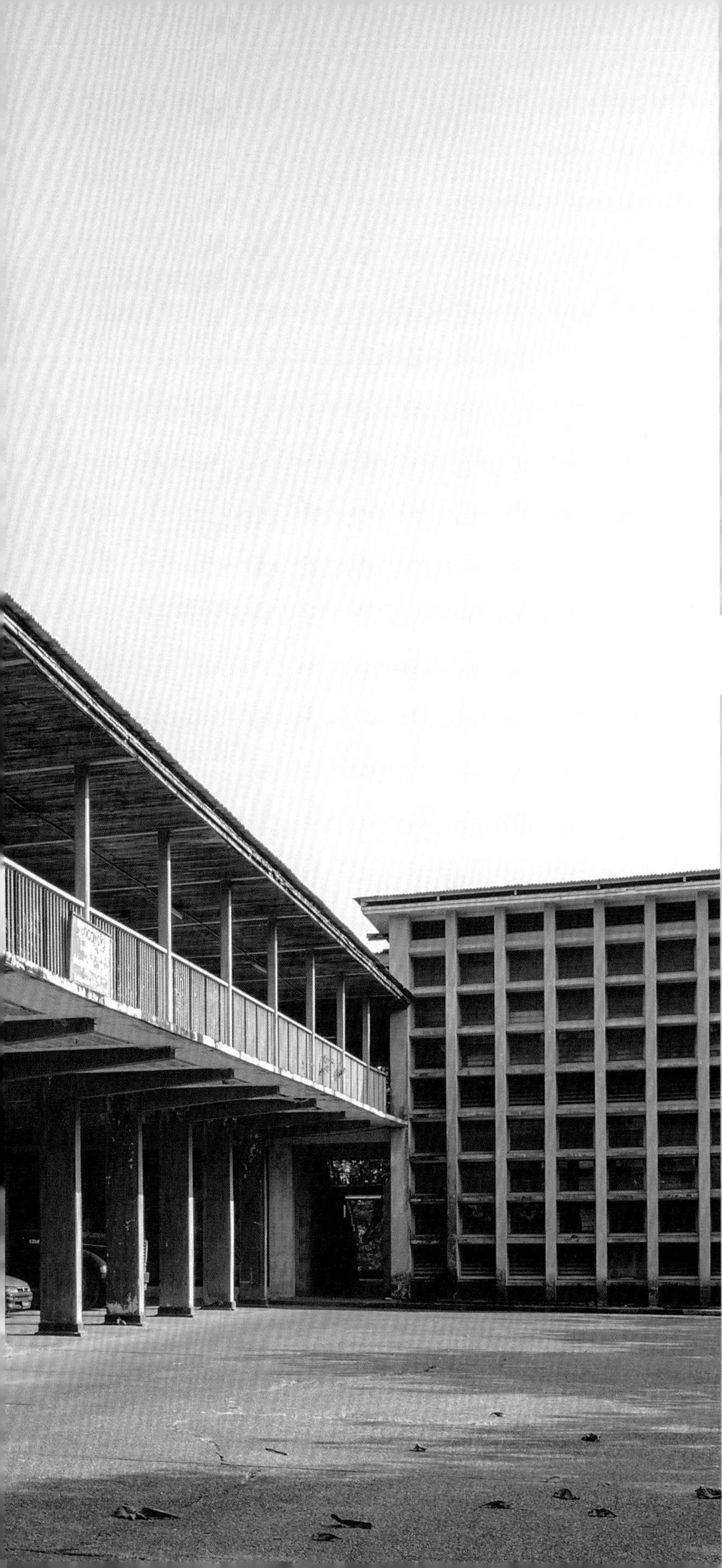

Technical High School

090 D

123 Natmauk Road
Raglan Squire
1954–1956

This simple, elegant school building lies in a sorry state today, although the Singaporean government plans to renovate it. Its history is not well known but tells of a time when, despite all its post-independence problems, Burma's future looked bright. Technical education for the young generations was a top priority of the new government and, thanks to extraordinary investments at the time, this high school became the country's pride and joy and the top vocational institution in Southeast Asia.

The school is a large, low-rise complex, with the main building standing just off Natmauk Road. The British architect, Raglan Squire, does not say much about it in his autobiography—perhaps because he thought the school paled in comparison to his Engineering College, today's **University of Medicine-1** 099 F. Interestingly, the most detailed description of the project is found in Soviet publications of the time, perhaps because the American "class enemy" was involved in plans for the school. (The Soviet Union would eventually send some of their best designers to Yangon to build the **Inya Lake Hotel** 103 F and the **Institute of Technology** 108 A.) The semi-circular roof elements and curved entrance canopy lend the street-facing main building an almost playful appearance. It contained the main assembly hall, designed for 600 people. Its parquet floor was made from local teak wood. For ventilation purposes, the windows were covered with louvres instead of glass. Other windows in the complex were simply covered with metal mesh. This simple design was perfectly suited to the climate. And to ensure that such openness would not lead to excessive noise pollution, the ceilings in classrooms and workshops were fitted with acoustic plates. Most inside walls were painted with distemper paint, only a few with oil-based paints. Some concrete surfaces were not painted at all. The rest of the complex adheres to a simpler and more sober form. The two wings containing the classrooms are raised on stilts, with car parks and a common area right beneath the western wing. Like the loggia-like corridors on the first floor, this was a way to accommodate the strong heat and regular torrential rainfalls during the monsoon. The fourth wing, completing the structure towards the north, housed vocational workshops, remnants of which are still visible. Further north were the hostels for boarders. Behind those, further north still, are two tall interconnected eight-storey tower blocks, seemingly housing boarding students as well. They are unusually high for Yangon's architecture of this period.

5

The whole school complex was mostly built using reinforced concrete. Be sure to admire the several large mosaic murals within the main compound, if you are able to enter. They portray idyllic and optimistic displays of traditional life in an independent Myanmar. Besides Squire's Engineering College (where, according to his autobiography, the murals were created at his behest), similar artwork also adorns the Government Technical Institute in Insein, the **Institute of Technology** 108 A and the University of Education. As most of the Technical High School lay abandoned at the time of writing, it is a small miracle that these important 1950s artworks remain in such good shape. Some of the artists involved in this initiative—Kyi Winn, U Khin Maung, U Nann Waii, Bagyi Aung So and U Thein Han— are among Myanmar's most celebrated artists of the 20th century. The Technical High School opened in July 1956. It was built with Burmese government funds and cost 2.5 million US dollars (or more than 20 million US dollars in today's money). The Ford Foundation paid for instructors from Dunwoody, a Minnesota vocational college, to help develop a curriculum. About 600 students, half of them boarders, combined artisanal vocational training with high school diploma programmes. The school was resolutely state of the art. The Ford archives reveal that the decision to support the school was the matter of some debate: could a project so ambitious, catering to a relatively small number of students, be replicated on a national scale? The Foundation's final report on the project tries to acquit itself thus:

"It was undoubtedly an extravagant undertaking—many Burmese admitted as much, and none expected that it would be duplicated on such a scale elsewhere in Burma. But the school was designed to enhance the reputation of technical education in Burma [... and] viewed in that light, the decision to commit such relatively great resources to a single school may not have been so unwise."

Later the high school was used as a branch of the Radiation Protection Department, an organisation under the Department of Atomic Energy. The Singaporean government has committed funds to renovate the school and return it to its original use as a vocational training centre. A tender was issued in late 2014. If successful, this project could help create awareness of post-independence architecture in discussions of the city's built heritage—a subject usually monopolised by the city's colonial buildings. And perhaps soon, the school may again produce very successful graduates. As Myanmar's economy roars ahead, skilled technicians and engineers may become in high demand.

Villa "Goethe"
(former AFPFL Headquarters)

091 D

8 Komin Kochin Road
Unknown
1920s

Off a short, sloping driveway stands this stately villa from the early 1920s. Judging by its overall appearance, the building was probably commissioned by a European—what we do know for certain is that a wealthy Chinese businessman, Chan Chaw Paing, acquired it shortly after its completion and added a number of Chinese characteristics. Chan Chaw Paing's wife was none other than Lim Chin Tsong's daughter. (Read more about the larger-than-life tycoon in the section about the **Lim Chin Tsong Palace** 095 F.) The villa was largely built from stone and steel and is hence in decent structural condition today. Goethe-Institut, the international German cultural organisation, has leased the property as a base for its growing activities in Myanmar. A full-scale renovation is planned, which will see the building restored to its former glory while becoming a multi-functional cultural space. It will also host a courtyard restaurant. The residence is set back from the street, at a good distance from the noisy thoroughfare. The exclusive feel of the villa is accentuated by the large *porte-cochère* in front of the main entrance. Inside the building, one finds details revealing the second owners' roots. There are Chinese characters on the entrance's half-round transom. The teak room dividers are also clearly Chinese. Above the *porte-cochère*, a generous balcony overlooks the leafy yard and beyond the tall palm trees, the tip of the **Shwedagon Pagoda** 075 E comes into view. On the second floor, a light well provides natural lighting to the spacious hallway connecting all rooms. The villa is a typical example of a wealthy residence built in this period. Colonial Rangoon was booming in the 1920s, leading to a lot of construction activity. Not much is known of its owners' later life. It can only be speculated that Chan Chaw Paing and his wife left Yangon with the onset of the war, before or during the Japanese invasion in early 1942. This was the case of many other ethnic Chinese residents who often crossed the land border into Yunnan province. Thousands decided to return to Burma after the war. They rebuilt their communities in Chinatown, where about a quarter of the housing stock was destroyed during war-time bombing. Many, however, did not come back. Perhaps they were lost in the vagaries of war, or found their fortunes elsewhere. The real historical significance of the Villa Goethe stems from its use at the end of the war and the immediate post-war period. General Aung San and the *Thakins*, or nationalist Burmese leaders, chose this building as the headquarters of their Anti-Fascist Organisation (AFO). The AFO was renamed the Anti-Fascist People's Freedom League (AFPFL) after the war. It became the main

political party working for Burmese independence. Under the leadership of General Aung San, it united the various factions into which Burma's independence fighters had by then split. It is said that General Aung San even lived in the building for some time, in the annex at the rear of the building. After his assassination, followed by independence, the AFPFL became the young country's main political party. Its leader U Nu was the country's prime minister for much of the immediate post-independence period. The group's headquarters were here, on what was then Churchill Road (now Kaba Aye Pagoda Road and its southern prolongation called Komin Kochin Road). The place remained a centre of Burmese political life until the liquidation of the AFPFL under General Ne Win in 1962. Around 1968, the building became the State School of Fine Arts and served as such until 2003. From that point, the former AFPFL headquarters was used for occasional art exhibitions organised by the Ministry of Culture. But the building gradually fell into disrepair and Cyclone Nargis in 2008 caused further damage. Thanks to some basic repairs led by the

Myanmar Artists and Artisans Organisation, art continued to be shown here. The Goethe-Institut was offered the property by the Ministry of Culture during negotiations on a cultural agreement between Myanmar and Germany. The house's historic aura, inviting location and beautiful grounds seduced the Institut immediately. The lease agreement was approved by President Thein Sein's cabinet in early 2015. The building was inaugurated by German President Joachim Gauck during a state visit in February 2014. The Goethe-Institut in Yangon offers German language classes at all levels and facilitates cultural exchanges between Germany, Myanmar and the world. With this new venue in the old villa, the institute also aims to provide young Burmese artists with a space for innovative forms of expression and creative experiments. It also offers training programmes and support for young people in the fields of music and film, as well as workshops about the use of media in education.

This book was made possible thanks in part to the Goethe-Institut's generous support.

5

Bogyoke Aung San Residence 092 D

25 Bogyoke Museum Lane
Unknown
1921

The Bogyoke Aung San Residence is a beautiful teak villa dating back to the early 1920s. Today it is a museum commemorating the father of Burmese independence. It is well preserved and a fine example of the houses built by the wealthy in what was then a suburb of Yangon, east of **Shwedagon Pagoda** 075 E. Down the street from the German Embassy, a covered outside stairway leads to the two-storey house, protecting visitors from the torrential monsoon rains that inundate the city for part of the year. The villa features a wide veranda on its front and an elaborate turret on the side, facing the entrance. Upon entering the museum, the visitor arrives in the dining room, adjoined by the reception and living rooms. The bedrooms and library are on the second floor, as is a small Buddhist altar room. The museum displays family memorabilia and photos from Aung San's short but tumultuous life. Aung San was born in 1915 in Natmauk, in central Myanmar. He left for Rangoon to study English Literature and History at the **University of Rangoon** 101 F and quickly became a prominent student leader. In 1938, he quit his studies to join the *Thakin*, a Burmese nationalist group founded in the early 1930s. The following nine years

of his life are a remarkable tale of cunning, courage and vision. He visited the Indian National Congress Assembly in Rangarh in 1940, where a protest against India's forced participation in the Second World War galvanised India's independence movement. While travelling in China in 1940 to seek assistance from Chinese communists, he was picked up (some say, apprehended) by the Japanese authorities and sent to Tokyo. Japan wanted to bankroll the Burmese nationalist movement and rout Britain out of the country, offering military support and assurances of independence. Aung San accepted. Between 1940 and 1941, Aung San and his now legendary "Thirty Comrades" received Japanese training and assistance in Hainan, China. With Japan's support, they became the Burma National Army, fighting alongside Japanese forces and growing in numbers as they invaded their own country from Thailand. In 1943–44, as the Japanese occupation strained under British counter-incursions, Aung San grew disillusioned with Japan's military ability, distrustful of their promises and unhappy with their treatment of Burmese forces. In 1944, he turned his back on Japan and threw his lot in with the Allied forces. Aung San's finest hour was perhaps his visit to London in January 1947, when he negotiated the terms for Burmese independence with British Prime Minister Clement Attlee. But Aung San was never to reap the fruits of his hard work.

On 19 July 1947, while he was sitting in the **Secretariat** 006 B with his provisional cabinet and no doubt running over preparations for Burma's official independence in January 1948, gunmen barged into the room and mowed everyone down with sub-machine guns. The entire cabinet was killed. The residence became a museum in 1962, the same year the first **Martyrs' Mausoleum** 074 E, later bombed, was inaugurated. Military dictator Ne Win, who was one of the "Thirty Comrades" himself, wanted the national narrative to place more emphasis on Aung San's companions, including his own role. Following the pro-democracy protests co-led by

Aung San's daughter, Nobel Peace Prize laureate Aung San Suu Kyi in 1988, the military junta decided to repress "the cult" of Aung San and neglected the building for years. After a major five-year renovation that saw walls strengthened and roofs and stairs repaired, it reopened to the public in 2012. Visitors can again walk freely inside the villa. The grounds feature a statue of Aung San doing gardening work. The small pond is where Aung San Suu Kyi's older brother drowned in 1953. This tragedy prompted the now-twice bereaved family to move to the famous house on University Avenue. This is where "the Lady" lives, and spent much of her life under house arrest.

5

Ngadatgyi Pagoda (Seated Buddha)

093 D

Shwegondaing Lane
Unknown
Early 20th century

You may want to approach this vast monastery complex (called Ashay Tawya) from the south, by following the Bogyoke Aung San Museum Lane. Its peaceful setting offers a respite from traffic-choked Yangon. Between its winding pathways and scattered buildings, visitors are likely to encounter monks in meditation. There are teak and stone buildings; one stone edifice is painted a striking pink. Inside the central Ngadatgyi Pagoda, the impressive seated Buddha statue rises 20 metres high (which explains why this Buddha is known as the "five-storey Buddha"). The statue has the Buddha doing the *Bhumisparsa Mudra* or "earth witness" hand gesture, which he made while achieving enlightenment under the Bodhi tree: at that moment, the demon Mara tried to intimidate the Buddha with an army of monsters; the Buddha made this gesture to beckon the Earth to bear witness to the moment. Mara cowered away and the Buddha realised enlightenment. The seated Buddha statue was at, or near, its current location when the pagoda was constructed in the early 20th century. A photo from 1895 shows it in a partially ruined state, surrounded by the pillars of a former pavilion. The pagoda and the Buddha statue were renovated during the early 1990s by the SLORC junta. The building or renovation of Buddhist religious structures was one of its favoured tools to try to mobilise public support.

5

Chaukhtatgyi Pagoda (Reclining Buddha)
Shwegondaing Lane
Unknown
1907–1912, 1957–1966

This massive structure houses one of the largest reclining Buddha statues in Myanmar, which dates back to the early 20th century. From Shewgondaing Road the red roof of this vast indoor structure is visible from afar, but the best views are probably enjoyed from around the nearby **Ngadatgyi Pagoda** 093 D as you arrive or leave. The enormous 65-metre long Buddha is in the reclining position of his last dying days. The donor of the original Chaukhtatgyi Pagoda and the Buddha statue was a man called U Po Tha. Born in 1857, he became one of the country's leading rice merchants and a generous benefactor. (His funds also built the northern main praying hall at the **Shwedagon Pagoda** 075 E.) The tall and shiny steel girders bear the inscription "Lanarkshire Steel", indicating that they were produced in Motherwell, just outside Glasgow. Steel produced in Britain was shipped halfway around the world and used in countless buildings of Rangoon. "Falkirk Iron Foundries", "Cowie Bros., Glasgow" and "Cargo Fleet, Middlesbrough" are only some of the inscriptions you find across town. Some steel was also cast locally, for example at DD Coath Foundry, which produced the steel staircases for archival stands

inside the legendary **Secretariat** 006 B. In this pagoda, the use of steel enabled a new Buddhist architectural style, bigger and utilitarian, making space for a Buddha statue of monumental dimensions. Major repairs and alterations to the Chaukhtatgyi Pagoda were carried out between 1957 and 1966. During that process, several metres were added to the statue, making it the third largest of its kind in today's Myanmar. Unusual for a statue of this size, this Buddha's eyes (measuring 1.7 × 0.5 metres) are made of glass. A one-day festival is held in the pagoda grounds every December. Instead of walking through the streets for alms, monks are brought food by the people living in the neighbourhood.

5

Main hallway, Lim Chin Tsong Palace

5

State Fine Arts School (Lim Chin Tsong Palace)

131 Kaba Aye Pagoda Road
Clark & Greig (contractors)
1915–1919

095 F

The State Fine Arts School now uses the palace built by Lim Chin Tsong, probably Myanmar's most famous business tycoon of the colonial era. He led a flamboyant life, obvious in this eccentric five-storey residence with its wild mix of Chinese and Western architectural elements. The tall pagoda-like central tower rises above a main reception hall. From there, a central staircase leads to rooms laid out in a star shape. The balcony above the grand portico overlooks Yangon—in 1919, Lim Chin Tsong would have enjoyed a view stretching all the way to the river. His family name is printed in Chinese above the balcony roof and a large teak wall divider, painted in red and gold and about 10 metres wide, separates the dome from the balcony area. Some of the walls feature large murals. These were painted by Dod and Ernest Procter in 1920. They mainly depict Chinese landscapes and, as Sarah Rooney notes in her *30 Heritage Buildings of Yangon*, these murals "are nicely executed but unremarkable, and contain no hint of the artistic talent the couple would exhibit in their later years". The interior was lavishly furnished and decorated. Allegedly Chin Tsong spent over 30,000 pounds sterling, or more

than 1 million in today's money, during a shopping spree at Harrods in London, where he also first met the Procters. The 1924 *Seaports of the Far East* (also quoted in Rooney's book) describes how

"the magnificence of [the house's] equipment in rare and valuable furniture, in statuary, pictures, articles of gold, silver, ivory, curios of every description and in the richness and novelty of its electrical illumination, is in keeping with (...) the carving of the woodwork, the marble floors and staircases (...) and the greatness of the perspectives of halls, corridors and noble apartments, where the old and the new, the East and the West are expressed of a harmony that is remarkable and unique".

Born to Chinese Hokkien parents in Rangoon in 1867, Lim Chin Tsong took over his father's rice trading business at the age of 21. Soon he would expand into many other sectors, most importantly oil. He became the main agent for the Glasgow-based Burmah Oil Company, causing frequent headaches at headquarters with his creative accounting techniques. Although he could not read or write Chinese himself, his company books were written in Chinese so as to evade the control of the Scottish company. Running behind on payments, his financial fortunes often hung in the balance. Sources from the BP Archive (as BP took over Burmah Oil, company files are in its possession) state that

5

"one week Chin Tsong would be desperately hard pressed, with the ominous word bankruptcy ringing in his ears; the next he would strike it rich with a big steamer freight—or the promise of one. On several occasions he was, said Rangoon, "at the height of his tether, shedding copious tears"; at other times he was in the millionaire bracket, entertaining lavishly at the Rangoon race track". He died from influenza in 1923. The legend goes that when the phone company threatened to disconnect his line for non-payments, the bedridden Chin Tsong finally expired in frustration. His funeral on 8 November brought out every community in Rangoon. Thousands lined the streets between his palace and the Hokkien cemetery. He was, the *Rangoon Gazette* wrote, "the most popular resident of Rangoon"—remembered not only for his lavish lifestyle but also for his philanthropy, notably a Lim Chin Tsong School.

After Chin Tsong's death, his wife continued to live in the palace. Perhaps due to a meagre inheritance from her husband, she was living there modestly by 1938. The Japanese ran a radio station from the palace during the war. The building escaped unscathed despite nearby fighting. After independence, the palace was used as a hotel and renamed the Kambawza Palace. It was also used as a ladies' hostel for students of the Institute of Economics. From 1971 to 1974, the commission that drafted the country's socialist constitution under General Ne Win used the building as its headquarters. This constitution was in force until the 1988 uprisings, then suspended, and the country went without one for 20 years. (The 2008 constitution is the source of huge public debate at the time of writing which, if nothing else, shows the political environment is freer than it has been for many years.) The palace was later repurposed as the Ministry of Culture. The minister's office was at the top of the tower. Following the government's move to Naypyidaw in 2005, the State Fine Arts school became the only remaining tenant, leaving much of the building unused and in need of repair. Fortunately, Lim Chin Tsong's palace received heritage status in September 2014. It is expected to receive a full renovation with government funds. Its heritage status may herald a public use for the building. Chin Tsong's legacy is bound up in other iconic buildings around the city. He was an alumnus (popular, naturally) of St Paul's English School, today's **BEHS 6 Botataung** 007 B. He also chaired the Rangoon Turf Club, today's **Kyaikkasan Race Course** 096 F.

Main stands, Kyaikkasan Race Course

5

Kyaikkasan Race Course (Rangoon Turf Club)

South Race Course Road
Unknown
1926

096 F

This racecourse was once home to the Rangoon Turf Club, a famous racing stable and social institution of the colonial days. It was founded in 1887, using a racecourse in Maidan, and moved to these facilities in 1926. Unlike virtually every other club established during the colonial administration, the Turf Club was open to non-whites—provided, of course, they were of a certain social status: Lim Chin Tsong, a larger-than-life ethnic Chinese tycoon who recurs throughout this book (you cannot miss his very own **Lim Chin Tsong Palace** 095 F) was at one point the club's chairman. Racing was a very popular source of entertainment in the colonial days. As a British publication reviewing the colonies' myriad delights wrote in 1910:

"There is now no lack of racing in Rangoon. The policy of the present executive has been to popularise the sport as much as possible, and extra meetings are held practically every fortnight throughout the year, with the result that (...) racing has never been so popular as at the present time."

But the racecourse gradually fell into disuse after the war, although the socialist regime that came to power after the 1962 coup used it for various official rallies, on Union Day (12 February), Peasant Day (2 March) and May Day. In those days, some of the buildings were used as conference halls for government representatives. When the remains of former UN Secretary-General U Thant arrived in Yangon in 1974, the coffin was placed here for "public" viewings—in reality, these were highly restricted by the military junta. When students protested against the lack of an official ceremony for U Thant, who was one of post-independence Myanmar's most cherished figures, they overran security at the Kyaikkasan Race Course and took the coffin to Yangon University. More about this incident, and its tragic aftermath, can be read in the section about the **U Thant Mausoleum** 077 C. You won't hear any galloping sounds or cheering crowds nowadays. Its most recent successor, the Yangon Riding Club, moved to new facilities in Dagon township in 1996. The vast grounds of the racecourse host student dormitories and sports facilities. The bowels of the stadium are now inhabited, possibly by the families of groundskeepers. The grounds are not open to the public and it can be difficult to charm your way inside, but the space's open-air expanse and overgrown colonial relics feel faintly magical. It would be a worthy candidate for a redevelopment project to return the place to large-scale public use.

"What Are Your Five Favourite Buildings in Yangon?"

Sarah Rooney,
author of *30 Heritage Buildings of Yangon:*
Inside the City that Captured Time

The Secretariat 006 B

It's impossible *not* to include this sprawling ruin on a list of favourite Yangon buildings; it is the centrifugal point for much of the country's modern history and looks as if it was materialised not from bricks and mortar, but from the pages of a novel by Charles Dickens. Though renovation efforts may clear away the cobwebs, the complex will always be an evocative monument to how the unforgiving decades of the 20th century shaped the contours of this former capital city.

Sofaer's Building 022 B

You know immediately from looking at this grandiose but dilapidated building that it is somehow still being held together by the ambitions and stories of its past inhabitants. Commissioned a century ago by a Baghdadi Jewish trader, it was once an emporium of imported wonders that became the extravagant swansong of a family empire on the verge of collapse. Today, as its rooms are selectively gentrified and its sagging walls are propped up by new inhabitants, this building's fortunes will chart the progress of a country's hopeful, but precarious, resuscitation.

Sule Pagoda 016 B

This spiritual site pre-dates everything else in downtown Yangon. I love the way it has become integrated into the modern city, locked in place by the ceaseless whirl of traffic, the pocket-sized shops that surround it, and the barefoot flow of monks and worshippers depositing their prayers. Spend a morning or an afternoon within its shaded enclaves and you get the sense

that all of life must, at some point in time, circumambulate this gilded miniature mountain around which Yangon's urban landscape came into being.

Surti Sunni Jamah Mosque 053 C

This splendid, wedding-cake structure seems impervious to the tremendous changes that are taking place around it. Yangon's oldest mosque is situated on what used to be Moghul Street, which was the setting of an informal pavement stock exchange during the economically parched Socialist era where people came to trade in illicit gems, gossip, and covert land or air routes out of the country. Walk along a line drawn any which way between these five buildings, lingering especially in the grid of streets around this mosque, and you will map a route

that takes you straight through the shifting sediment of the city's historical core.

Former Myanmar Railways Company 057 B

Once the headquarters of the Burma Railways Company, which laid the tracks that stitched together the disparate parts of the British colony, this building has been derelict for as long as I have been visiting Yangon. Under the SPDC regime, its U-shaped floor plan made it ideal for hiding a battalion of riot police that remained on standby should any disturbances threaten the enforced peace. The building has a tenacious and utilitarian beauty; as the much-publicised centrepiece of Yangon's most high-profile property development, it will surely become emblematic of this new and unfolding chapter in the country's history.

Inside the Secretariat's western stairwell

Kamaryut

6

Inside the main dining room at House of Memories

House of Memories (former Burmese Independence Army Headquarters)

097 E

290 U Wizara Road
Unknown
Unknown

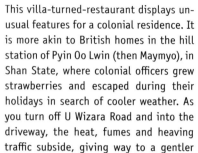

This villa-turned-restaurant displays unusual features for a colonial residence. It is more akin to British homes in the hill station of Pyin Oo Lwin (then Maymyo), in Shan State, where colonial officers grew strawberries and escaped during their holidays in search of cooler weather. As you turn off U Wizara Road and into the driveway, the heat, fumes and heaving traffic subside, giving way to a gentler aura: when the authors of this book arrived for an afternoon drink, staff were enjoying a leisurely game of five-a-side football in the courtyard at the front. The house displays many of its original features, save for the makeshift roofing which suggests repairs prompted by weather damage. The house was at one time known as the "Nath Villa" (a sign at the front gate still bears that name) and belonged to Mr Dina Nath—Chairman of the Indian Independence Army's chapter in Burma—and his wife, Caroline. The Nath family still owns the house and as their grandson, Richie, explains: "I thought about renting it out, but I couldn't do it." Instead, they converted the spacious house into

a pleasant restaurant which, as the name suggests, doubles up as a homage to the Nath family and their heirlooms. A number of private dining rooms are named after Nath family members, save for one on the first floor which features a grander name still: it was the office of none other than General Aung San. Indeed, and like in a number of other properties around town, General Aung San struck up quarters here for a time. The Naths, also active in the anti-colonial struggle, gave Aung San a room in 1941. Dina Nath also brokered meetings between the Indian Independence Army and Aung San. The IIA's leader, Subhas Chandra Bose (who, like Aung San, colluded with the Japanese at the start of the war) stayed here during clandestine visits to meet with Burma's independence leader. As the Nath family recount on the restaurant website, Dina Nath was subsequently imprisoned for a year by the British, in 1947, for his role with the IIA. Rajiv Gandhi, prime minister of India (1984–1989), later honoured Nath's role in the independence struggle. The house features many photos of Nath's momentous life. The house is well preserved but clearly delicate. The staff politely ask you not to run or jump on the first floor's teak floorboards. (And as the authors were writing this text on the first floor's airy terrace, a small piece of the roof came crashing to the ground.)

6

Drugs Elimination Museum 098 E

Kyun Taw Road
Unknown
2001

In a city full of surprises, this may be one of Yangon's more surreal buildings. First there's the premise: an entire permanent exhibition dedicated to class-A drugs and Myanmar's (frankly dubious) triumphs in stopping their production. And then there's the building itself: impossibly vast and imposing, with vague allusions to pagoda architecture, especially the tiered roof design and the canopy—although bizarrely, this one is held up by Roman Doric columns. The overgrown and empty surroundings, colonised by stray dogs, are rather haunting. The façade is tiled a creamy beige. The logo of the Central Committee for Drug Abuse Control—a hand setting fire to opium poppies—adorns the alternate spaces between the three storeys' mirrored windows. The logo also appears on the entrance's heavy wooden doors. But nothing prepares the visitor for what they find inside: first a deathly silence, ominous enough to discomfort even the most hardened drug users. (Presumably.) The entrance features a vast portrait of Myanmar's erstwhile leader, Than Shwe, surrounded by adoring officials. By the picture he is quoted announcing that his government would do its "utmost with whatever resources and capability we have in our hands to fight this drug menace threatening the entire humanity". Throughout the museum's never-ending floors, visitors are treated with detailed descriptions of the global drug trade and the basics of industrial drug production. Fake ecstasy pills are pinned to the wall and itemised, like rare butterflies. You will also find photos of apprehended producers and traffickers and victims in the advanced stages of addiction. Haunting paintings adorn the walls, illustrating the medical and figurative torments of drug abuse along with captions like "From insanity to death". After the bloodbath of 1988, the junta reeled from international condemnation and sought ways to boost its international profile. In an article about the museum, *Vice*, an American magazine (with a loud, proud and liberal take on recreational

6

drug consumption) notes that there were "650 square miles of opium-producing fields scattered throughout Myanmar, and 80 per cent of New York City's street heroin arrived by way of Southeast Asia's notorious Golden Triangle" in the 1990s; the bizarre museum showed a government "desperate for good PR", in *Vice*'s words. Today the problem is far from eradicated. Myanmar is the largest producer of methamphetamine and a mixture called *yaba* (methamphetamine and caffeine) is ravaging the country's youth in many impoverished areas. While Myanmar's war on drugs did appear to make some headway until the mid-2000s, poor farmers are returning to heroin production for lack of other options. Poppy cultivation nearly tripled between 2006 and early 2015.

Library façade details, University of Medicine-1 (former Rangoon College of Engineering)

6

University of Medicine-1 (Rangoon College of Engineering)

Pyay Road
Raglan Squire
1954–1956

The architectural profession in post-independence Myanmar began with the introduction of a degree programme at Rangoon University in 1954. It took another four years for the first five students to graduate. U Tun Than, who designed the **Children's Hospital** 069 C in Dagon township, was in that first small cohort. Back then, all the students knew Raglan Squire. Squire was born in London in 1912 and read architecture at Cambridge in the interwar years. He founded his first practice in 1937, but would soon serve with the Royal Engineers during the war. He was an influential member of the Royal Institute of British Architects (RIBA) Reconstruction Committee during the rebuilding of London after the war. His conversions of townhouses into apartments on Eaton Square, in Belgravia, are especially notable. Squire was chosen to build the new Engineering College of Rangoon University. This was evidence of the government's desires to attract a forward-looking, international architect to post-independence Yangon. Squire

first came to Rangoon in November 1953. For the Brit, the "contrast to fog-bound, cold London, was too much". He was taken on a night time drive through the streets of Yangon and, in his autobiography, writes that he fell in love with Burma and the Burmese that night. His plans for the complex delighted the government, who pushed him to start building as soon as possible—Prime Minister U Nu came to lay the foundation stone. Squire brought a large team of experienced architects and engineers from the UK. The total payroll exceeded 100 people, although it was bloated by extensive domestic staff employed by the expats. Just like Squire's **Technical High School** 090 D, this was a comparatively expensive building for impoverished post-independence Burma. Funds were made available via the Colombo Plan and were therefore indirectly provided by the Americans. For those countries in the region that had strong domestic communist movements, accepting aid outright from the United States was politically contentious. It was also the aspiration of many newly independent nations in Southeast Asia to be perceived as non-aligned. Therefore, accepting funds and technical assistance from a multilateral mechanism like the Colombo Plan was an expedient loophole. As you approach the complex, the main library building sits

perpendicular to the street and is visible from far down Pyay Road. Note the canopy covering the entrance area. A large rectangular window on the street-facing side appears like the only opening of the tall building's façade. Raglan Squire said of the Library building, the tallest in Yangon at the time:

"The Library building would be multi-storey and, therefore, presented different problems. I finally decided that I would clad the whole of this building with precast, coffin shaped, panels; into these panels I would fit different coloured glass strips assembled in the form of louvres. The result would be a building that would be gently ventilated, through the louvres, along its total length and which would receive, through the different coloured glass, a kind of dappled daylight effect like the lightning in a tropical jungle."

The rest of the complex consists of lower building wings containing more lecture theatres and classrooms. In a time before air conditioning, the overarching design inspiration was the extreme climate (a recurring feature in this book, as you may have noticed). Squire personally commissioned Burmese artists to design various murals and bas-reliefs in the courtyard; these have been very well preserved. Just like the ones installed at the Technical High School, they portray idyllic and optimistic displays of traditional life in a (newly) independent Burma. It is worth exploring the entire compound, which at 60 years of age exudes the same forward-looking modernity of its younger days.

Raglan Squire regarded this commission as the high point of his career (which continued until his retirement in 1981). What earned him the most attention internationally were not the concrete buildings, but a structure that has since disappeared. Indeed, Squire also designed a wooden assembly hall, which locals quickly dubbed "Laik Khone" ("back of the tortoise") due to its peculiar shape. It was a remarkable piece of timber engineering, its stability testimony to the quality and resilience of Burmese teak. In some places of the concave assembly hall's structure, eight layers of wood were stacked on top of each other, made possible by advances in timber design techniques. Better adhesives, timber connectors and novel prefabrication methods contributed to the achievement too. Unfortunately, the maintenance of the hall proved cumbersome and expensive. Amid the economic hardships of the post-1962 socialist period, the structure deteriorated and was eventually torn down around 1980. Squire initially planned for the hall to be built of reinforced concrete. Had that been done,

would it still be standing today? The opening ceremony in 1956 was a notable event in post-war Rangoon. Raglan Squire describes it the following way:

"The Library building I lit from the inside so that all the little coloured glass, coffin-shaped windows sparkled like a Christmas tree. The Assembly Hall was brightly lit inside and we arranged for a gentle flow of lighting outside; the roof looked like the humped back of a giant turtle. The buffet tables each had their own oil lamps, the pweis glittered as on the street on my first night [in Rangoon]—and the whole complex was alive with happy, laughing people. The crowds were so great that we held up the traffic for hours on the main Prome [Pyay] Road out of Rangoon. It was a great day and great evening. I went to bed happy—yet with a little tinge of sadness. Could anything quite so magnificent ever happen again for me, personally, in the rest of my life? I have had many great days since but, truly, never one quite like that."

In 1961—only five years after it had moved into the brand new building complex—the architecture department was again relocated. This time, the move took it from the indirectly US-funded and British-designed facilities into the newly built **Institute of Technology** 108 A which—tellingly—was donated by the Soviet Union. Squire

had left Burma a long time before then. Subsequent assignments took him around the world, including the Middle East where he built the Tehran and Bahrain Hilton hotels, an airport in Baghdad and a town-planning scheme for Mosul. Squire had a long retirement and passed away in 2004. His son Michael is the principal of the London-based architectural firm Squire and Partners, whose most notable projects include the Chelsea Barracks and the Shell Centre redevelopment, both in London. His firm should not be confused with the Singaporean heir to Squire's name, RSP (short for Raglan Squire & Partners, which Squire founded shortly after leaving Burma). The firm continues to be involved in Yangon today, but makes no reference to its founding father on their website. RSP built the **Sule Shangri-La** 009 B in the 1990s and participates in the proliferation of rather nondescript mixed-use developments around Yangon, such as the planned Gems Garden project west of Inya Lake. While RSP may have strayed, it seems, from the grand designs of its founder, we hope this guide can at least help put to rest a worry that Squire recounts in his autobiography, as he departed from Burma in the 1960s: "I wanted to do something great. I knew I had done a good job in Rangoon but, with Burma slipping into self-imposed obscurity, who on earth would ever see my buildings there?"

6

U Soe Lin's Residence 100 F
80c Inya Road
U Soe Lin
2014

Although his major works are further south (**City Hall** 018 B and **Myoma National High School** 081 C), Myanmar's star architect U Tin and his descendants have had a profound influence on this part of the city, which recurs frequently over the remaining pages of this chapter. U Soe Lin is one of U Tin's grandsons. His modern residence stands adjacent to the old master's own house (which unfortunately is off-limits these days). Like many in his family, U Soe Lin followed in his grandfather's footsteps. He read architecture in the USA in the 1970s, at the University of Oklahoma and at the Catholic University in Washington DC; his practice today is also located in the US capital. U Soe Lin has mainly worked in the United States but makes frequent trips back home, and has built here too. Notable structures include the Pun Hlaing International Hospital, which was finished in 2005. With the boom in Yangon today, he is seeing a rise in assignments in his native Myanmar. Another noteworthy project is the Royal Textile Academy Museum in Bhutan. U Soe Lin's Yangon residence is currently rented out to the Danish ambassador. This building perpendicular to Inya Road is one of dualities. It reflects the architect's roots in Burma as well as his Western training. Being residential, the front of the building is kept private with a gate and stone wall shielding the living quarters. Behind that wall, the house opens up to a landscaped garden with an open terrace. The functional spaces and bedrooms are located in the modern masonry structure, made of reinforced concrete. The side wall features narrow windows. A pavilion area, visible from the outside and covered in glass, contains the living room. Exposed steel supports it, covered by a wooden roof with subtle nods to vernacular temple architecture. It towers above the building section like an umbrella.

6

ရန်ကုန်အနောက်ပိုင်းနည်းပညာတက္ကသိုလ်
ပဥ္စမအကြိမ်အင်ဂျင်နီယာတွဲ,/အင်ဂျင်နီယာနည်းပညာတွဲ.
တွဲ.နှင့်လ ဘ င်အခင်းအနား
၂၅·၂·၂၀၀၄

Inside the Convocation Hall, Yangon University

6

Yangon University
(University of Rangoon)

Yangon University Estate
Various architects
Established 1920

101 F

Yangon University is one of the most complex and contested spaces in Yangon, one of immeasurable political importance for the history of the city. It is where successive generations of the country's brightest minds have come together to imagine a better future for themselves and their peers. For that reason, it was also the theatre of many moments of upheaval during Myanmar's fraught 20th century. The campus is nestled between Inya Lake and a long stretch of Pyay Road, with some of the more notable buildings concentrated in the area's northernmost quarter circle. Most tourists drive down Pyay Road on their way from the airport and can make out the set-back buildings through the university's leafy surroundings. Other buildings, like the **University of Medicine-1** 099 F, are right along the road. A stroll around the campus is highly recommended. The university consists of a large number of lecture halls and faculty buildings, student hostels, sports facilities, library buildings, a Christian chapel, the Buddhist Congregation Hall as well as a large **Convocation Hall**. The latter was built in 1927. It sits at

the end of a long driveway and serves as a focal point for the sprawling campus. The Hall's symmetrical shape, with a stepped back roof and three arched doorways in the centre, creates a stately impression. Both sides of the building feature colonnaded walkways. A large lecture theatre is flooded with natural light, thanks to its glass dome. It was here that US President Barack Obama gave a speech on his state visit to Myanmar in 2012. (In 2014, he delivered a speech in the Diamond Jubilee Hall, also on the campus.) The architect of the Convocation Hall was none other than Thomas Oliphant Foster, who had already designed several buildings in Yangon, some with his junior partner Basil Ward. Ward also helped with work at the university until his return to London in 1930. Besides the **Old Library Building** (1927), it is likely that Foster and Ward also designed the **Science Hall**: note its large cantilevered entrance canopy, similar to the National Bank of India's on Pansodan Street, today's **Myanma Agricultural Development Bank** 026 B. **Judson Chapel** was built in the early 1930s. Its architectural language is similar to that of the Convocation Hall and has clear Art Deco leanings. Its tall tower is the university's other main landmark. It is named after Burma's first Baptist missionary, Adoniram Judson (more on him can be read in the **Bible Society of**

Myanmar section 012 B). John D Rockefeller, Jr. donated 100,000 rupees for the chapel's construction. Burma's most famous architect, U Tin, also left his mark here—albeit not directly within the university premises. His **Buddhist Congregation Hall**, opposite University Avenue, is set back from the street and not easily found. Built in trademark U Tin style, it was donated by a wealthy Burmese merchant to offer a Buddhist place of worship to the students. A key keeper is usually around and can let you in. More modern buildings include the **Universities' Central Library** 102 F, built by one of U Tin's grandsons. Another of U Tin's progeny, his youngest son U Kin Maung Thint, built the **Recreation Hall** around 1960 together

with architect and planner Oswald Nagler. The university was founded by the British as Rangoon College in 1878, then an affiliate of the University of Calcutta. It later became independent and was renamed University College, and later Rangoon University in 1920 after merging with the Baptist Judson College, which gave its name to the aforementioned Judson Chapel. Teaching at the University was modelled on Oxbridge, as was the case for elite institutions across the British colonies. As historian Jan Morris describes in *Stones of Empire: The Buildings of the Raj*:

"The greater universities established by the British in India, notably those in the Presidency towns, deliberately set out to transfer British ideas and values to the Indian middle classes, if only to create a useful client caste. Their curricula were altogether divorced from Indian tradition—no more of those thirty-foot kings—and their original buildings were all tinged somehow or other with architectural suggestions of Cam or Isis [these are rivers flowing through Cambridge and Oxford, respectively; the authors]."

This notion easily applies to Rangoon University too. Except that by summoning the country's brightest minds, it eventually attracted young men who became the leading cadres of the Burmese nationalist movement. Aung San, Ba Maw, U Nu and U Thant all studied here, to name but the most famous examples.

Major strikes took place at the university in 1920, 1936 and 1938. (The 1920 strike is described in some detail in the section about **Myoma National High School** 081 C.) The campus suffered significant damage from bombings during the Second World War. In 1949, the Karen (who occupy Karen State on the Thai border) made incursions into Rangoon—a sign of post-independence Myanmar's fragility—and the University was closed down for a time. After Ne Win's coup in 1962, a new generation of students were quick to rise up, in July of the very same year. Ne Win was quick to react: he dynamited the student union building in retaliation. The University was put under a military directorate—it was previously run by the professors themselves—and the default language of instruction changed from English to Burmese. While the change to a vernacular and non-elite language could have become a positive development in itself, the military's rigid and inept approach led to a drastic fall in academic standards. In 1974, the campus was again the theatre of major student protests when the coffin of U Thant, the former UN Secretary-General, was snatched from **Kyaikkasan Race Course** 096 F and brought to the university. This was an outraged reaction to the regime denying him an official funeral. More about this incident, and its tragic aftermath, can be found in the section on the **U Thant Mausoleum** 077 C. Students from Yangon University were also central to the 1988 uprisings. Undergraduate

degrees were scrapped after student protests in 1996 and only resumed in 2013. The university continues to be a tense political space where students test the limits of authority. In November 2014, hundreds of students protested against an education bill that, they felt, did not give universities the independence previously promised. The education bill continued to spur discontent across the country: in January 2015, around 100 students took part in a two-week march from Mandalay to Yangon—a distance of 650 kilometres. There was controversy too in December 2014, when around 300 students from Yangon University were not granted diplomas because they did not have "scrutiny cards", or ID papers—a problem that disproportionately affects Muslim students from Rakhine State, whose right to Burmese citizenship is ferociously contested by the authorities. (The government similarly denies the existence of the ethnic label of "Rohingya", which many Muslims from Rakhine State self-identify as.) The UN Special Rapporteur for Human Rights in Myanmar, Yanghee Lee, said at the time that she was "shocked" to hear that these students were unsure of receiving their degrees. At the same time, Myanmar's opening-up has allowed the University to foster new and encouraging international ties. Notably, a partnership with the University of Oxford is helping it to "develop and implement a strategic plan that will transform the way they teach and research," according to the British institution.

6

Universities' Central Library 102 F

Yangon University Estate
U Kin Maung Lwin
1976

This modern building, adjacent to the older university library, was designed in 1973 and was due for completion in early 1975. However, the U Thant funeral crisis rocked Rangoon University in 1974 and led to a delay in construction. Students looted the building site, equipping themselves with bricks and other building materials to build a tomb for the remains of U Thant on the grounds of the former Students' Union building, which was destroyed by the Ne Win Government in 1962. The library building brilliantly showcases "architecture of scarcity", or the ingenuity of local architects making do with very limited means. Note the windows with their many grilles—large glass was very hard to come by. Simple iron angle bars support the teak stairs. The marble is sourced from inside Myanmar; this local variety is not as shiny as its Mediterranean equivalents.

The floral pattern on the outside of the building was supposed to be permeable, allowing for more natural light; but again those plans were shelved as the production proved too cumbersome. The shafts underneath the roof were designed to hold the air conditioning units that, alas, were never procured and fitted. An inner courtyard was repurposed as a light shaft, allegedly because the university authorities wanted to avoid providing a cuddling spot for amorous students. All the while, the building's airy layout was accomplished successfully. The folded roof is particularly notable and should be renovated in the coming years. The inverted pyramid layout is best appreciated from the first floor. The library design also took great care to preserve many of the local *gangaw* trees that stood on the site. In the end, only nine were felled, leaving more than 40 standing and offering plenty of shade today. The wide staircase was designed to provide informal seating for the students during their breaks. Although only designed to hold 280,000 books, the library today possesses 600,000 in the building's air-conditioned basement. The ground floor is split between a reading room and an administrative office. The first floor contains further post-graduate reading rooms as well as some of the library's prized antique possessions, including palm leaf books, some more than 500 years old. The library's architect U Kin Maung Lwin (or Ronnie, as he is widely known) is a grandson of U Tin, Myanmar's most famous architect. Together with his friend Dr Kyaw Lat (today YCDC's chief consultant on urban planning issues), Ronnie studied architecture in Dresden, Germany, setting off first to London by a Bibby Line steamship in 1960. While Dr Kyaw Lat returned permanently to Myanmar in the 1970s, Ronnie settled in West Germany, working for universities and major construction company Holzmann until his retirement. Today he splits his time between his two homes in Yangon and Wetzlar, north of Frankfurt. His grandfather had several children and grandchildren, who include many architects working across the globe in the US, the UK and, in Ronnie's case, Germany.

6

Sule Pagoda Road as seen from the pedestrian overpass at the corner of Anawratha Road (photo taken late 2014)

Remoulding the City after 1988

Upon assuming power, the State Law and Order Restoration Council (SLORC) tried to rewrite Yangon's urban geography. The measures had one overall goal: to prevent a repeat of the 1988 anti-government uprisings that almost toppled the military order.

Ne Win's road to socialism not only led Burma towards international isolation, it ruined the country's economy. Real economic growth is believed to have been just 1 per cent per year from 1962 to 1988. Neighbouring Thailand, and farther afield, Indonesia and Malaysia, also had authoritarian governments but their economies grew much quicker. The lack of growth had a profound impact on Yangon's cityscape. Simply put, there was little demand for new buildings and the old ones remained. Yangon did not share the same fate as many East and Southeast Asian metropolises, which began to grow spectacularly during that period. In 1980s Yangon, time was standing still.

But momentous change soon followed. In 1987, the authorities devalued the kyat for the third time, having already done so two years before, in 1985, and previously in 1964. This time, the impact was devastating. It practically demonetised the country and 75 per cent of all banknotes were declared worthless overnight. The ensuing scramble for anything of intrinsic value—and the general distrust of paper money—led to rampant

inflation and rice shortages the following year. It was in this climate that protests by students from the **Institute of Technology** 108 A erupted in late 1987, and again in early 1988. By August 1988 the discontent swelled into a mass movement for democracy, shutting the city down for weeks and eventually leading to the military's brutal crackdown. Hundreds if not thousands died. Many residents of Yangon could recall shocking episodes of bloodshed they witnessed at the time, filling the streets with traumatic memories. One student (now a prominent activist), Khin Ohmar, described a scene near Inya Lake to journalist Benedict Rogers:

"There was blood everywhere. Some people jumped into the lake, some were kicked into the lake. I saw a little boy in his white and green school uniform, maybe eleven or twelve years old, probably in the area by accident, being beaten up and dragged into a truck. I kept screaming. It was like hell."

The crackdowns had a visual impact on the cityscape itself, with several buildings burnt or otherwise damaged.

Overpass at Thein Gyi Market, across Shwedagon Pagoda and Mahabandoola Roads

The entrance gate to Aung San Suu Kyi's home on University Road, by Inya Lake

As the protests died down, one of SLORC's first orders to the populace was a large public cleaning initiative "to wash the city with sweat", picking up trash and covering buildings with a new lick of paint. Journalist Bertil Lintner shares this colourful, so to speak, anecdote about the decree:

"The army was soon seen cleaning the capital's shabby streets and painting houses everywhere. The SLORC set a deadline for private buildings as well; all houses had to be painted before the end of the year, or power and water would be cut. People had to use whatever paint they could find—white, green, red, blue and pink—and Rangoon soon looked like a patchwork quilt. A joke doing the rounds in Rangoon had a man waiting alone at a bus stop who kept pacing back and forth. Asked why, he replied: 'If I stand still, someone might paint me.'"

Yangon's municipal body, the Yangon City Development Committee (YCDC), was founded by the SLORC regime in 1990. It is responsible for urban planning, the city's limits, taxation and foreign economic relations. The top echelons of the city's administration, including the position of mayor, are staffed with senior army officials; however, the nine members of the committee were appointed in (controversial) elections for the first time in December 2014.

After 1988, SLORC formulated an "Urban Works Programme" as a direct response to the unrest. It was so sweeping and ambitious that UN Habitat, in one of its early assessments, called it internationally unprecedented. Whether the authorities implemented every aspect is another question—but the vision was to transform Yangon, erase the trace of 1988 and, in the regime's eye, remove the conditions that made the uprisings possible.

A huge—and hugely controversial—part of the programme involved forced evictions and relocations, moving droves of people away from the centre to 10 newly created townships in Yangon's outskirts. Some estimates put the number of relocated inhabitants (both forced and unforced) at up to 500,000, or about 20 per cent of the city's population at the time. The stated intention was to modernise the way people lived. Indeed, many of those relocated had previously lived in slum-like dwellings around the city's monastic complexes. But often there was no infrastructure in these new environs. People were physically and economically cut off from the city centre. That they were, for a large part, from areas that saw massive protests was no coincidence. Middle-class communities were also singled out for eviction, often because they had sheltered protesters.

Under the pretence of infrastructure investments, Yangon's downtown streets were widened and the width of pavements reduced. The most notable example is Lower Pansodan. Here even the wide porticos of old colonial buildings disappeared. Large thoroughfares such as Bogyoke Road and Sule Pagoda Road were divided down the middle by fences to prevent jaywalking. Instead, pedestrian overpasses were built. Critics deemed these changes to be crowd-control measures: indeed, it is harder to demonstrate if there are no pavements and when crossing the street becomes physically impossible. It is also easier for the military to shoot into the crowd from the comfort of a pedestrian bridge.

The new Dagon University was created in 1993, far from the city centre and separate from the city, preventing students from mixing with the general population. Meanwhile, **Yangon University** 101 F became close to deserted, as it could no longer offer undergraduate degrees.

The junta closed down many spaces connected to the days of nationalist struggle, should anyone try to use them subversively—the **Martyrs' Mausoleum** 074 E being just one example. Meanwhile, efforts to mould a new Myanmar identity as a tool of nation-building culminated in projects of varying eccentricity, such as the **National Museum of Myanmar** 067 C,

the **Drugs Elimination Museum** 098 E and the National Races Village outside Yangon. The brutal crackdown on the demonstrators caused international outcry and led to (mainly Western) sanctions. Their effectiveness has always been contested. Some of the country's most important trading partners, especially China, Thailand and Singapore, continued to do business openly with the regime. Japan, too, remained an uneasy partner of the military junta. Public and private money from these countries was invested into construction projects in Yangon. These feature extensively in this very book and—on the surface at least—defy the idea that Myanmar was "isolated" in the 1990s. The junta became ever more dependent on foreign direct investment into the extractive industries, chiefly oil and gas as well as timber and jade. While these business deals created a wealthy and well-connected class of oligarchs, they failed to spur broad-based economic growth. Liberal economic policies only went so far as the inward-looking, at times paranoid junta would allow.

That, too, had its impact on Yangon's cityscape. There was no large middle class. Most of the population could barely make ends meet. At the same time, sanctions

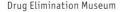

Drug Elimination Museum

increased the scope for kickbacks. A parallel exchange rate, import licences and other restrictions on trade led to windfalls for a tiny minority of super-rich cronies. For visitors to Yangon in the 1990s and early 2000s, one visible manifestation of this was the scarcity of modern cars on the streets.

One of the most profound changes to Yangon occurred when the junta unveiled a brand new and purpose-built capital, Naypyidaw, in 2005 (see the section on page 372). Although Yangon was and remains the undisputed commercial heart of Myanmar, the city was never central to the ancient Burmese kingdoms that formed the backbone of the generals' new narrative. The 1988 democracy protests further alienated the regime from their capital, and the major urban transformation programme never really put the junta leaders' minds at rest. (With good reason, as the 2007 Saffron Revolution went on to show.) The move to the Burmese heartland (or hinterland, if you prefer) cost the country billions of US dollars and explains the sorry state of many of Yangon's downtown heritage buildings, which were left vacant by the government. The move also explains Yangon's lack of public works from the early 2000s onwards.

The post-1988 era also led to a deterioration of public policy. The seeds were sown when Ne Win nationalised the education system, in effect sinking the standards of higher education. (See **Yangon University** 101 F for more details.) The large-scale and forced resettlement of hundreds of thousands of skilled ethnic Indian and Chinese inhabitants led to a glaring shortage of human capital. Finally, misguided economic policies drove many of the country's brightest minds abroad. Post-1988, the junta proved incapable of addressing these problems. Worse still, the army became so intertwined with the running of the country that obedience and military hierarchy practically replaced merit and critical thinking in the corridors of power. As yet, this problem remains.

Further reading:

Seekins, Donald. "The State and the City: 1988 and the Transformation of Rangoon." *Pacific Affairs* 78.2 (2005): 257–275.

UN Habitat. *Human Settlements Sector Review: Union of Myanmar*. 1991.

Rogers, Benedict. *Burma: A Nation at the Crossroads*. Random House, 2012.

Lintner, Bertil. *Outrage: Burma's Struggle for Democracy*. Weatherhill, 1995.

Insein and Mayangone

Inya Lake Hotel seen from lakeside shore

7

Inya Lake Hotel

37 Kaba Aye Pagoda Road
Viktor Andreyev and
Kaleriya Kislova
1958–1962

103 F

The former First Secretary of the Communist Party of the Soviet Union, Nikita Khrushchev, presented the government of Burma with three gifts when he visited the country in 1958. One of these was the Inya Lake Hotel. Secluded from the traffic of the main street, its location on the shores of Inya Lake makes this a tranquil oasis. It is built in the style of a typical "sanatorium", the rest and recreational centres you still find everywhere across the former Soviet Union. Soviet workers were allocated places in these state-run vacation centres, often located by the sea or big lakes. The architects transported this architectural concept several thousand kilometres east to post-independence Burma, with the brief to build a resort up to international standards. Burma back then lacked a modern hotel. The **Strand** 036 B had seen better days and the **Thamada** 085 B only opened in 1964. The Inya Lake Hotel has only two features that distinguish it from most Soviet sanatoria of the same period: first, the entrance is larger than usual and features a large portico above the parkway. Perhaps this is explained by local climatic realities, requiring a larger rainproof area by the main entry. Second, the imitation of a steamship funnel on the building's

top gives the hotel a peculiar, cruise ship-like impression, a playful maritime association along the lakeshore. At the back of the hotel, an annex building houses events and banquets. Its decorated, high-ceiling walls are worth observing: this would have been a "House of Culture" in the Soviet Union. These were the main public spaces for people to gather and enjoy sanctioned culture and celebrations outside their usually austere apartments. The hotel used to feature large "Inya Lake Hotel" letterings, both above the entrance and on the steamship funnel around the back. Viktor Semyonovich Andreyev (1905–1988) was a successful Soviet architect born in Kharkov, today's Kharkiv in Ukraine. (Kharkiv preceded Kiev as the Ukrainian SSR's capital.) He graduated from its architecture faculty in 1930. Kharkov's Avant Garde and Constructivist architecture was very prominent, the main example being the Gosprom building complex, dating from the latter half of the 1920s. Many architects from Kharkov moved to Moscow and constituted a strong faction in the architecture profession there. Like other foreign architects introduced in this book, Andreyev's Burma assignment was just one of several international jobs. He built USSR exhibition pavilions in Vienna and Beijing (the latter is now the Russian Embassy in China) and the Soviet Embassy in Prague. At home in Moscow, he built the Chinese Embassy among many other projects. Andreyev enjoyed

high social status in the USSR. He was the recipient of many prizes: two orders of Labour Red Banner, a Stalin Prize of Third Grade, and most importantly perhaps, the People's Architect of the USSR Prize in 1978. Sadly, not much is known about the second architect, Kaleriya Dmitriyevna Kislova. She is the only female architect featured in these pages and deserves as detailed a portrait as our research could muster. Her name appears in a 1950 Soviet illustrated magazine called *Ogonyok*. The article interviews several women in successful careers, and Kislova is shown in her design bureau, explaining that she thoroughly examined every flat in the buildings constructed according to her designs. Together, Kislova and Andreyev built the House of Political Education of the Soviet Union's Communist Party in 1979, in Moscow. It was demolished after the Union's collapse, perhaps because it symbolised the "poisoned" air of Communism, as historian and journalist Petr Kozma explains. Today, the same plot is occupied by an office centre that is "a tremendous monster, much uglier than its allegedly poisoned predecessor," in Kozma's judgement. The Inya Lake Hotel was renovated and upgraded by hotelier Adrian Zecha in 1990. It was a reluctant assignment imposed on him, as we describe in our descriptions of the Strand Hotel and the Thamada which he also renovated. Zecha dismissed the Inya Lake Hotel as a "Russian bunker". The hotel has been kept in good shape and, although it may be a little far from downtown to constitute an entirely practical place to stay, you are well advised to enjoy a cold beverage in the garden cafe overlooking the lake.

7

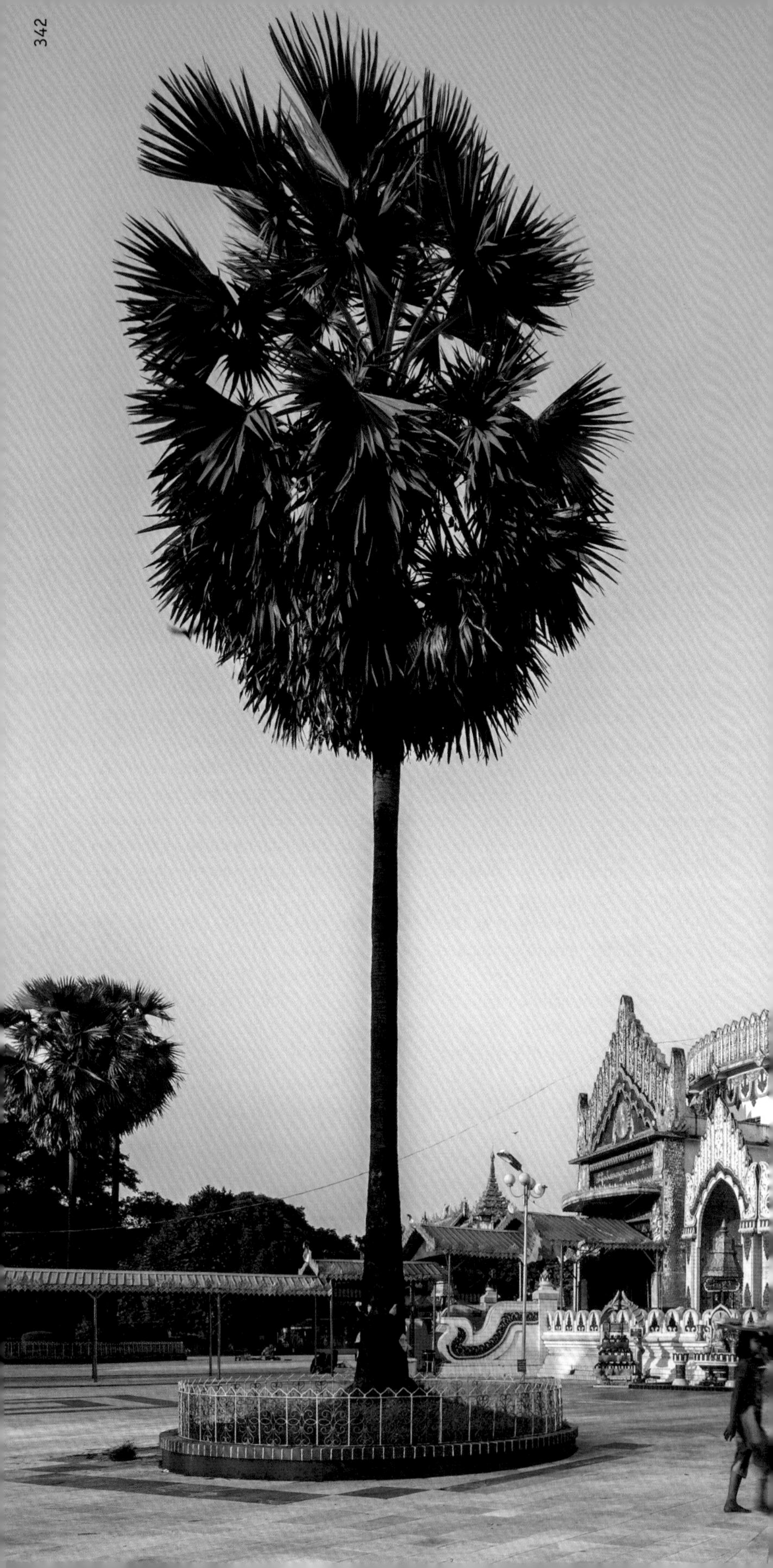

Kaba Aye complex
Kaba Aye Pagoda Road

Burma's first prime minister, U Nu, was a devout Buddhist. Buddhism was also an obvious tool of nation-building after independence since an estimated 90 per cent of the country is Buddhist. In this vein, one of U Nu's abiding legacies was his convening of the Sixth Great Buddhist Synod. This council brought together 2,500 monastics from countries practising the Theravada branch of Buddhism, including Cambodia, Laos, Myanmar, Sri Lanka and Thailand, to review and recite the scriptures written in the ancient Pali language. The synod was convened for two years, between 1954 and 1956, its conclusion coinciding with the 2,500th anniversary of the last Buddha's demise. This sizeable religious compound was built for the synod. Centred around a massive man-made

cave, it comprised a pagoda, a library, a hospital and hostels for the monastics. The hostels, immediately to the west of the cave, are still used by Myanmar's most venerable monks. There was very little major construction taking place in the early independence period—a civil war was ravaging much of the country, even reaching the outskirts of Yangon, until it ebbed away in 1950. This makes the Kaba Aye complex's scale all the more impressive. The Burmese parliament passed the relevant motion in 1951, stating that material improvements are "not sufficient to solve the problems of society and that measures for the spiritual and moral well-being of man could alone be effective". Forty hectares of land were allocated to the project and 1 million pounds sterling, a stately sum for the cash-strapped country, were set aside for the construction. When the synod began in May 1954, 200,000 pilgrims gathered

in the rain outside the cave to listen to the broadcast of the first day's proceedings. Dignitaries from the participating countries sent their messages. Even two German-born monks attended the proceedings, perhaps the first non-Asians to do so in Buddhism's long history.

Kaba Aye Pagoda (World Peace Pagoda)

104 F

Unknown
1952

Of the buildings within the complex, the pagoda remains the most used today. Best begin your exploration here, as taxi drivers will have no problem finding it. Just like at the **Shwedagon Pagoda** 075 E, it is advisable to keep your shoes in a plastic bag and inside a backpack before entering the pagoda, as you will likely exit from another side if you venture elsewhere within the complex.

When built in 1952, the Kaba Aye stupa was a complete break from the past: worshippers were able to enter the hollow pagoda. Usually stupas were solid, with the relics buried underneath them, just like at the Shwedagon Pagoda. The Kaba Aye Pagoda's innovation was made possible by modern construction techniques and supporting steel structures. The principle was later replicated at the **Botataung Pagoda** 001 B and the **Maha Wizaya Pagoda** 076 E. Even the Shwedagon Pagoda's duplicate in Naypyidaw, the Uppatasanti Pagoda, is hollow. At the Kaba Aye Pagoda, the relics inside an inner chamber consist of the remains of two of the Buddha's disciples. Before being brought to Burma, they lay in London's Victoria and Albert Museum. The Kaba Aye Pagoda's dimensions are rather modest: it is 34 metres high and has about the same diameter. Leave the pagoda towards the north to reach the Maha Pasana Guha.

7

Maha Pasana Guha (Great Cave)

Unknown
1952-1954

105 F

The convention of the synod was held here, a cave inside an artificially created rock. Its construction consumed 12,000 tons of cement and 380 tons of steel. The dimensions are equally impressive: the outside structure is 140 metres long and 110 metres wide. Inside, the assembly hall is 70 metres long and 40 metres wide. This created capacity for about 7,500 spectators to join the 2,500 monastics. Six entrances admitted people back then, signifying the Sixth Great Buddhist Synod.

The cave was completed in 14 months, thanks in no small part to thousands of volunteer labourers. Allegedly, U Nu was inspired to commission the cave as the centre of the synod following an earlier visit to the Satta Panni Cave in India, where the First Great Buddhist Synod was held the year after the Buddha's passing. Today the cave is surrounded by trees. When the synod was held, however, it was almost entirely bare and its scale therefore easier to appreciate. The cave can be visited, the main entrance is on the southern side. It is still used for religious ceremonies. Given the precious little traffic around here, locals use the road surrounding the cave for their workout routines.

Pitaka Taik
(Tripitaka Library)
Benjamin Polk
Circa 1956–1961

106 F

Despite being part of the complex, few visitors venture far enough north to find the most interesting building of the whole complex, fenced in and looking somewhat out of bounds. In front of it is an oval pond and manicured, hilly landscape. The Burmese word "Pitaka" derives from the Pali "Tripitaka", which translates as "Three Baskets" and denotes the canons of Buddhist scriptures. U Nu wanted a library that would store the Pali texts from the respective Theravada Buddhist countries alongside other religious writings that would emerge from the synod. For this, he commissioned an American architect. Benjamin Polk (1916–2001) had come to India in 1952 with his wife. He set up practice with fellow American Joseph Allen Stein (1912–2001) in New Delhi in 1955. (Stein had left the US due to the politically and culturally oppressive atmosphere of the McCarthy era.) The two men were later joined by Binoy Chatterjee and ran one of the largest architectural practices in Asia at the time. Together they built all over India. (Lodhi Road in New Delhi is sometimes referred to as "Steinabad" in recognition of the many buildings Stein designed there.)

7

Polk also took assignments abroad, in Nepal for example, where he built the Royal Palace, and of course in post-independence Yangon. Prime Minister U Nu asked Polk to incorporate a number of highly symbolic elements and numbers into the library design. Note for example the radial design (which follows stupa architecture, above all that of the Sanchi Stupa in Madhya Pradesh, India), the building's three storeys (after the Three Baskets of Wisdom, or Tripitaka) and the numerous lotuses. The building was to last 2,500 years, until the end of the next Buddhist epoch—quite a brief for a Modernist Western architect! But happily Polk was no dogmatist, so to speak, and proved highly sensitive to the structure's religious and spiritual components. The material of choice was reinforced concrete. He found that the medium served the spirit of modern Burma and would allow for the building to become an heir to the architectural practices of ancient Bagan (formerly known as "Pagan"). As he explained:

"The traditional Burmese pointed arch from Pagan would now partake of the nature of reinforced concrete with its capacity to resist tension in bending. It would incorporate the structural continuity of reinforced concrete tank design, but cantilevered. Thus the interior arches of the Library could be bound in the central position of the building like the stamen and pistil forms of a flower. Here the uniformly pyramidal silhouettes of Pagan would be punctuated with the cantilever, partially hidden, but giving the weight of the building a dynamic upward and outward thrust behind the encircling walls. Perhaps there is something 'primitive' here."

The library was designed with three wings, containing a public library, an auditorium and a religious museum respectively. The central core of the building would be reserved for scholars and monks of the institute, as a sanctuary for study and meditation. An Indian site manager named Visvanath Jhanjee oversaw the construction process. It was to take five years and ran into its own set of problems. An ethnic Chinese carpenter foreman was murdered. The first site engineer had to be removed from the job after he was found to have a drinking problem. The "political vicissitudes" of the times also plagued U Nu's pet project, as Ne Win replaced him as prime minister between 1958 and 1960. We therefore date the start of the construction between 1955 or 1956 (the latter being the end of the Sixth Synod) and 1960 or 1961, by which time U Nu had won back this prime ministerial post. U Nu was also present at the inauguration ceremony and served the architects the first two dishes of its banquet. A Soviet publication at the time credits the library to both Polk and Stein, although Polk makes no mention of his partner's involvement in Yangon. This building is magical. With its bold architectural design, it conveys the bygone optimism of a young Buddhist nation.

Nawaday Cinema

Kaba Aye Pagoda Road
Unknown
1990

107 F

Near the **Kaba Aye Pagoda complex** 104 F, the Nawaday Cinema is an arresting example of SLORC-era architecture for the entertainment industry. The contrast with the handful of cinemas downtown—from the colonial **Waziya** 011 B to the 1950s and 1960s-built cinema/hotel, the **Thamada** 085 C, for example—could not be starker. If the architectural feel of those theatres immediately evokes the colonial era, in the case of the Waziya; or the enterprising optimism of the 1950s for the Thamada, then the Nawaday Cinema's isolated location, self-contained park, expansive dimensions and swaggering golden statue reflect an entirely different vision of the city and the built environment. In that sense, the Nawaday Cinema was clearly a SLORC production. Its construction required the resettlement of more than 20,000 people that lived on the large complex, according to some sources. The cinema's vast, rectilinear atrium and lobby would not look out of place in Naypyidaw. The trappings of government officialdom are clear in the grandiose statue out front too—a large replica of the Myanmar Academy Awards trophy. (On the other hand, the pediment crowning the building owes more to the city's colonial heritage.) A private operator has been leasing the venue since 1997. A Chinese restaurant specialising in shark-fin soup also occupies the premises.

Yangon Technological University (Rangoon Institute of Technology)
Insein Road
Pavel Stenyushin (architect)
1958–1961

This major university campus was another gift from the Soviet Union. The Engineering College of Rangoon University moved here upon its completion in 1961. Prior to that, it was housed in the Engineering College, today's **University of Medicine-1** 099 F designed by Raglan Squire, which had only been finished a few years before in 1956. Interestingly, the biographies of both Squire (1912–2004) and the Soviet architect, Pavel Stenyushin (1904–1971), have significant parallels. Stenyushin and Squire were each involved in their countries' reconstruction efforts after the Second World War. Squire planned the conversion of townhouses into apartments in London's Belgravia, while Stenyushin worked for *Mosarkhitektura* and designed the city centre of Kursk, a Soviet city almost completely razed during the war. In Kursk, Stenyushin built two pompous buildings on the central Red Square, a hotel and the City Council; both have Neoclassical and more pure Stalinist architectural features. Before the war, Stenyushin also designed a massive "General's House" on Moscow's Leningrad Avenue. And just like Squire, he made a name for himself abroad. His Technological University in Yangon preceded later international assignments including the Polytechnic University in Kabul. Political systems and architectural styles divided these men, but their work took eerily parallel paths. Both brought their aesthetics to Burma but had to adapt to local climatic realities. This led to some similarities in their work, for example the covered walkways and exterior-facing corridors. The main building of the Technological University features an imposing colonnade and large protruding roofs. This peculiar shape explains why some students called this the "university under the table". Its slightly concave form harmonises with the circular plaza which it concludes towards the north, featuring a large water fountain at its centre. A series of courtyards and open staircases create an airy atmosphere inside the various buildings. Perforated walls perform a similar function. Plaques in Russian and Burmese are placed inside the central columns of the colonnade and commemorate the laying of the foundation stone by former Burmese President U Win Maung on 21 April 1958. Three years later, students moved to this location, rather far away from the centre. Some felt sentimental about the new setting. As one of them—U Myint Khine—recalls:

"On our first day, with renewed hope and vigour, and a feeling of great anticipation, I made my way through the huge, lofty columns of the main entrance. But, I must confess, in all honesty, that I felt a little bit disappointed. The architecture was, if anything, imposing. It was extremely functional, but to me, it was a bit too sterile. The old Faculty of Engineering buildings we

left behind were somewhat airy and light in comparison. The Burmese murals decorating the various façades were a joy to behold during our classroom breaks. The whole aspect was aesthetically very pleasing. All this flashed through my mind as I entered [Rangoon Institute of Technology], but I quickly put it out of my system. Whether pleasing in appearance or not, as I remarked before, it was still functional and solidly designed. If this is the 'altar' where I must gain my final 'rites of passage' into the world of Engineering, so be it. I will grow to love it and indeed I truly did in the end."

The Soviet Union was among the first countries to recognise independent Burma. But things got off to a rocky start as the Soviets backed communist anti-regime forces in their fight against the government in Yangon. Embassies in both countries only opened in 1951. By 1955, relations had warmed considerably. Prime Minister U Nu went on a two-week tour of the Soviet Union and Eastern Europe, signing trade deals and technical cooperation agreements. Burma pledged to support Soviet foreign policy, including backing Communist Chinese membership of the UN (at that time,

Taiwan still represented China there). A high-level Soviet delegation visited Burma in 1955 and Rangoon's population was told to line the streets and cheer the motorcade. It was during this visit that the agreement to build the Rangoon Institute of Technology was agreed in principle. Three years later, on Khrushchev's next visit, it was officially presented as a gift of the Soviet people. Burma's embrace of the Soviet Union was pragmatic. It was finding it difficult to sell large quantities of surplus rice on the world markets, and the Soviet Union was an important buyer—although payment was often in kind. US intelligence was worried that "Communist trade, Communist experts and Communist-designed and erected buildings could be followed by Communist arms, Communist ideas, and ultimately, Communist control of this country". When Ne Win took over power in a military coup in 1962, the socialist period of Burmese post-independence history dawned. But in its Ne Win vintage, this socialism took the country on an inward-looking and isolationist path.

Yangon Correctional Facility (Insein Prison)

Main entrance on
Hlaing River Road
Unknown
1887 (with later additions)

109 A

Despite the government's claims to have released the country's remaining political prisoners (which is disputed—in fact, the UN Special Rapporteur for Human Rights in Myanmar believes they are jailing new ones), this building retains the haunting aura of its darkest days. Many pro-democracy activists were incarcerated here after the 1988 uprising, often in inhumane and squalid conditions. Insein Prison became known throughout the world as the ultimate symbol of the junta's repression. The origins of the correctional facility go back to the late 19th century. By that time, Insein was still only a small town, about 15 kilometres north of downtown Rangoon. The new prison here was intended to relieve the Rangoon Central Gaol ("gaol" being the more commonly used British spelling for "jail" during the period), which was reaching full capacity. By 1908, both Insein and Rangoon jails were by far the biggest in British Burma, with more than 2,000 inmates each.

The Inspector-General of Prisons in Burma at the time reported proudly that growing inmate populations were proof of effective law enforcement. But by the 1920s, Burma had developed a reputation for being the most violent part of British India. With a population of 13 million, the government sent about 20,000 men to prison each year (women were also imprisoned, but their numbers usually stayed below 5 per cent of the total number of convicted men), which was four times the average of British India as a whole. This, needless to say, led to overcrowded prisons and further building works were needed to extend their capacity. By 2009, Insein Prison had space for about 5,000 to 6,000 inmates; however, an estimated 10,000 prisoners were being held here. The architecture of Insein Prison closely follows the so-called Pentonville model, based on the late 18th-century theories of Jeremy Bentham, who proposed penitentiary designs hiding the jailer from the prisoners' sight, encouraging "the sentiment of a sort of omnipresence". Located in north London and built in 1842, Pentonville Prison revolutionised correctional facilities in 19th-century Britain, with reverberations across the Empire. Confronted with a growing inmate population and a move away from the idea

of "punishment" towards the "reform" of prisoners (whether that was systematically achieved in practice is another question), the main features of these new-generation prisons were: a structure of building wings revolving around a central observation tower; walls between prison cells hindering communication between inmates; and workshops allowing prisoners to learn a trade while in confinement.

The Rangoon Central Gaol was demolished some time after the war (its former site is where the New General Hospital is located now, just north of Bogyoke Road) and Insein Prison became the main correctional facility for the capital region. Its notoriety grew with the government's growing reputation for brutality. During Ne Win's reign (1962–1988), undesirable political opponents were regularly put away here—including architect U Kyaw Min, who built the **Thakin Kodaw Hmaing Mausoleum** 080 C among many other projects. Later, with the student protests, these numbers swelled dramatically. The horrors experienced by the inmates are difficult to fathom. Punishments included solitary confinement for extended periods, torture and denial of medical care. Sanitary conditions were unbearable. Several former political prisoners have discussed their experiences in writing. One former political prisoner, Dr Ma Thida, named her memoirs *Sanchaung, Insein, Harvard* to illustrate her trajectory from a Yangon youth to the prestigious halls of an Ivy League university—and the traumatic years in between, from 1993 to 1999, when she became a *cause celebre* of human rights groups. Other former political prisoners work full-time to expose injustices in the regime's penal system. Based in the border town of Mae Sot, Thailand, the Assistance Association for Political Prisoners (Burma) (AAPP) lobbies to support political prisoners and honours the memories of those who died behind bars. Their offices contain a replica of an Insein jail cell and a miniature model of the correctional facility. Insein Prison is, of course, inaccessible to outsiders. The main gate leads to several checkpoints visitors must pass before reaching the compound. But you may get a chance to study the prison's layout from your aeroplane seat. If leaving Yangon by plane in a westerly direction, those sitting on the right may well catch a glimpse of the prison beneath them, even at night. Its radial design stands out. In early 2015, the AAPP estimated that there were still about 160 political prisoners in Myanmar, most of them within the walls of Insein Prison.

7

"What Are Your Five Favourite Buildings in Yangon?"

Zaw Lin Myat, Graduate Student of Architecture and Historical Preservation, Columbia University

**Mahabandoola Garden,
formerly Fytche Garden**
The Mahabandoola Garden has been my favourite spot downtown ever since I was a child. The Independence Monument, fountains and greenery, surrounded by the majestic **High Court** 021 B and **City Hall** 018 B, create a true urban oasis in downtown Yangon. Especially in the hot summer, the park is a nice place to hang out in the evening as a breeze from the river cools down the day. In the 1990s, there were merry-go-rounds and Ferris wheels for children to enjoy. I vividly remember those times when I ran around the park and rode these attractions each week. Unfortunately, they have been replaced with not-so-attractive public bathrooms.

Ministers' Building (Secretariat) 006 B
The former Secretariat is shrouded in mystery for a Millennial like me. Majestic as it may seem from the sidewalk, the Secretariat is off-limits for the general public other than you-know-whos doing you-know-what behind the layers of security, fences and thick vegetation. Until recently, I have only vicariously experienced it through the historical accounts of General Aung San's assassination, and the independence ceremony shortly thereafter, when the Union Jack was retired and the six-star Union of Burma flag was raised. The building holds so much historical and architectural importance for British Burma as well as independent Burma. When you know its history, it can overwhelm you as you pass by on the crumbling sidewalk.

Karaweik Palace 089 D
A big boat in the form of two mythical birds can be attractive to any child. Famous ice cream on the boat added to the excitement of the place when I was little. A royal barge, it is in fact a concrete structure anchored firmly on the bank of Kandawgyi Lake. Perhaps it's a Burmese counterpart to Venturi's postmodern duck—except it is more elaborate in the form of a mythical bird, painted gold. Very Burmese. It makes a statement on the lake, and it is lovely to enjoy the scenery from its platform, facing the venerable **Shwedagon Pagoda** 075 E as if you were royalty on a pilgrimage.

Chinese Shophouses in Latha Township
Architecturally unique from all other parts of downtown Yangon, these two-to four-storey shophouses are home to the Chinese community which make up Yangon's Chinatown. The wooden louvre windows, *dougong* brackets, some quite detailed, recall the Chinese heritage you find throughout Southeast Asia. These buildings might not be as grand as many colonial buildings but they make the fabric of vibrant Chinatown. Although they are largely intact on the lower block of Latha Street, they can be spotted throughout Latha Township and are always great to look up at as you navigate its bustling streets.

**Warehouses at the end of
Sule Pagoda Road**
These long, windowless brick structures span along the Yangon River and stand imposingly at the end of Sule Pagoda Road. The architecture is clearly utilitarian. The warm-orange brick walls that make up these warehouses, arranged in a uniform and orderly fashion, have become iconic of Yangon's port. When you walk along Merchant Road and look towards the river from the numbered streets, their presence is hard to ignore and can be appreciated in the light of the setting sun.

Mahabandoola Garden, one of Yangon residents' favourite public spaces

Thanlyin

8

Star City

Star City

Kyaik Khauk Pagoda Road
Dragages Singapore
(contractor for Zone B)
2010–2016 (estimated for Zone B)

Sitting on 170 hectares of land on the banks of the Bago River, this master-planned gated community is the most extensive residential project to date on Yangon's real estate market. It stands in Yangon's periphery, in Thanlyin, which is a town in its own right: it was only connected to Yangon in 1993, when a bridge across the Bago River was built. The deep sea port of Thilawa is just 15 kilometres to the south, placing Star City in a strategic position between Yangon's centre and this new major special economic zone. The development is split into several phases. The first one is now complete and largely occupied. Its five star-shaped residential blocks of eight to 12 storeys will each be complemented by an identical set of buildings to the west.

A recreational complex will be placed between them. Zone B will open in 2016; it is being built by Singapore-based Dragages, a member of the French Bouygues construction group. Future phases may include more apartment blocks. Eventually, developers expect this area to be able to house more than 20,000 people. The development's architecture and layout is so generic it could be anywhere in the world. The buildings' star-shaped layout and similar orientation means many units ended up facing one another, rather than offering views of the lake and river. The use of central hallways prevents cross-ventilation for most units. Despite these design shortcomings, the development is popular with the growing upper middle class. Construction quality is reportedly sound, and the apartments' specifications are modern. A golf course partially surrounds the compound towards the undeveloped riverfront. Landscaped courtyards and tree-lined streets provide further greenery.

Depending on their size and orientation, apartments sell from anywhere between 80,000 and 450,000 US dollars. A ferry service will soon connect this site with central Yangon, reducing transit time. For now, the only road connection to Yangon is a two-lane highway that appears to be over capacity already. Despite the short distance, getting downtown can take up to one hour. Given the breakneck speed at which Yangon is developing, Star City is visionary in several aspects. For one, it heralds the development of the river's opposite bank. Thanlyin and Yangon's Dala township are natural expansion areas for Yangon. A major new bridge is expected to connect the latter with the downtown area in several years, bringing relief to the more than 30,000 daily commuters, but also causing a real estate frenzy in Dala. (For the time being Dala still feels like a world apart from Yangon. It is a popular tourist destination for day-long motorbike rides through the countryside.) Star City also suggests Yangon's wealthy will prefer to live in these gated communities, commuting to their jobs in the centre or in Thilawa, and requiring ever-greater infrastructure investments to accommodate the resulting flow of traffic.

8

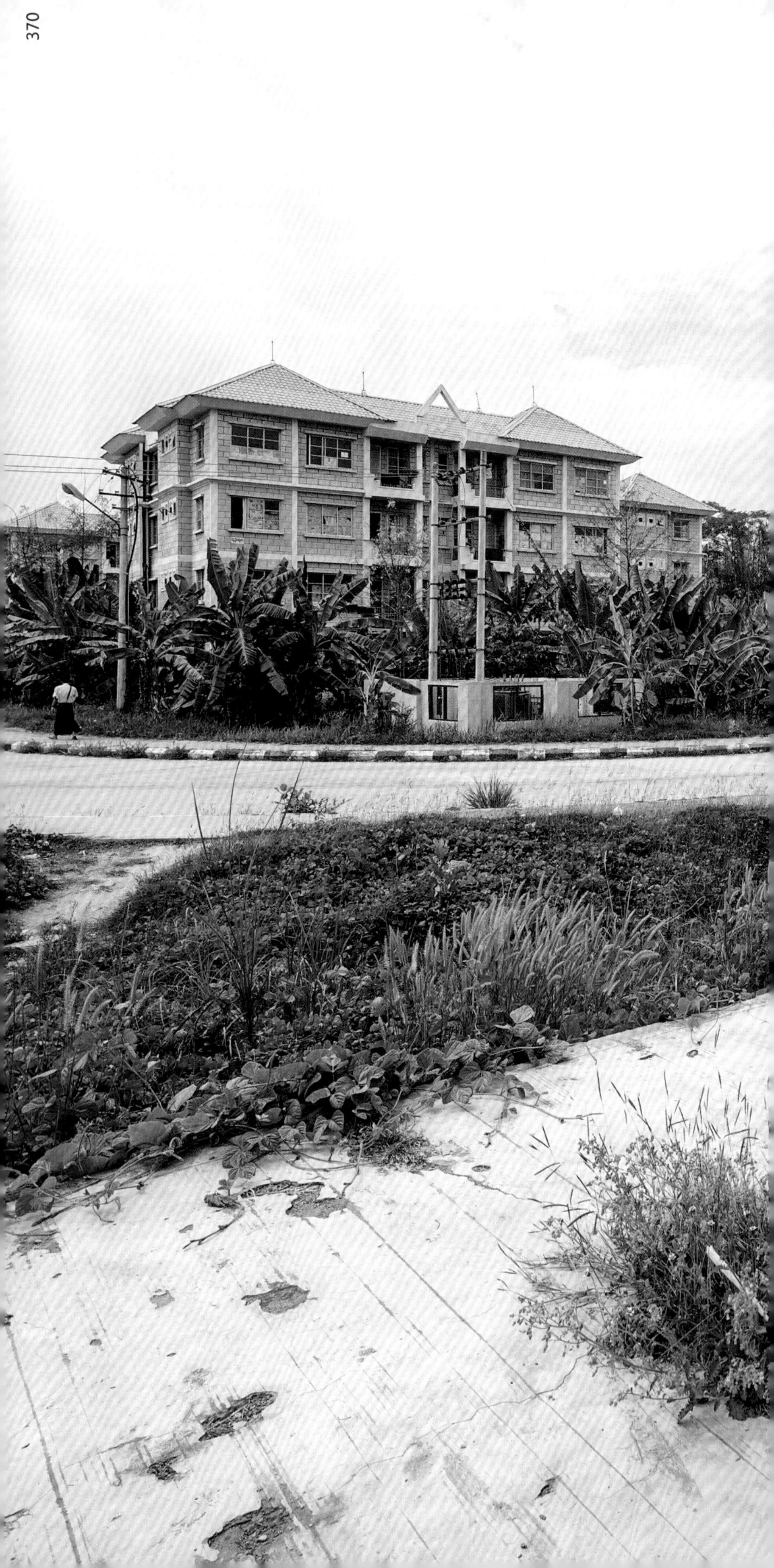

Naypyidaw: Built by Lonely Kings

Naypyidaw is Myanmar's new, shining and purpose-built capital. Empty highways connect its huge and often baffling buildings. Bearing signs of the regime's uneasy relationship with Yangon, the city shows a conscious desire for strategic isolation and a new national narrative. But can it grow into the role?

Although there had been rumours, the news still caught many people unawares. Practically overnight, on Sunday, 6 November 2005, the military authority moved the country's entire government from Yangon to a new, purpose-built city 320 kilometres to the north, about halfway up the road to Mandalay. Its name was Naypyidaw, or "abode of kings". An almost virgin site was chosen for this bold experiment, west of a small town called Pyinmana. The terrain was so remote that few people grasped its scale. Nearby residents reported seeing Chinese contractors in Pyinmana's tea shops as early as 1999. Some observers expected a major new *Tatmadaw* (army) headquarters here. But early on that Sunday morning, a large convoy of trucks loaded with the contents of entire ministries started their engines and left Yangon, heading north.

Naypyidaw transformed the country's political geography. Since the British occupied Lower Burma in 1852, and Upper Burma in 1885, Myanmar's centre of gravity had moved to the south, away from the historic Burmese heartlands of its former capitals, Amarapura, Ava, Mandalay and Pagan. Under British rule the hitherto quiet and swampy Yangon became the country's economic and political heart. As we discuss in the section on post-1988 Yangon, when the military enacted urban planning policies in response to the pro-democracy movement (see page 332), the changes they eventually imposed on Yangon failed to

give the generals much peace of mind. Instead the junta continued to distance itself from the city; the generals deemed it an unnatural capital. But with Naypyidaw, they didn't just create a physical distance from Yangon, or indeed any other city—they also insulated themselves from their people.

Many saw this as a defensive move. Naypyidaw is far from the coast, where it could fall victim to a foreign invasion. Naypyidaw is on a hill. Naypyidaw is closer to the country's conflict areas where episodic violence has flared between ethnic minority armed groups and the *Tatmadaw*, although a draft national ceasefire was signed in April 2015. Whatever the motivations, the cost of building a city from scratch in one of Asia's poorest countries is—ultimately—indefensible: the government has spent an estimated 4–5 billion US dollars on Naypyidaw already. And judging from construction activity and the city's scale, the total invoice will continue to grow.

Naypyidaw's urban layout bears a strong resemblance to American suburbs and strip malls. Economic, residential and even hotel zones are strictly segregated. The hotel district lies adjacent to the (largely undeveloped) diplomatic housing compound. Predictably, given the dearth of city life, most diplomatic missions have chosen to remain in Yangon so far. The ministry area is 10 kilometres to the north. As a city built exclusively for motor vehicles, it doesn't provide for pedestrians outside gated shopping

The old road connecting Yangon and Mandalay

and hotel complexes, which often offer golf carts for transportation given their vast dimensions. This is a city without an easily discernible centre—perhaps no accident. The symbols of power, above all the gigantic parliament building, are not easily accessible. No public space surrounds them. Whether these are conscious security measures or results of poor urban planning is a matter of debate. In the eyes of journalist Siddharth Varadarajan, Naypyidaw "will always lack the urban cadences and unpredictable rhythms that characterise city life in Rangoon or Mandalay. And this is precisely what makes the new capital so attractive to the generals."

Large sporting venues had been built for the Southeast Asian Games that were held here in 2014. In a city full of curiosities, the Wunna Theikdi and Zeyar Thiri sporting complexes may be the most revealing: they are perfectly and eerily identical, despite being 35 kilometres apart. They both contain an outdoor stadium, three indoor stadiums, a swimming complex and indoor halls. (The contractor in both cases was Max Myanmar, one of the country's largest and best-connected conglomerates.) These are not the only surreal copycats. The new capital's City Hall is a replica of Yangon's. The Uppatasanti Pagoda is almost an exact copy of the **Shwedagon Pagoda** 075 E. It is one foot shorter and its base is hollow, but from the outside the illusion is almost perfect. This complicates our earlier point about Naypyidaw symbolising a clean break from Yangon. In these cases, the intention may be to overwrite the originals or take away from their unique symbolic and political power.

Myanmar International Convention Centre

Myanmar International Convention Centre 2

The gigantic Myanmar International Convention Centre was built by Chinese contractors and with Chinese money. If you aren't visiting the city for a major event or conference there, you may feel very lonely in Naypyidaw's vast airport. As of early 2015, the only international connections include Kunming (in China's Yunnan province), Kuala Lumpur and nearby Bangkok. It was designed by Singaporean CPG Corporation and built by Myanmar conglomerate Asia World.

You will waste no time in traffic jams here: Naypyidaw boasts what is probably the most under-used ten-lane highway on earth. You may see water buffalos having a snooze right in the middle of it, which tells you how often they've felt confronted by passing cars. The highway is especially wide in front of the *Hluttaw (parliament)*. Maybe history will prove

these ambitious highway planners right. Until then, the experience remains surreal, enhanced by the beautifully manicured flowerbeds at a number of equally massive roundabouts.

Leave Naypyidaw for one of the surrounding towns, the closest being Pyinmana, just behind a crest from Uppatasanti Pagoda, and you return to ordinary Myanmar with bustling traffic, vibrant street life and a scale shrunk back to human proportions. A tree-lined road alongside the railway tracks used to be the only connection to Yangon before the construction of the Yangon-Mandalay Expressway. Follow this road to the south and it intersects with the arterial road which links Naypyidaw International Airport with the new capital.

In being a new and—to start with at least—artificial capital, Naypyidaw has

Pyidaungsu Hluttaw (National Assembly)

various precedents around the world. Besides historical examples in the United States, Australia, Russia and Canada, there were prominent capital relocations more recently in Brazil (from Rio de Janeiro to Brasilia), Kazakhstan (Almaty to Astana), Belize (Belize City to Belmopan) and Nigeria (Lagos to Abuja). It takes decades to judge their success. Of those examples, Naypyidaw is not the only purpose-built capital created for military and strategic reasons.

The opening-up of the country is also changing Naypyidaw and the way we may come to think about it. The grotesquely huge parliament building (*Pyidaungsu Hluttaw*) has played host to, in some eyes, surprisingly vibrant debates on new laws and regulations. The opposition National League for Democracy (NLD) has had MPs here since a by-election in 2012, including opposition leader Aung San Suu Kyi. And while we cannot guess for certain the outcome of the 2015 elections, the oft-quoted democratisation process will doubtless shape the city's dynamic. It presents a fascinating case of a place planned by authoritarian rulers for the purpose of spatial isolation, confronted with the imperative now to grow into the deserving capital of an aspiring democracy—although the speed, depth and sustainability of that purported transition is contentious.

Much media coverage of Naypyidaw will no doubt focus on the oddities resulting from its undemocratic and secretive genesis: a zoo boasting an air-conditioned penguin house, deserted highways and bulky government buildings—these will be Naypyidaw's trademarks for years to come. For now, its abiding legacy is anyone's guess.

Naypyidaw International Airport

Uppatasanti Pagoda

Star World Hotel

City Hall

Wunna Theikdi Pool

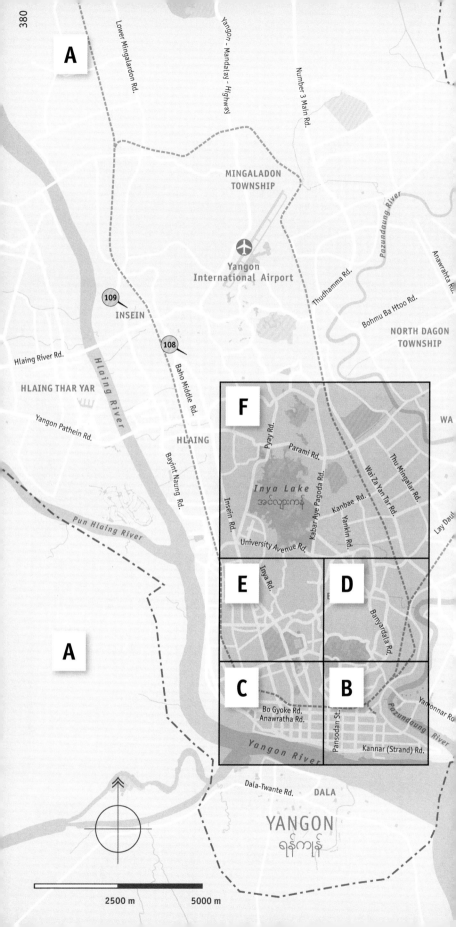

A

MINGALADON
TOWNSHIP

Yangon
International Airport

109
INSEIN

108

Lower Mingalardon Rd.

Yangon - Mandalay - Highway

Number 3 Main Rd.

Pazundaung River

Thudhamma Rd.

Bohmu Ba Htoo Rd.

Anawrahta Rd.

NORTH DAGON
TOWNSHIP

WA

Hlaing River Rd.

HLAING THAR YAR

Yangon Pathein Rd.

Hlaing River

Baho Middle Rd.

HLAING

Bayint Naung Rd.

Pun Hlaing River

A

F

Pyay Rd.

Parami Rd.

Inya Lake
အင်းလျားကန်

Insein Rd.

Kabar Aye Pagoda Rd.

Kanbae Rd.

Yankin Rd.

Wai Za Yan Tar Rd.

Thu Mingalar Rd.

Lay Daul

University Avenue Rd.

E

Inya Rd.

D

Banyardala Rd.

C

Bo Gyoke Rd.
Anawratha Rd.

B

Pansodan St.

Yamonnar Rd.

Pazundaung River

Kannar (Strand) Rd.

Yangon River

Dala-Twante Rd.

DALA

YANGON
ရန်ကုန်

2500 m

5000 m

Notes

Yangon's downtown area is best discovered on foot. While we have not
included walking routes, these maps
can help plan your itinerary. There are many different ways to trans-
literate Burmese spellings into the
Latin alphabet, but rarely any con-
sistency in how these are applied—
equally, this book does not restrict
itself to one system throughout.

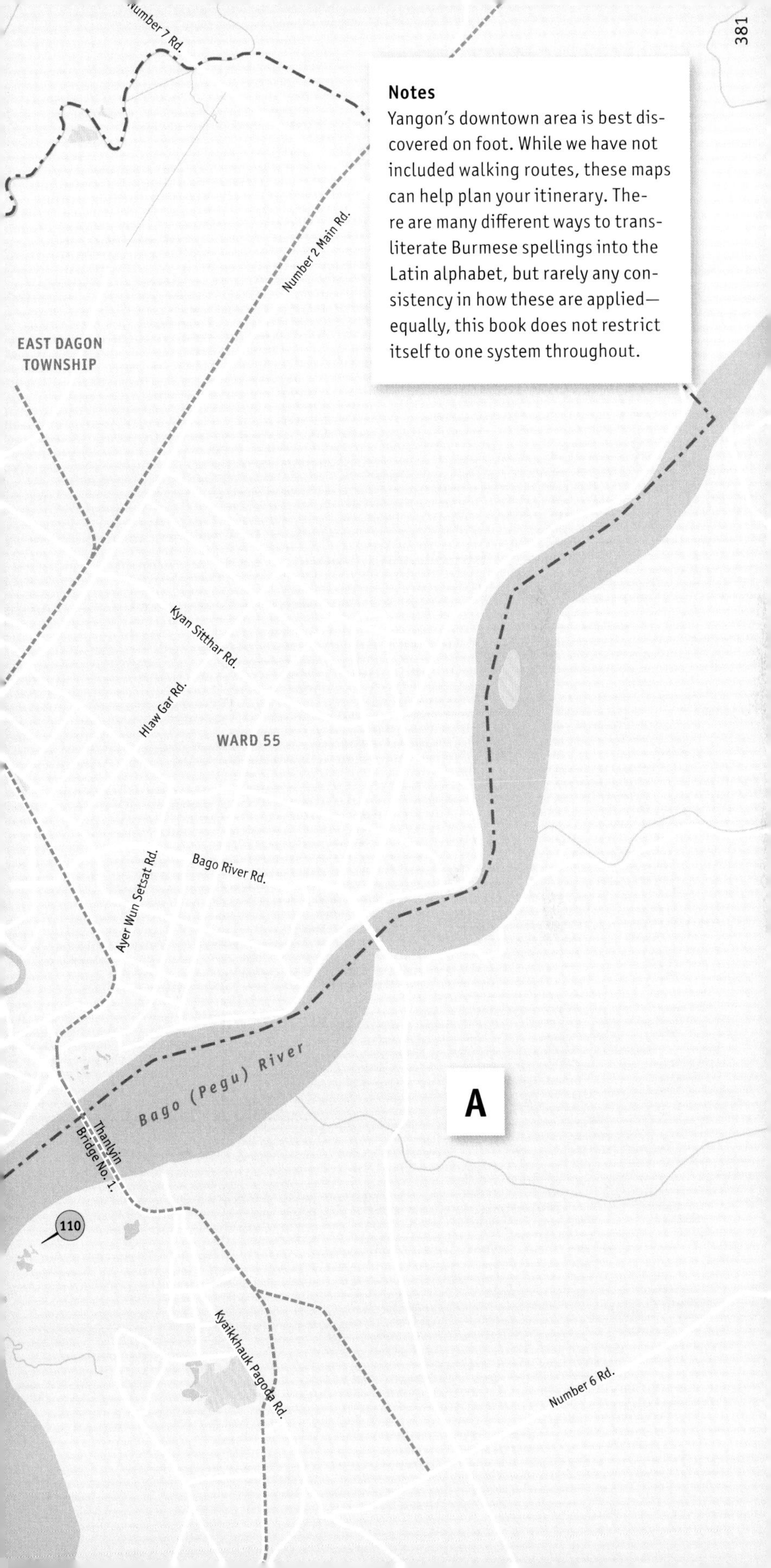

Number 7 Rd.

Number 2 Main Rd.

EAST DAGON
TOWNSHIP

Kyan Sitthar Rd.

Hlaw Gar Rd.

WARD 55

Ayer Wun Setsat Rd.

Bago River Rd.

Bago (Pegu) River

A

Thanlyin
Bridge No. 1.

110

Kyaikkhauk Pagoda Rd.

Number 6 Rd.

Pazundaung

Upper Pazundaung Rd.

Lower Pazundaung Rd.

Pazundaung River

Maha Bandoola Bridge

54th St.
55th St.
56th St.

Bazaar Rd.

Merchant Rd.

54th St.
55th St.

Kannar (Strand) Rd.

250 m   500 m

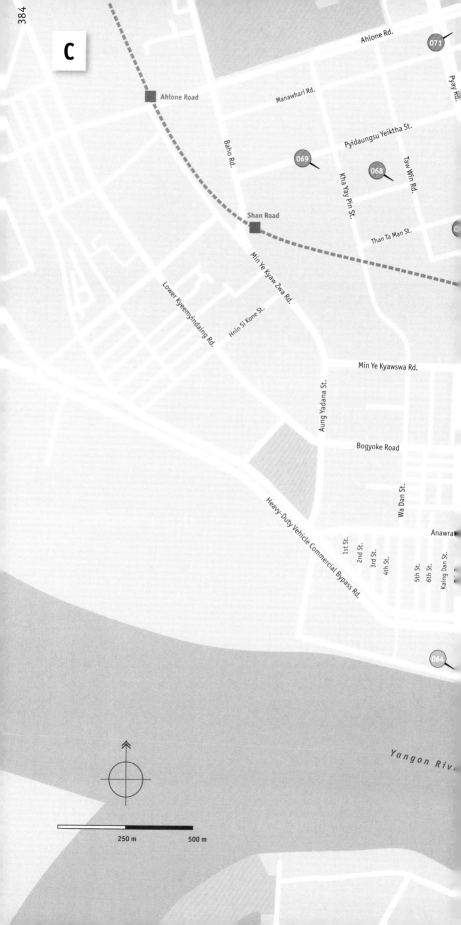

C

Ahlone Rd.

071

Pyay Rd.

Manawhari Rd.

Ahlone Road

Pyidaungsu Yeiktha St.

Baho Rd.

069

068

Taw Win Rd.

Kha Yay Pin St.

Than Ta Man St.

Shan Road

Min Ye Kyaw Zwa Rd.

Lower Kyeemyindaing Rd.

Hnin Si Kone St.

Min Ye Kyawswa Rd.

Aung Yadana St.

Bogyoke Road

Wa Dan St.

Anawra

Heavy-Duty Vehicle Commercial Bypass Rd.

1st St.

2nd St.

3rd St.

4th St.

5th St.

6th St.

Kaing Dan St.

064

Yangon Riv

250 m

500 m

D

094

Shwegondaing Lane

Banyar Dala Rd.

093

Ngar Htat Kyee Pagoda St.

092

Nat Mauk Lane 1

Pho Sein Rd.

091

Komin Kochin Rd.

Bahan Rd.

090

Nat Mauk Rd.

Kandawgyi Park

089

Kan Yeiktha

Kandawgyi Lake

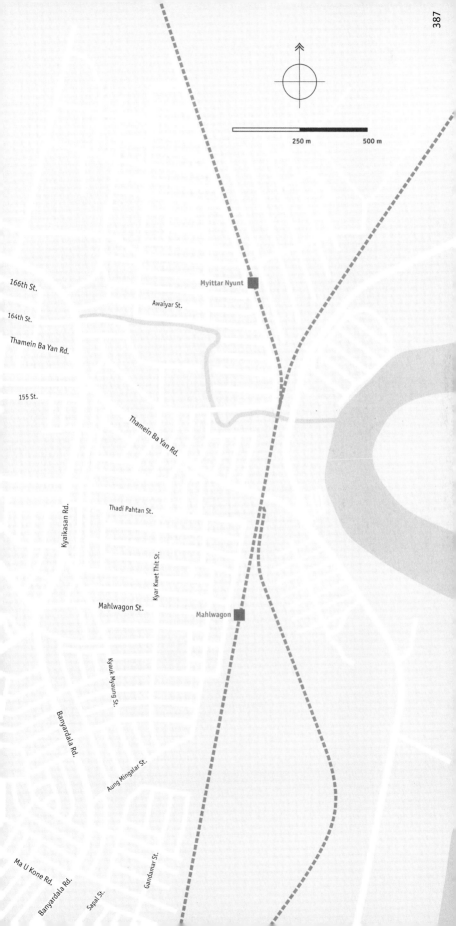

250 m   500 m

166th St.

Awaiyar St.

164th St.

Thamein Ba Yan Rd.

Myittar Nyunt

155 St.

Thamein Ba Yan Rd.

Kyaikasan Rd.

Thadi Pahtan St.

Kyar Kwet Thit St.

Mahlwagon St.

Mahlwagon

Kyauk Myaung St.

Banyardala Rd.

Aung Mingalar St.

Ma U Kone Rd.

Banyardala Rd.

Sapal St.

Gandamar St.

E

098

097

U Wizara Road

Ma Kyee Kyee St.

Kyun Taw Rd.

Maha Myaing St.

Pyay Rd.

Shan Kone St.

Dhammayone St.

Bargaya Rd.

Sanchaung St.

Dhammazedi Rd.

People's Park

Shin Saw Pu Rd.

Pyay Rd.

Panhlaing Road

Baho Rd.

070

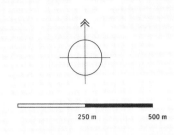

250 m   500 m

Inya Myaing Rd.

Shwe Taung Kyar St.

Kabar Aye Pagoda Rd.

Inya Rd.

Dhammazedi Rd.

Dhammazedi Rd.

Shwegondaing Lane

074

Old Yay Tar Shay St.

U Wizara Road

Thein Gottara
Park

075

U Htaung Bo Rd.

076

073

Ahlone Rd.

F

Military Golf Course

Parami Rd.

Pyay Rd.

ပါရမီလမ်း

Parami Rd.

Pyay Rd.

103

Inya
Lake
Lovers
Hill

101

Inya Lake
အင်းလျားကန်

102

Inya Rd.

Adipati Rd.

Hledan Rd.

University Avenue Rd.

Inya Place

University Avenue Rd.

Hledan

100

095

Nar Nat Taw St.

Pyay Rd.

Inya Rd.

099

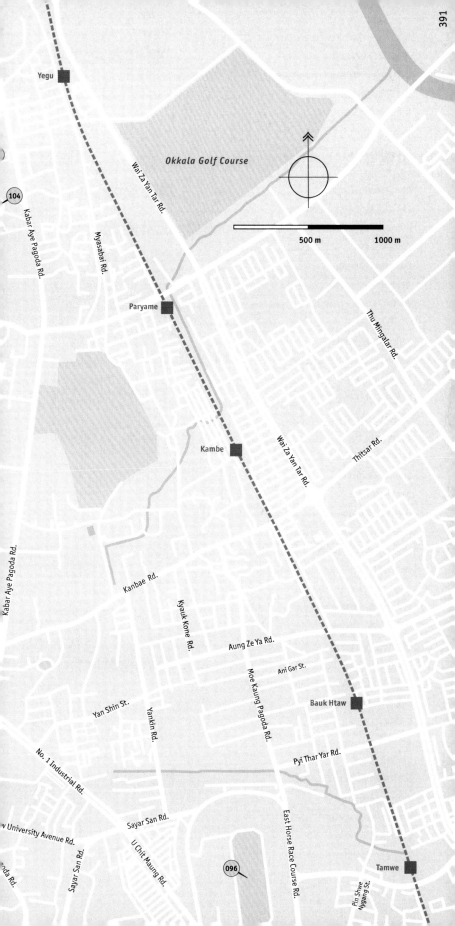

Yegu

104

Kabar Aye Pagoda Rd.

Myasabai Rd.

Wai Za Yan Tar Rd.

Okkala Golf Course

500 m   1000 m

Thu Mingalar Rd.

Paryame

Thitsar Rd.

Kambe

Wai Za Yan Tar Rd.

Kabar Aye Pagoda Rd.

Kanbae Rd.

Kyauk Kone Rd.

Aung Ze Ya Rd.

Ani Gar St.

Yan Shin St.

Yankin Rd.

Moe Kaung Pagoda Rd.

Bauk Htaw

No. 1 Industrial Rd.

Pyi Thar Yar Rd.

University Avenue Rd.

Sayar San Rd.

Sayar San Rd.

U Chit Maung Rd.

096

East Horse Race Course Rd.

Tamwe

Pin Shwe Nyang St.

Building Index

Bibliography

Afsheen, S. *Under Five Flags: Life Like a Turbulent River Flows*. Xlibris, 2001.

Andrus, James Russell. *Burmese Economic Life*. Stanford University Press, 1947.

Amrith, Sunil. *Crossing the Bay of Bengal: The Furies of Nature and the Fortunes of Migrants*. Harvard University Press, 2013.

Burmistrenko, Nikolai Alekseevich. *Stroitel'stvo i Arkhitektura Birmy*. Library of Congress, 1957.

Butwell, Richard. *U Nu of Burma*. Stanford University Press, 1969.

Fong, Kecia. "Imagining Yangon: Assembling Heritage, National Identity and Modern Futures." *Australia ICOMOS Historic Environment*, 26.3 (2014): 26-39.

Frasch, Tilman. "Tracks in the City: Technology, Mobility, and Society in Colonial Rangoon and Singapore." *Modern Asian Studies*, 46.1 (2012): 97-118.

Fredman Cernea, Ruth. *Almost Englishmen: Baghdadi Jews in British Burma*. Lexington Books, 2007.

Ghosh, Amitav. *The Glass Palace*. Random House, 2001.

Grant, Colesworthey. *A Rough Trip to Rangoon in 1846*. Orchid Press Publishing Limited, 1995.

Japan International Cooperation Agency, JICA. *Yangon Urban Transport Master Plan: Major Findings on Yangon Urban Transport and Short-Term Actions*. 2014.

Kamdar, Mira. *Motiba's Tattoos: A Granddaughter's Journey Into Her Indian Family's Past*. Public Affairs, 2000.

Kraas, Frauke, Gaese, Hartmut, Mi Mi Kyi. *Megacity Yangon. Transformation Processes and Modern Developments*. LIT Verlag Münster, 2006.

Lamprakos, Michele. "The Idea of the Historic City." *Change Over Time*, 4.1 (2014): 8-39.

Le Fleur, Sybil and Blanche, with Derek Flory. *Torn Apart: How Two Sisters Found Each Other After Sixty-Five Years*. Random House, 2011.

Lintner, Bertil. *Outrage: Burma's Struggle for Democracy*. Weatherhill, 1995.

MacMillan, Allister. *Seaports of the Far East*. Collingridge, 1924.

Moore, Elizabeth Howard. "Unexpected Places at the Shwedagon." *A Companion to Asian Art and Architecture*. Eds. Rebecca M. Brown and Deborah S. Hutton. Wiley-Blackwell, 2011.

Moore, Elizabeth Howard, Osiri, Navanath. "Urban Forms and Civic Space in Nineteenth- to Early Twentieth Century Bangkok and Rangoon." *Journal of Urban History*, 40.1 (2014): 158-177.

Morris, Jan and Winchester, Simon. *Stones of Empire: The Buildings of the Raj*. Oxford University Press, 2005.

Myint-U, Thant. *The River of Lost Footsteps: Histories of Burma*. Farrar, Straus and Giroux, 2008.

Myint-U, Thant. *Where China Meets India: Burma and the New Crossroads of Asia*. Farar, Straus and Giroux, 2012.

Ozhegov, SS. *Arkhitektura Birmy*. Nauka Moscow, 1970.

Pearn, BR. *A History of Rangoon*. Rangoon Municipal Corporation, 1939.

Polk, Benjamin. *Building for South Asia: An Architectural Autobiography*. Abhinav Publications, 1994.

Popham, Peter. *The Lady And The Peacock, The Life of Aung San Suu Kyi of Burma*. Rider, 2012.

Rogers, Benedict. *Burma: A Nation at the Crossroads*. Random House, 2012.

Rooney, Sarah. *30 Heritage Buildings of Yangon: Inside the City that Captured Time*. Serindia Publications, 2012.

Seekins, Donald. "The State and the City: 1988 and the Transformation of Rangoon." *Pacific Affairs*, 78.2 (2005): 257-275.

Seekins, Donald. *Historical Dictionary of Myanmar (Burma)*. Scarecrow Press, 2006.

Seekins, Donald. *State and Society in Modern Rangoon*. Routledge, 2014.

Skidmore, Monica (ed.). *Burma at the Turn of the Twenty-First Century*. University of Hawaii Press, 2005.

Singer, Noel. *Old Rangoon: City of the Shwedagon*. Kiscadale Publications, 1995.

Spate, OHK and Trueblood, LW. "Rangoon: A Study in Urban Geography." *Geographical Review*, 32.1 (1942): 56-73.

Squire, Raglan. *Portrait of an Architect*. Colin Smythe, 1984.

Stadtner, Donald M. *Sacred Sites of Burma*. River Books, 2010.

"Studio Yangon" project description, Hong Kong University, 2014. Available at studioyangon.wordpress.com

Thanegi, Ma and Broman, Barry Michael. *Myanmar Architecture: Cities of Gold*. Times Editions - Marshall Cavendish, 2005.

Tong, Chee-Kiong. *Identity and Ethnic Relations in Southeast Asia: Racialising Chineseness*. Springer, 2011.

Turnell, Sean. *Fiery Dragons: Banks, Moneylenders and Microfinance in Burma*. Nordic Institute of Asian Studies, 2009.

UN Habitat. *Human Settlements Sector Review: Union of Myanmar*. 1991.

Wright, Arnold. *Twentieth Century Impressions of Burma: Its History, People, Commerce, Industries, and Resources*. Lloyd's Greater Britain Publishing Company, 1910.

Wright, Ashley. *Opium and Empire in Southeast Asia: Regulating Consumption in British Burma*. Palgrave Macmillan, 2013.

Yegar, Moshe. *The Muslims of Burma: A Study of a Minority Group*. Schriftenreihe des Südasien-Instituts der Universität Heidelberg, 1972.

Acknowledgments

This book would not have been possible without the help of many people. They deserve a note of gratitude. Above all, we would like to thank Franz Xaver Augustin and the Yangon Goethe-Institut for their enthusiasm and generous support. Kecia Fong provided patient mentorship and invaluable help with heritage-related questions. Heinz Schütte generously read the entire manuscript and provided valuable feedback. Zaw Lin Myat supported the project from the start and helped wherever he could. In U Hpone Thant (Harry) we found a most helpful resource to answer many of our particular questions about Yangon's post-independence history, and where it unfolded. In Yangon, many people helped us with their expertise, during interviews: U Tun Than, Daw Moe Moe Lwin, Dr Kyaw Lat, U Sun Oo, Maki Morikawa, Masahiko Suzuki, Amelie Chai and Stephen Zawmoe Shwe deserve a special mention. Special gratitude must also go to U Kin Maung Lwin for taking the time to take us around Yangon University. U Soe Lin provided valuable insights into Burmese architecture in Washington, D.C. Patrick Robert encouraged this project from the beginning and unlocked usually off-limits buildings for the authors, connecting them with many other individuals along the way. We are indebted to Graham and Charmaine Lewis for kindly translating and paraphrasing a Burmese article about the Martyrs' Mausoleum. Bob Percival has been a great supporter and friend of the authors, enlivening their time in Yangon with wisdom and good humour. Takashi Kamiyama's logistical help was greatly appreciated. Sarah Rooney, Melissa Cate Christ, Petr Kozma, Susmit Banerjee, Laetitia Millois, Ilaria Benini, Ben White, Bram Steenhuisen, Ben Wolford, Stewart Traill, Elizabeth Rhoads and Oliver von Braun-Dams provided valuable feedback or helped with individual research-related questions. Special thanks to Kasita Rochanakorn for copy-editing the manuscript. The usual caveats apply.

Illustration credits

All photos taken and copyrighted by Manuel Oka (www.manueloka.com), except for:

Photo on pages 16–17 provided by John Tewell and reproduced with permission
All three photos on page 19: Philip Adolphe Klier
Four photos on pages 18–21: Nick DeWolf
Photo on pages 22–23: Don Oppedijk
Illustration on page 122 provided by DP Architects and reproduced with permission
Photo on page 285: Christian Schink
Two photos on page 320: Arkar Win

Authors

Ben Bansal (1981, Berlin)
is an economist with degrees from the School of Oriental and African Studies (SOAS) in London and Cambridge University. Ben has worked in finance for most of his career, as an economist, fund manager and banker. Since going freelance a few years ago, several of his assignments have dealt with Myanmar's economic transition, bringing him to Yangon and piquing his interest in the city. His academic research interests include the economic history of post-war Tokyo and contemporary urban development issues in South and Southeast Asia.

Elliott Fox (1987, Paris)
is a media adviser in the international development and human rights sectors. He studied politics and communications at SOAS, the London School of Economics and City University's Graduate School of Journalism. He started working on Myanmar issues while interning at the United Nations in 2008. Since then he has traveled to Myanmar regularly: as a press officer for visiting former heads of state and Nobel Peace Prize laureates, as a tourist and—of course—to write this book. Between trips, he awaits good Burmese food in east London.

Manuel Oka (1983, Munich)
is a freelance architect and photographer. He has been commissioned to photograph the buildings of numerous architects and his images have been published internationally in books and magazines. Manuel graduated in architecture from Vienna Technical University and went on to study in Yoshiharu Tsukamoto's graduate studio at the Tokyo Institute of Technology. He worked for architectural firms Fumihiko Maki and KMDW in Tokyo before joining Erich Gassmann in Munich. Manuel spent several months researching the book and shooting in Myanmar.

The *Deutsche Nationalbibliothek* lists
this publication in the *Deutsche
Nationalbibliografie*; detailed bibliographic data are available on the Internet
at http://dnb.d-nb.de.

ISBN 978-3-86922-375-9

Copy-editing
Kasita Rochanakorn

Proofreading
Mariangela Palazzi-Williams

Final corrections
Clarice Knowles

Design
Manuel Oka

Maps
Katrin Soschinski

QR codes
Christoph Gößmann

Image processing
Tiger Printing (Hong Kong) Co., Ltd.
www.tigerprinting.hk

Printing
Spindulio Spaustuvė, Kaunas
www.spindulys.lt

Kindly supported by the
Goethe-Institut in Myanmar